HEINEKEN IN

OLIVIER VAN BEEMEN

Heineken in Africa

A Multinational Unleashed

Translated by
BRAM POSTHUMUS

HURST & COMPANY, LONDON

First published in the United Kingdom in 2019
By C. Hurst & Co. (Publishers) Ltd.,
41 Great Russell Street, London, WC1B 3PL
Copyright © 2018 by Olivier van Beemen
Originally published in 2015 by Uitgeverij Prometheus, Amsterdam,
as *Heineken in Afrika*
English translation © Bram Posthumus, 2019

This paperback edition, 2021
All rights reserved.
Printed in Great Britain by Bell and Bain Ltd, Glasgow

A Cataloguing-in-Publication data record for this book
is available from the British Library.

ISBN: 9781787384880

This book is printed using paper from registered sustainable
and managed sources.

www.hurstpublishers.com

This book was published with the support of the Dutch Foundation for Literature

**N ederlands
letterenfonds
dutch foundation
for literature**

'Transparency is beautiful if you have nothing to hide'

Heineken's advertising slogan in Sierra Leone

CONTENTS

FOREWORD

IT WILL HAPPEN HERE

Iceri ceza umutima. Léandre closes his eyes and lifts his hands skywards. 'Beer enchants the heart,' he translates. He seems to be entering a trance-like state, thoughts travelling far, far away from the drab concrete building on a mud road where I interview him:

> We worship beer. Beer is part of each important moment in life and every ritual. It starts with birth. A new-born child receives a few drops to become strong. And don't forget the mother. While she's pregnant, she doesn't drink too much, but after she has given birth she drinks a lot. It improves her milk.

To illustrate his point, he puts his hand on his chest and squeezes it tenderly. 'Then you get the first communion, the first day at school, university, marriage, the funeral, first remembrance of the deceased, second remembrance ... There is always Primus or Amstel. Young girls praise its benefits. It's sacred froth to us.'

Léandre Sikuyavuga is the deputy director at the *Iwacu* newspaper in Burundi. His love for beer is far from exceptional. With a grin on his face, he retells the story about how the Libyan leader Gaddafi once suggested to his Burundian colleague to have the brewery in the capital Bujumbura replaced with a milk factory. 'That was something the colonel really hadn't thought through. Doing such a thing here is political suicide.'

Burundi, a densely populated country wedged between Rwanda, Tanzania and the Democratic Republic of Congo,[1] breathes beer. Crossing the border from Rwanda, the first thing you see is a large wooden billboard sporting the image of a traditional drummer, a national symbol. Look more closely at the space where his drum is, and you will find another national symbol: a glass full of beer carrying the Primus logo. Welcome to Burundi, the message reads. A little farther down the road, another billboard features the same brand: 'One history, one beer, Burundi's pride'.

On the mountain road from the border to the capital, cyclists struggle with their heavy loads. One man manages to carry an unbelievable fourteen crates of Primus while seated on his bicycle. Those who do not own a bike, mostly women and children, carry one or two crates on their heads.

Who brews all that beer? Heineken, lord and master of the local beer market, in good times and bad, for more than sixty years.

Africa is the beer industry's new paradise. Africans love their beer, even though sales remain modest. But here is the good news: purchasing power is rapidly increasing for many people, and the continent's prospects are bright. The brewers have made their calculations, and the conclusion is that the African markets will see explosive growth.

In the battle for the continent, Heineken's starting position is excellent. The Dutch multinational has more than forty breweries in sixteen countries and exports its product to virtually every other market. The company is highly experienced: the world's second-largest beer brewer (after AB InBev) has been exporting its products to Africa for more than a century. It started brewing locally as early as the 1930s.

FOREWORD

International business considers Africa 'the final frontier', where enormous profits are to be had for daring entrepreneurs with stamina. Since the turn of the century, many national economies have picked up, and the birth rate is unstoppable. There is now a growing urban middle class who, to the delight of the brewers, consider drinking light-coloured lagers an important part of their newfound status.

Moreover, Africa represents far more than a golden promise, and Heineken is keenly aware of that. There is so little competition that in a lot of countries one small bottle of beer is no cheaper—or even more expensive—than in Europe, while production costs are lower. Beer in Africa is almost 50 per cent more profitable than anywhere else. Some markets, like Nigeria, are among the most lucrative in the world.[2] Heineken CEO Jean-François van Boxmeer, an old Africa hand, calls the continent 'the international business world's best kept secret'.[3] With this book, I attempt to uncover that secret.

The beer trade in Africa may be profitable, but it is far from easy. Most of the continent's people are still poor, bad infrastructure turns the distribution of your crate of beer into a major challenge and there is a dearth of qualified staff. While wars, *coups d'état* and famine occur less frequently than during the disastrous 1980s and '90s, many countries are still looking for that elusive political and economic stability. Almost all economies continue to rely on commodity exports. When the oil price falls, Africa's economic giant—Nigeria—falters.

Recent history in Sierra Leone offers another example of how vulnerable a country and its local beer market can be. At the end of a long and exhausting civil war, this West African nation was going through a period of impressive growth when it was suddenly hit by the deadliest Ebola epidemic on record. Years of progress were wiped out in a matter of months.

FOREWORD

Obstacles are not only commercial; doing business in Africa leads to ethical dilemmas that can no longer be dismissed. Back in beer-crazy Burundi, Heineken works closely with an autocrat who binned his country's constitution in 2015 by refusing to step down after his second and last term of office. As we will see, the regime's survival is intricately bound up with Heineken. The United Nations has recorded crimes against humanity committed by the regime, and yet Heineken agrees to have a high-ranking judge appointed president to the Board of Directors of its Burundi subsidiary. How should a business deal with such dilemmas? And where do the boundaries lie?

Six years of research have gone into this book. I have visited every African country—except Ivory Coast—where Heineken runs breweries in which it has a majority shareholding: Algeria, Tunisia, Egypt, Sierra Leone, Nigeria, Ethiopia, Congo-Brazzaville, the Democratic Republic of Congo, Rwanda, Burundi, South Africa and Mozambique. And I went to Kenya where Heineken has an export office. I combed through the company archives, read all the literature I could get on the subject and spoke with 400 sources in and around the company. I also received confidential documents and USB sticks brimming with information.

The Dutch version of *Heineken in Africa* was published in November 2015. Until then, Heineken had refused all interviews, and the company elected not to react to the manuscript I had sent prior to publication. They shunned all contact until early 2017, when the main actors had a change of heart. Suddenly, they were prepared to talk to me. The current director for Africa and two of his predecessors made themselves available, and I interviewed the managers involved in corporate responsibility issues, legal matters, production chains and human rights.[4] And I got to talk—extensively—with CEO Van Boxmeer.

FOREWORD

This reworked and updated version of my book, the first to be available in English, includes many fresh revelations and insights. In Nigeria, for instance, I discovered an elaborate corruption case, and in the same country I had a candid interview with a former top manager, who told me that on his watch Heineken had used thousands of prostitutes for a publicity campaign. I also discovered that in Rwanda the company had been more entangled in the 1994 genocide than I had realised. In Congo, my research played a part in a recent settlement involving employees who had been made redundant during the civil war. The existence of the first Dutch version has also enabled me to demonstrate how Heineken has responded to critical reports and which strategies the company has employed to defend itself and limit reputational damage.

Heineken has responded to the passages in this new edition with which it disagrees. In the words of spokesperson John-Paul Schuirink: 'We don't do this line by line, because that would imply in a sense that we're authorising the book, which we don't want to do.' Presumably, Heineken wants to maintain to the outside world that one should take my work 'with a pinch of salt', as Van Boxmeer suggested during a debate.[5]

'Don't turn this into a crusade against Heineken. You're too young for that,' the CEO warned me during our first meeting. I can reassure him. This is not an indictment of Heineken specifically but a piece of thorough research into the ways of a multinational in Africa, the continent many see as the next big thing for business. As far as I have been able to determine, the Dutch beer brewer's behaviour resembles that of its competitors and other Western companies in many respects, and I do not consider it my mission to show where Heineken performs slightly better or slightly worse than the rest.

I consider it far more important to highlight the problems confronting a company like Heineken in Africa and to show the true effects of its own actions. Unlike many other journalists and analysts covering the corporate world in Africa, I have gathered most of my information on the spot. It comes from people who have worked (or continue to work) for the company—or for whom dealing with Heineken has been part of their daily lives.

This approach seemed self-evident to me when I started my research, but I have learned over the years that the very opposite is true. What has struck me during conferences, in debates and reading the literature is that virtually all available information about multinationals comes from the companies themselves. Academic research and policy-making are routinely based on reports and briefings the companies have either published or commissioned. It stands to reason that these reports emphasise the positive benefits of corporate activity and avoid highlighting the negative aspects.

With this book, I want to show that darker side and provide a true-to-life image of the company that likes to blow its own trumpet regarding this supposed African success story, a story for which it has been lavishly praised. On a visit to Ethiopia, Dutch Queen Máxima lauded the company for a local agriculture project. Prime Minister Mark Rutte regaled the United Nations General Assembly with an animated tale about 'the world famous Dutch beer brewer'.[6] Readers of the right-wing Dutch daily *De Telegraaf* sing the company's praises; to them, this is an enterprise in the best traditions of the VOC (the Dutch East India Company). They use this qualification, not as an accusation of neo-colonial practices but as a compliment for its boundless entrepreneurial spirit.[7]

Why on earth would someone spend six years of his life studying Heineken in Africa? There were more than a few people I spoke with who wondered whether I was on the payroll of SABMiller (now AB InBev) or another competitor. In Africa, I was sometimes suspected of being ... a Heineken spy.

FOREWORD

I must disappoint the conspiracy theorists. It does not happen often that a journalist gets his hands on a single subject that brings together two long-held passions: Africa and beer. For five years, I have been absolutely convinced that nothing is more fun and more satisfying than being a thorn in the side of Heineken in Africa. (I do not think this sentiment is mutual.)

Heineken appeared on my radar in 2011, when I was covering the Jasmine Revolution and the fall of President Ben Ali in Tunisia for the Dutch business daily *Het Financieele Dagblad*. It emerged that the beer brewer had been working with a businessman who was closely connected to the deposed dictator and his clan. Heineken denied having been aware of this when the partnership began, but I knew this to be a lie: the company hoped to benefit from the connection.[8] My journalistic instinct was on high alert. It was a relatively small news story—after all, most foreign companies were doing business with the clan around the president and his wife. But if Heineken was clinging so tenaciously to its lies about the matter, would it behave any differently in other countries ruled by controversial regimes or hampered by a difficult business climate?

I started working on *Heineken in Africa* just over one year later, in the expectation that the subject would keep me busy for two years at the most. But after the first publication in Dutch, the subject kept trailing me. I received fresh tip-offs, got to know and understand the company better. From my work as a correspondent in France, I know that journalists must often cover a wide range of subjects, rendering specialisation difficult. Often you know far less about a subject than the person you are interviewing. Today, I can declare that while there is still a lot I could learn about Heineken's African business empire, at least the company no longer gets away with trite declarations and fanciful tales. I believe I am getting closer to the core.

My research has produced a book of fifteen chapters with an emphasis on Africa south of the Sahara, Heineken's priority zone. Each country chapter is followed by a thematic one, in which I attempt to add depth and context to the observations. I want to show, for instance, that the company's African history, now more than a century old, serves as an important foundation for its current commercial success. I will also argue that Heineken has almost limitless freedom to sell its product. I trace the impact the beer brewer has on local economies and societies and subject the company's corporate social responsibility policy to a critical examination. How does Heineken behave as an employer? Expats have little to complain about, but does the same apply to local staff? There will be no shying away from the difficult stuff, the really tough ethical questions. What considerations compel a company to continue brewing beer in times of war or under a dictatorial regime that oppresses its people?

As a journalist, you'd like your readers to reflect on what you have written. Publication in the Netherlands did just that: within and outside Heineken, there were vigorous debates. Questions were asked in the Dutch and European parliaments, and the Dutch Ministry of Foreign Affairs began to doubt the wisdom of working with the world-famous beer brewer. My book is used in Dutch universities, and Van Boxmeer himself has said that its publication has led to corporate soul-searching, whatever that may mean.

In Africa itself, meanwhile, it remains largely business as usual. In many countries, sales are increasing as the quest for further expansion continues unabated. Nigeria fell on hard times following the drop in the oil price and the devaluation of the naira, the country's currency. However, the Dutch brewer knows that growth in Africa is rarely linear and there is still ample opportunity for expansion. There was good news from Ivory Coast where a new brewery went into production and the new brand, Ivoire, grabbed one-third of the market in a matter of months.[9] Ethiopia was another country where 'robust growth' was reported.

Let us start our journey of discovery there, in Africa's Beer Nirvana.

ETHIOPIA

TURBULENT BEER PARADISE

Imagine a country where the population is rapidly expanding to 100 million. A country where people's purchasing power is rising fast, where beer is much loved but still little consumed. This is Ethiopia, every brewer's dream, with year-on-year growth expected to be 15 per cent.[1]

While economic growth in many African countries appears to exist mostly on paper, in the Ethiopian capital Addis Ababa, the *rising Africa* narrative is clearly visible. The skyline consists of concrete skeletons surrounded by wooden scaffolding: future hotels and office blocks. Roads are being tarred and enlarged at a brisk pace while sewage systems are added—unfortunately not always in a smooth sequence. Modern trams, made in China, traverse the metropolis, and you will find a thriving scene of restaurants and coffee bars in areas where the new middle classes have settled. Ethiopia has pride, its own alphabet and its own calendar. At the end of the nineteenth century, the Italians attempted colonial conquest but were defeated by Emperor Menelik II and his troops. In the twentieth century, Emperor Haile Selassie led

Ethiopia into steep decline. Selassie, who ruled from 1930 to 1974, wanted all power for himself, so much so that he personally appointed the country's beer brewers.[2] The nation then fell into the hands of a communist regime, and Ethiopia became a byword for bad governance, hunger and misery.

Democracy is still a distant ideal, but there is no denying the economic recovery. Ethiopia has pivoted towards other emerging economies and the West, especially the United States, home to a large part of its diaspora. Since 2003, the government has been presenting double digit growth figures almost every year; this is a 'growth machine'.[3]

Dozens of previously nationalised companies were returned to private ownership, including the breweries. The French giant Castel struck first: in 1998, it bought the Saint George Brewery and became market leader in record time, using modern marketing methods and new brands. In 2011, Heineken paid 163 million dollars for two small provincial breweries, one in Bedele in the west and another in Harar in the east. A former Dutch employee never saw the point: 'How could they spend so much money—on that?'

A little later, the last remaining state brewery, Meta Abo, became part of the British Diageo company, well known for its brand Guinness. Ethiopia has thus become a battleground of titans, the only country where three out of the four African top guns are waging war with more or less equal means (AB InBev is the only one absent). The fight has been joined by four smaller actors: Ethiopian beer brewers Dashen and Raya, Unibra of Belgium and the Dutch family enterprise Bavaria.

There was drinking and dancing

I decide to investigate Heineken in the town of Harar. To get there, I must first go to Meskel Square, a giant asphalt area in the shape of a crescent, ideal for the revolutionary parades of the communist age. Today, a giant billboard on top of an office block tells me: HEINEKEN, ON TOUR SINCE 1873. From here, buses depart to all major towns around the country. It is 5 a.m., it is cold and it is raining—this city lies some 2 kilometres above sea level. The darkness has not yet lifted when the bus leaves the capital, on its way to the green highlands with its acacias.

Harar is more than 1,000 years old, and Jugol, the walled inner city, has been placed on UNESCO's World Heritage list. It is a labyrinth of streets and squares. There are more than eighty mosques; their mint green minarets rise above the adjacent white houses. For some, Harar is Islam's fourth holy site, after Mecca, Medina and Jerusalem; others mostly regard it as a regional centre of commerce.

Despite its devotion, Harar is known as a place of tolerance. Nineteenth-century visitors encountered a series of veritable bacchanalia. 'Even though they are very devout believers, they violate the rules of the Qur'an when they indulge in drinking sprees, consuming their self-made beer. They drink frequently and excessively, like brutes,' according to a visiting Italian engineer.[4]

Beer and mosque have been going well together in Harar for a long time. In fact, their relationship is so good that in the 1980s the Ethiopian government decided to build a new brewery here. Help was at hand from the communist international that Ethiopia belonged to at the time, more specifically from the world's premier beer country, Czechoslovakia. Ethiopians got a good lager, with a fine bitter taste.

The Harar brewery organises tours, a custom dating back to pre-Heineken times. There is great transparency—perhaps involuntarily. A whiteboard marks the objectives and the results, amounts of beer lost and the number of employees, drastically axed in a short period of time. The guide is not allowed to comment, but this is clearly a touchy subject. Another statistic gives

3

the number of days the factory has been accident-free, only twenty-one. It is mid-September when I visit, and there have already been four accidents this year.

Still, union leader Teshome Daba says that the brewery is performing much better since Heineken took over. Things are run more professionally. Heineken has also made an arrangement with a local hospital: when there is an accident, an ambulance will come; in case of an emergency, the patient will be flown to Addis Ababa, expenses paid by the employer.

The downside of all this is a worsening mood on the shop floor. Daba:

> The pressure has increased and the joy has gone. In the old days, the brewery was home, now our place of work resembles a prison, because management wants to solve everything by punishing people. Our collective agreement used to say that whenever someone was late or took a small thing home they would receive a warning. That was then, as they say. Now there is punishment, preferably immediate dismissal. They want to get rid of people.

He recalls how the director, Johan Doyer, called all staff to a meeting in the large function hall of the company canteen, a few months after the takeover. Doyer had good news. According to those who attended, he said: 'We have come to this place to deliver better quality and a higher market share.' The Dutch wanted to get to work with the existing staff, including management. Former brewing master Tesfaye Wolde Mariam remembers: 'When the meeting was over, everyone was happy. There was drinking and dancing. Everyone considered this a promise that there would be no layoffs.'

One year later came the bolt from the blue: the cleaners and caretakers were to be sacked because their jobs had been outsourced. Indignant workers went on hunger strike on the company premises, but management called in the army, which stopped them. And that was only the beginning. Heineken's arrival in Ethiopia eventually meant the forced dismissal of 600 workers.[5]

Heineken appointed a new director at Harar: Tadele Abebe, a man with a formidable reputation. 'They love him at Heineken,' says a former director. He thinks that the new man's policies are a tight fit with those of his Dutch predecessor:

> Doyer took every form of contestation as if it were resistance. Previously, he had worked in Rwanda, Burundi and Congo. Perhaps in those places they are used to a white man playing boss, issuing orders that the black staff then execute. That does not work here. I think he's got some kind of a hang-up. When we had an important meeting I would often be the first person to be greeted. Johan then just had to demonstrate that he was the boss. It looks as if he's jealous.

My sources are struck by the fact that the new Ethiopian managers at Heineken are all Tigrayans, from the north of the country. They form a 6 per cent minority of the national population but are a force to be reckoned with, thanks to the major role the Tigrayan People's Liberation Front (TPLF) played in removing the communist regime, a coup that propelled Meles Zenawi, a Tigrayan, to power in the early 1990s. The TPLF is the backbone of the ruling Ethiopian People's Revolutionary Democratic Front (EPRDF), which occupies a large majority of the seats in the country's parliament. Although the current Prime Minister, Abiy Ahmed, is not from the north, the Tigrayans remain influential in Ethiopia.

'It could be a coincidence that they all belong to the same group,' says Wolde Mariam, 'but it does not look that way. I am hearing constant rumours that Heineken is keen to develop political connections.' The former director, for his part, thinks that Doyer was advised to work with the Tigrayans. 'Heineken seems to steer a political course. Some no longer see the company purely as an investor. I don't think that is smart. What happens when the government falls?'

A short-lived Journey of Love

It may have been a figment of the imagination or a genuine worry on the part of the former managers, but here is a bit of history: Heineken's Ethiopian adventure has already included a walk through an ethnic minefield. When it wanted to promote its Bedele brand in 2013, the company engaged the services of the immensely popular singer Teddy Afro and aligned itself with the artist's Journey of Love Tour.

Teddy Afro has fans in Ethiopia and beyond. He belongs to the Amhara, numerically the country's second-largest ethnicity. Their language is also the country's official language, which is only spoken by a quarter of the population. Most Ethiopians, more than 30 million, are Oromo. They inhabit a large region in the west, south and centre of the country and feel oppressed by both the Tigrayans and the Amhara.

Teddy Afro is critical of the authorities and prefers to sing about the heroics of Emperor Menelik II, whom many Ethiopians revere owing to his victory against the Italians in 1896. But the emperor is also controversial because of his expansionism. He doubled the size of Abyssinia, as the country was then called, by conquering large areas and imposing the Amharic language and culture on the peoples he had subjugated. There is little solid historical research, but there are reasons to assume that these conquests were accompanied by large-scale campaigns of murder and mutilation; some even call it genocide. Most of the victims were Oromo.[6]

Unsurprisingly, then, admiration for Menelik II among the Oromos is, shall we say, rather restrained, and when Teddy Afro compared the conquest of their land with a 'holy war', they'd had enough. They called for a boycott of Bedele that would last until Heineken ended its sponsorship of the singer. Like all modern activists, they started their campaign on social media. A

Facebook group attracted more than 30,000 followers in record time, and #BoycottBedele started trending on Twitter. A poster appeared on the internet depicting Hitler, Menelik II and Teddy Afro side by side, standing on a pile of skulls covered in blood pouring from bottles marked Heineken and Bedele. The caption read: 'Boycott Bedele Beer & Heineken. Stop glorifying genocide.' The influential station Radio Oromo reported on the campaign and there were plans to occupy the brewery.[7]

The singer denied having made the controversial remark—it was all a plot brought by others bent on sullying his reputation. Initially, Heineken refused to yield under pressure, but when the movement kept growing, the company changed tack.[8] It was a short-lived Journey of Love. There are no known figures describing the extent of the damage the boycott caused, but the Dutch brewer's image was definitely tarnished.

Spending scarce foreign currency on Heineken or medicines?

Heineken was not discouraged. A few months before the controversy, the construction of a brand new brewery was officially launched in Kilinto, a suburb near Addis Ababa. In the blazing sun, Doyer laid the first stone, together with the Dutch minister for foreign trade and development cooperation, Lilianne Ploumen. The minister, in a beige pantsuit and high heels, had earlier been given the red carpet treatment, flanked by a welcoming troupe of dancers. Doyer made an assessment: 'There are certainly pitfalls in fast growing markets. You must be able to take a few hits here and there.'[9]

Thanks to the new brewery, Heineken tripled its production capacity in Ethiopia. The company introduced a new brand, Walia, named after the Walia Ibex, the national football team's symbol. The message, not to be missed: Heineken exists for all Ethiopians.[10] It was an instant success. Six years after the Dutch had bought two dilapidated state breweries, they became the country's largest beer producer.

There were still a few worries though in early 2018. For instance, how could Heineken repatriate its profits from a country that had a large foreign currency deficit? A thorough analysis in the weekly *Addis Fortune* revealed that the company had developed such good relationships with the local authorities that it could claim priority when foreign currency was allocated. Ethiopia did not have the money to purchase the basic necessities for survival, but Heineken was allocated around 50 million dollars for new investments. A local bank manager was shocked: 'We have been given the order to prioritise the needs of beer producers, to the detriment of those who import life-saving medicines.'[11]

2

HISTORY

THE CONQUEST OF AFRICA

Heineken has a rich African history, which began at the tail end of the nineteenth century when it was shipping crates of beer to a few port cities. Since the 1930s, the company has been brewing beer locally. The knowledge and experience gained during all those years have laid the foundation for its enduring commercial success.

The continent has rarely disappointed the Dutch. In the 1950s, West Africa was one of the world's principal markets, and even during the disastrous 1980s and '90s, Africa kept making money for the brewer's Head Office. Heineken's secret? A tenacity few others can match. The company has proved to be inventive and able to adjust in order to circumvent the obstacles put in its way. Where others saw mainly destitution, it never lost sight of Africa's potential. But Heineken also resorted to commercial practices that even in those early days were considered controversial—or were, quite simply, illegal.

HEINEKEN IN AFRICA

Bier soll sein!

Seen from a small place like the Netherlands, the rest of the world is very large. Fame and money await those who think big and go abroad. That was certainly the conviction of Gerard Heineken when he established 'Heineken's Bierbrouwerij Maatschappij' in 1873. In short order, his beer, made in Amsterdam, was served in the grand cafés and theatres of Paris, considered the most cultured city on earth in those days. In the last decade of the century, small quantities of Heineken's beer were sent to the Dutch East Indies, Singapore, Brazil and the Caribbean.

Africa first made contact with Heineken at the Cape, run by the British at the time. Then came other European colonies, including Egypt and Algeria. Initially, exporting to the continent failed to be profitable. The quality of the beers was mediocre after the long sea voyage, it was sold in small quantities and there were countless problems, like broken bottles, theft and fierce competition from other European brewers.[1]

The importance of exports increased when crisis stalked large parts of Europe in the 1930s: dozens of breweries went bankrupt, and these far-flung foreign markets offered some respite. Exported beers were primarily to be consumed by the colonial elites, but beer merchants saw no need for discrimination: if the great and the good could afford it, they would sell it to anyone with money.

But the European authorities saw things quite differently. Until midway through the last century, Africans in British East Africa were barred from drinking imported beer, and until the 1960s black South Africans were limited to drinking what was called 'kaffir beer', an opaque drink that was only sold in the so-called beer halls.[2] Paternalism had a lot to do with it: the African had to be protected from himself and from ill-intentioned vendors, and he should not spend all his money on alcohol. But self-interest was also involved: drunkenness could lead to disorderly behaviour or awaken colonised minds. And another, rival element of self-interest raised its head: tax revenue. The colonial authorities were expected to pay for their own upkeep, and alcohol levies were an excellent way to fill the coffers.[3]

Heineken's Africa ambitions went further than just that. The company benefited from technology that enabled it to brew beer in almost any climate, thanks to the genius of Henry Pierre Heineken, the son of company founder Gerard, and a chemical engineer.[4] The first time the Dutch brewer actually set foot on the continent was in 1930, when it bought a stake in a Swiss investment firm founded by the French banker René Gaston-Dreyfus. With this move, Heineken took joint ownership of one Moroccan and two Egyptian breweries.

A little while later, Interbra went on sale. This was a Belgian holding company with breweries in France, Belgium, the Belgian Congo and Angola, among other places. Interbra was also the parent company of Cobra, an investor who had stolen Heineken's thunder by establishing a brewery in the Dutch East Indies, something the Dutch had been keen to do themselves.[5] Heineken had to make a hard choice: Was it better to take over insolvent breweries serving the domestic market or seek growth abroad? Its director at the time, Dirk Stikker, opted for the international adventure, and in 1935 his company, Gaston-Dreyfus and a Belgian partner took control of Interbra and Cobra.[6]

Disagreements arose early. Stikker held the view that his partners' opinions counted for less, since the breweries' continued operations relied to a large extent on Heineken's technical know-how. Most especially, the top manager had it in for Gaston-Dreyfus, who was—he claimed—unreliable.[7]

Matters came to a head during the Second World War. With their country under German occupation, Dutch brewers were allowed to continue producing their beer on the condition that they supplied the occupiers, in adherence to Hitler's order: *Bier soll sein!* (There must be beer!). Stikker began questioning the presence of two Jews on Cobra's Board of Directors, Gaston-Dreyfus and his French compatriot Paul Dreyfus de Gunzburg, a situation he considered undesirable. In 1940, Heineken asked the two men to relinquish their posts, which they reluctantly did.[8]

The feud between Stikker and Gaston-Dreyfus continued when the latter returned to Cobra's Board of Directors. Stikker, who was to become the Dutch foreign minister and secretary-general of NATO, was far less the diplomat in private when describing his Jewish partner: 'I had lost the memory of his fantastic nose and [I noticed that] his despicable habit of using his hands and handkerchief to constantly mess with that splendid piece of equipment had not disappeared.'[9] At the end of the 1940s, the director finally got his way when Gaston-Dreyfus surrendered his stake in the business.[10]

Underdeveloped and promising

When the German occupation of the Netherlands came to an end in 1945, Heineken had no idea how its African breweries had survived the intervening years. Surprisingly well, as it turned out. Damage was limited, and some places had done a roaring trade. In Egypt, for instance, production had more than quintupled, thanks to thirsty Allied Forces. 'Beer and oil kept the war machine going,' it was recorded.[11]

Heineken used the unexpected windfall to build a new brewery in Lagos, the capital of British Nigeria. In tandem with United Africa Company (UAC, a Unilever subsidiary), Heineken created Nigerian Brewery (singular at first, later plural: Nigerian Breweries), and in 1949 the first bottle of Star left the premises.[12] The new brand became a huge success, and Heineken/UAC decided to build more breweries in Kumasi (Gold Coast, today's Ghana), Freetown (Sierra Leone) and Moundou (Chad).

The Belgian Congo also brought good news. The Belgian colonists who were running the brewery in Leopoldville, which was to become Kinshasa, claimed that the local Primus beer tasted so good that 'anyone importing beer from Europe would find life pretty difficult here'.[13] Appreciation of the local beer stood in stark contrast with how the local population was viewed, as Heineken deemed the Congolese to be extremely underdeveloped:

> Whatever one's opinion on the matter, the negro is, on a cultural scale, at a much lower level than the Javanese. ... Whatever work there is, the women perform it. They are entirely second tier, similar to the time of the Batavians ... Whenever the man goes to work, it is only for his own pleasure, not in respect of the work itself but because of the pay he receives. And because this pleasure largely consists of drinking beer, breweries consider this the promised land. It is said that in the rural stores 70 percent of trade now consists of beer and ... that 25 per cent of the negro's income is spent on beer.[14]

This was incentive enough for Heineken to build three more breweries in the vast colony. Elsewhere in the region, new factories opened in Gisenyi and Usumbura (now Bujumbura) in another Belgian colony called Ruanda-Urundi, Brazzaville in French Congo and in Luanda, capital of Portuguese-run Angola.[15]

After the war, Heineken's export markets looked decidedly bullish. In large European countries, brewers found it hard to satisfy their domestic markets; smaller nations tended towards export—the Danes, for instance, sent almost all of their Carlsberg and Tuborg to the rest of Europe. German competition had been destroyed in the war or struck by an export ban.[16] Heineken, another exporter from a diminutive European country, benefited from its collaboration with the illustrious duo Norman Eastwood and Bill Sharples. These two were every inch the stereotypical colonial Englishmen, with the khaki tropical costume, the pith helmet in the blazing sun and, of course, the stiff upper lip.[17] In the early 1950s, the company sent more than 100,000 hectolitres to Nigeria and the Gold Coast, more than six times its exports to the United States. This was the time when half of all the profits made on exports came from Africa. Just 15 per cent of the returns still came from the Netherlands.[18]

Heineken had to maintain its guard against fresh competition. Earlier than expected, the Germans returned with their popular brand Beck's. In Nigeria, the company responded adequately. 'We must immerse ourselves in a country where we sell such a large proportion of our product,' an internal report said. 'The only way this can be done is with an organisation of our own.'[19]

That organisation arrived in 1958, headed by the flamboyant Gerard van Os van Delden, well known for his 'phenomenal thirst' and 'unrivalled beer-selling abilities'. A former colleague claims that he was such a smooth talker he could sell a crate of Heineken to a total abstainer. He created a system of mobile brigades, some fifty African salesmen driving Volkswagen Beetles with the mission to recapture the coastal cities. This was meticulously done. They 'worked' every neighbourhood, every street, every shop, which meant that everything and everybody in the area was covered in the green Heineken paraphernalia; parties lasted well into the night. By 1960, Heineken had regained its position as top importer.[20]

There were other worries, though, such as the so-called surfboats. These were rowing boats that carried the beer ashore from the big ships of the *Holland West-Afrika Lijn* anchored in shallow ports. There was no shortage of theft and damage. A clearly astonished export manager reported:

> The negroes in the surfboats do not lift our crates from the platforms, they shove them and then throw them down. ... I had heard about theft in the surfboats, but what I saw in reality was ten times worse than I had imagined. ... There was no supervision, apart from one

misshapen, short-sighted negro who was supposed to fulfil that role but who lacked the character to put an end to this state of affairs.

A Dutch compatriot working for the shipping company had once tried to get the police involved, but 'the net result had been that these policemen arrived on shore completely drunk'.[21]

Notwithstanding occasional setbacks such as these, Heineken's strategy materialised bit by bit: the Dutch were brewing a perfectly consumable mass product on African soil, like Primus in Central Africa, Star in the Western region and Stella in Egypt. The population, having grown up with local beverages, became acquainted with clear European beer and would—as soon as purchasing power permitted—be charmed into consuming Heineken, handing the company huge margins on its sales. This strategy, still in place today, put Heineken ahead of the competition.[22]

Obstinate 'black rascals'

In the mid-1950s, the Dutch were riding high, but then they were confronted with a new phenomenon: Africa for the Africans. From reading the reports, it becomes clear that Heineken was at best lukewarm about the independence movements. The beer brewer feared a drop in living standards in Belgian Congo, and in Kenya the company complained bitterly that Nairobi, 'a virtually perfect European city', had fallen prey to robberies and violence. 'That small group of black rascals is making Kenya very unsafe,' was the reference a sales representative made to the Mau Mau Rebellion of the Kikuyu people against British colonial rule. He made allusions to a solution: a tough colonial response, if not genocide. 'Curious to find out whether the English will ever prevail without exterminating the one and a half million Kikuyus (it's what they're doing but only on a limited scale because the Labour Party is against it).'[23]

In the Portuguese colony of Mozambique, company representatives noted the absence of the 'colour bar', so evident in neighbouring South Africa. 'Still, one hardly sees Negroes in the European establishments,' one of them wrote. 'The population has been kept in a backward state and is extremely poor, so the financial side of things ensures automatic segregation, which is, after all, the desired state of affairs.'[24] Heineken applauded the regime of dictator António Salazar, who held on to the colonial empire until the bitter end:

> The political calm that reigns here can be gratefully attributed to the strong hand with which Portugal governs its colonies. The Portuguese troops provide ample proof that the country has no intention to simply release its colonies and instead wants [Mozambique] to be a bulwark against the surging black race, together with Rhodesia, South Africa and Angola.[25]

Yet Heineken was unable to halt the march of history. One by one, the colonies declared independence, and the multinational looked on wearily as young nations took protectionist measures, designed to rapidly develop their domestic industries. High duties were imposed to discourage imports, and sometimes they were banned outright, which meant—in Heineken's terms—the end of the 'golden export story'.[26]

The emphasis shifted to local production, where there were opportunities. Many a new leader found that part of being an independent nation was having your own beer brand. After all, two of them had emerged from the beer industry: Julius Nyerere, the president of Tanzania, and Patrice Lumumba, Congo's prime minister.[27] The latter was a commercial director at Bracongo, Heineken's competitor, in the mid-1950s. 'Patrice would give away bottles of beer in popular neighbourhoods,' writes Belgian author David Van Reybrouck. 'He brought beer and promised freedom. He sated the masses and made them thirsty for more. Emancipation started with a free glass of beer.'[28]

While it was true that the new breweries were managed by Europeans and continued to produce their lager following European recipes, the young nations still saw it as *their* beer. It is ironic that in countries that had freed themselves from the colonial yoke, clear European beer became a symbol of modernity and progress, while the local non-transparent brew was dismissed as old-fashioned.

So Heineken could continue brewing its beers in Africa but was facing pressure to smash the colonial structure. The new governments were of the view that the era of an all-white management issuing orders to an all-black staff had to come to an end. Shortly after its independence, Ghana established a quota for expats, but Heineken refused to cooperate. 'Perhaps bribery would work, but then on a fairly large scale,' one employee suggested.[29]

As Heineken was considering paying bribes in a manner that suggested this was routine (even though it was forbidden in the Netherlands), the authorities adopted *Africanisation* as their new battle cry. Some governments demanded participation; in Nasser's Egypt and Mobutu's Zaire, the end point was wholesale nationalisation. These developments in the 1960s and '70s compelled many Western companies to say goodbye to Africa.[30] Heineken, on the other hand, adapted. The company brought African talent to the Netherlands for training and internships, making sure that they could fill the top jobs in their own countries.

'Pumping' illicit money from Africa

There were more adjustments. Shortly after independence, a system was set up that enabled illicit money to be siphoned off. This happened within Interbra, where following Gaston-Dreyfus' departure Heineken was working with the Belgian Banque Lambert. Interbra used a system that consisted of two types of profit: one part that was officially declared to the local revenue authorities and the rest, often much larger, which was hidden. Out of sight of the authorities, this larger part was then transferred to a holding in fiscally attractive Switzerland.[31] As a result, the breweries continued to be highly profitable throughout the wave of independence declarations, while the new African governments were swindled out of much-needed tax revenues.

Sometimes, the local tax authorities attempted to strike back. In the early 1970s, the top manager at Bralima, a Congolese subsidiary, needed an entire month to balance the books. He had to rewrite parts of the administration to avoid being caught, as an audit was forthcoming. 'The major problem is finding acceptable explanations for the amounts of money Bralima has transferred to Interbra,' a memo says:

> He now has attributed these transfers to (technical) fees, compensation paid to Interbra for the use of the Primus brand name based on a (fictitious) royalty contract that has been backdated to 1963, charges incurred by Interbra etcetera. The fiscal balance now fully reflects transfers abroad, even though there is still the distinct possibility that the tax authorities will refuse to accept some of these expenses. However, there is no longer any fear of being accused of fraud.[32]

Every accounting trick in the book was used to hide these fraudulent practices.

In the 1960s, the size of revenues channelled away from Africa became a problem. 'The enterprise is very profitable,' wrote the director of Heineken International. 'Apart from the results declared on the balance sheet, significant sums arrive in Switzerland by way of the *marché parallèle*; it is impractical to pay these out to the shareholders'[33] (fig. 1.3). In 1962, Bralima's coffers contained 20 million guilders (the equivalent of 65 million dollars at today's exchange rate) in 'spare' money, four times the profits the company made worldwide during that financial year.[34]

Heineken was studying ways to convert the illicit money, as they put it, from 'Swiss black into Belgian white'. External Interbra shareholders were also a cause for concern. Taken together, the three firms, Heineken, Banque Lambert and Unilever, which acquired a small stake in the holding in 1965, held a minority of the total capital.[35] The majority was thus freely transferable, which not only rendered the enterprise vulnerable to takeover bids but also forced it to be transparent during shareholder meetings.[36] It was of the utmost importance to Heineken that Interbra continued to function as a 'smokescreen' between the opaque practices conducted in Africa and the main company.[37] Unilever, on the other hand, disagreed entirely with these 'manipulations' and feared that they could prejudice the relationship with the Congolese government.[38] Congolese palm oil was an order of magnitude more important to Unilever's interests than the brewery.

It was an attitude that upset Heineken. '[According to Unilever] everything should be done within legal boundaries: dividends, technical and/or commercial remunerations,' a board member wrote in 1967. 'I immediately pointed out that our organisations in Brussels and Rotterdam would not exist were it not for the money we had pumped in from Congo over the years. It is therefore unthinkable that this state of affairs be changed'[39] (fig. 1.2). He was probably referring to Interbra in Brussels and the Technical Overseas Management Department (Technisch Beheer Buitenland), which in 1963 had been merged with Heineken's Rotterdam-based Technical Management.[40] It leaves the impression that two important internal organisations at that time owed their existence to illicit financial flows from Africa, an indication of their importance. Unilever subsequently withdrew. Heineken and Lambert went on to have a candid conversation about their whitewashing practices with André Oleffe of the Belgian Banking Commission. The regulator was 'perplexed'

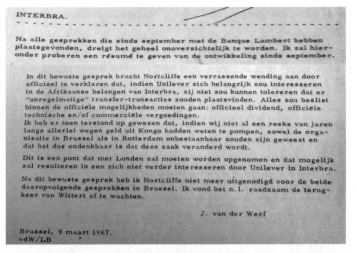

INTERBRA.

Na alle gesprekken die sinds september met de Banque Lambert hebben plaatsgevonden, dreigt het geheel onoverzichtelijk te worden. Ik zal hieronder proberen een résumé te geven van de ontwikkeling sinds september.

In dit bewuste gesprek bracht Nortcliffe een verrassende wending aan door officieel te verklaren dat, indien Unilever zich belangrijk zou interesseren in de Afrikaanse belangen van Interbra, zij niet zou kunnen tolereren dat er "onregelmatige" transfer-transacties zouden plaatsvinden. Alles zou beslist binnen de officiële mogelijkheden moeten gaan: officieel dividend, officiële technische en/of commerciële vergoedingen.
Ik heb er toen terstond op gewezen dat, indien wij niet al een reeks van jaren langs allerlei wegen geld uit Kongo hadden weten te pompen, zowel de organisatie in Brussel als in Rotterdam onbestaanbaar zouden zijn geweest en dat het dus ondenkbaar is dat deze zaak veranderd wordt.

Dit is een punt dat met Londen zal moeten worden opgenomen en dat mogelijk zal resulteren in een zich niet verder interesseren door Unilever in Interbra.

Na dit bewuste gesprek heb ik Nortcliffe niet meer uitgenodigd voor de beide daaropvolgende gesprekken in Brussel. Ik vond het n.1. raadzaam de terugkeer van Wittert af te wachten.

J. van der Werf

Brussel, 9 maart 1967.
vdW/LB

"[According to Unilever] everything should be done within legal boundaries: the dividend payments, technical and/or commercial fees.

I immediately pointed out that our organisations in Brussels and Rotterdam would not exist were it not for the money we had pumped in from Congo over the years."

1. Wat Interbra voor ons betekent:

Interbra is een houdstermaatschappij, waarin zijn ondergebracht:

als 100% deelnemingen:
- Brasseries, Limonaderies et Malteries du Congo "Bralima"
- Brasserie de Brazzaville
- Brasserie et Limonaderie de Burundi "Brarudi"
- Brasserie et Limonaderie de Rwanda "Bralirwa"

als 80% deelneming:
- Bouteillerie de Kinshasa "Boukin"

als 27% deelneming:
- Nova Empresa de Cervejas de Angola "Nocal"

alsmede een 2% deelneming in:
- Armement et Pêche Maritime - Matadi.

De onderneming is zeer winstgevend.
Naast de op de balans gedeklareerde resultaten komen via de "Marché parallèle" aanzienlijke bedragen, die bezwaarlijk aan de aandeelhouders kunnen worden uitgekeerd, in Zwitserland binnen.

Als gevolg van deze situatie ontstond gaandeweg een dispariteit tussen de beurskoers van het aandeel Interbra en de eigenlijke waarde ervan.
Door over het boekjaar 1969 een geconsolideerde balans te publiceren, is deze dispariteit belangrijk verminderd.

"[Interbra] is very profitable. Apart from the results declared on the balance sheet, significant sums arrive in Switzerland by way of the *marché parallèle*; it is impractical to pay these out to the shareholders."

Fig. 1.1–1.2: Two internal memos on Interbra (1967 and 1970)

when he was told that there was a plan to integrate Interbra in a Belgian oil company, only for Heineken and Lambert to buy it back later. Oleffe made it clear that 'the Commission would consider such an operation exceptionally improper'.[41]

In the end, Interbra was incorporated into Compagnie Lambert, the parent company of the Belgian bank. The advantage of the move was that—'with a deftly edited statement and a well-managed meeting'—Interbra's shareholders' would be rendered 'virtually powerless'.[42] Not only could they forget about a large chunk of Interbra's African profits; they were also more or less forced into selling their shares, thus ensuring that Interbra and its accounting tricks no longer had to suffer the presence of prying eyes.

The operation completed, Heineken and Lambert then divided their African possessions among themselves, each getting half. In 1971, these two halves were merged and became Ibecor. At the helm was the very influential Paul Bodart, father-in-law of another Belgian who would become a powerful force within Heineken: Jean-François van Boxmeer. Ibecor probably constitutes the most secretive contribution to Heineken's profitability. More on this shortly.

According to apartheid's letter and spirit

But first, to 1960s South Africa, where European dominance was showing no signs of weakening. Heineken was smelling opportunities there, but it knew that investing would be controversial, especially since the Sharpeville massacre of March 1960. Sharpeville was a township to the south of Johannesburg, where white police had violently repressed a protest against far-reaching limits to the freedom of movement for non-whites. The police killed sixty-nine demonstrators and wounded 180. The world was finally confronted with apartheid's true face, and the United

Nations called for a trade boycott. The West largely ignored this call, but Heineken was of course aware that investing in South Africa at this particular moment would be risky.[43]

For a moment, Heineken was in doubt about attaching its own name to the project, 'in view of the country's current reputation because of racial discrimination'. However, this would mean that in the upcoming partnership with Whitbread of Great Britain and a local businessman the firm would play a minor role; this prospect appealed even less to the Dutch.[44]

In December 1963, more than a year after the call for a boycott and only a few months after the incarceration of ANC activist Nelson Mandela on Robben Island, Whitbread South Africa was established. Heineken took a minority share and negotiated a fee for technical support. Optimism prevailed:

> The economy is moving and the standard of living is rising for all races. We must realise, though, that there is hardly any country in the world that has not declared itself opposed to the current regime in South Africa and that the countries closest to home [in north-western Europe] are its most fervent opponents.[45]

Heineken built the brewery in total compliance with apartheid's regulations. There were separate canteens, medical posts and dressing rooms. The toilet blocks were split into three: white men, white women, blacks. White salaries far outstripped those of the black workforce. In 1965, Heineken's executive belaboured the point: 'Be careful not to act in opposition to the letter/spirit of apartheid!'[46] In the meantime, Mandela and seven other ANC activists had been sentenced to life in prison, triggering more international indignation and louder calls for sanctions.

The South African adventure ended in failure. Cooperation between the partners did not go well, and the competitor, South African Breweries (SAB), proved a tenacious adversary on the domestic market—half a century later, Heineken would once again witness SAB's doggedness. Not at all in keeping with their character, the Dutch decided to call it a day earlier than they had planned. And that, with hindsight, may well have been the silver lining because shortly after their inglorious departure the economic sanctions against South Africa started to bite, and Western companies were put under serious pressure to divest. If Whitbread and Heineken (perhaps using its own global brand name) had succeeded in positioning themselves more firmly, it would have been difficult to dissociate, and Heineken's reputation would likely have sustained damage similar to what eventually happened to other companies, like Shell, BP and Barclays.

Still, the beer brewer continued doing business in South Africa because SAB produced the Amstel brand, property of Heineken, under a licence agreement. In this way, the company contributed to the regime's fiscal revenue and—according to critics—its international standing. The Dutch brewer deliberately failed to mention the licence in its annual reports, in order to avoid attracting attention. But the World Council of Churches blacklisted Heineken, and the Dutch trade union umbrella FNV did away with its investment in the company. In 1987, Heineken almost gave in: it agreed to rescind the licence or donate the income to charity. In the end, though, the company considered the risk acceptable and allowed SAB to continue producing Amstel.[47] Early this century, Heineken re-entered the South African market and wanted to take back its Amstel brand, but the people at SAB did not see the point of returning the household name they had created. We will cover the ensuing battle later.

Brewing beer for the Mobutu clan

As more African countries gained independence, Heineken shifted its attention towards Western markets, although at the beginning of the 1970s the continent still represented one-third of its overall beer production.[48] Almost ten years later, the company's assessment was that Africa continued to 'contribute significantly to profits' through dividends, technical fees and licences. 'Our policy must therefore be to hold on to these participations and maximise revenues from technical fees.'[49]

Easier said than done. One of the most difficult ordeals the company went through was Bralima's nationalisation under Mobutu, in the early 1970s. Buoyed by high commodity prices, Congo was doing very well under his strict rule. Kinshasa was alive, and there was beer aplenty. In 1974, the city hosted the legendary boxing match between Muhammad Ali and George Foreman (*The Rumble in the Jungle*), and that same year the breweries reached peak production—5 million hectolitres, a volume that would only be equalled forty years later but with a population that was three times larger.[50] Heineken rejoiced: 'Congo's economic situation is excellent and Mr Mobutu's leadership seems to be exemplary.'[51]

Joseph-Désiré Mobutu, 'the Leopard', was keenly aware that more wealth would not suffice to keep this vast and fragmented country together. The nation needed self-confidence and had to shed its colonial past. In 1971, he changed his country's name, its currency and its largest river into Zaire and adopted the name Mobutu Sese Seko Kuku Ngbendu Wa Za Banga for himself: Mobutu the indomitable warrior who goes from victory to victory.[52]

These symbolic changes failed to affect the dominance of international business, and Mobutu, the indomitable warrior, decided to grasp that particular nettle. He opted for nationalisation. The state first demanded a small stake in Bralima, basically a fine for the earlier accounting fraud. Heineken director Dr A. Miedema was incensed, but his case was very weak. 'I did not want to pursue the matter because Bralima is far from clean but I also wished to mention that this is a rather strange way to establish state participation in a private enterprise.'[53]

Bralima attempted to placate the government by nominating two Zairians to the Board of Directors—'just for the *couleur locale*', as the Head Office in Amsterdam reassuringly said—but in the end it was all in vain.[54] In 1975, Mobutu took possession of the entire enterprise and appointed a certain Litho at the top. Few at Bralima will forget his first week in office. On Monday, he requisitioned the top manager's office, but when he discovered that the office of the brewery director was larger, he installed himself there instead. On Tuesday, he decided to stop talking with expats and would henceforth rely on Zairean managers to pass down his orders. On Wednesday, he relegated all expats to the rank of advisors, whom he would rarely consult. On Thursday, he terminated all bank accounts used for payment of imported commodities and spare parts, an important source of revenue for Heineken. And on Friday he forced out the distributors in Kinshasa who ensured the arrival of 3 million crates of beer per month at their destinations.[55]

This new way of doing business was no success. Heineken, meanwhile, had understood that Litho was none other than the leader of the Ngbandi, Mobutu's ethnic group. In terms of hierarchy, he was placed above the indomitable warrior. 'The latter considers Mr Litho as his uncle, to whom he owes some sort of obedience. It should be clear, then, that Mr Litho is a very powerful man.'[56]

Heineken realised that thanks to Litho the Bralima brewery was now located firmly 'within the Mobutu clan's interest group, the group of families who for several years have been exploiting Zaïre for their own benefit'.[57] Within one year, according to the Dutch, Litho misappropriated almost 10 million zaires of company money, or a little less than 50 million guilders (the equivalent of 70 million current dollars). It is unknown how much of that money he channelled to Mobutu or the Zairean Army—the company suspected that both cashed in.[58] The Dutch brewer could have ended operations there and then and taken its losses but instead allowed itself to be used by a dictatorial megalomaniac, hoping for better days.

'This regime will come to an end,' wrote Miedema in a memo that oozed desperation:

> It can take a few years but this cannot possibly endure. Our biggest interest is, I think, to work towards keeping the company in the best possible state without losing money—preferably with some profit for us—so that when times change we and our partners can begin afresh from the cleanest possible point of departure.[59]

That was 30 May 1975, twenty-two years and three months before the Leopard's fall.

The difficulties of making money legally

The 1960s and '70s were a mixed bag: hope and a certain level of affluence in many parts of the continent, dictatorial rule and war in others. The Portuguese colonies and Zimbabwe were still fighting for their independence. Ruthless dictators like Idi Amin of Uganda, 'Emperor' Bokassa of the Central African Republic and Guinea's Sékou Touré killed thousands. Civil war reared its head, and the deadly failed secession of Nigeria's Biafra region caught the attention of the world. But the mood and the physical reality were mostly upbeat, symbolised—for instance—by hugely ambitious building sprees in many of the continent's capitals.

This began to change dramatically in the 1980s and '90s as more bad news (dictators, civil wars, mass kilings) occurred, from Sierra Leone and Liberia to Somalia's collapse and the genocide in Rwanda. The outside world no longer perceived Africa as a place of promise, but rather as a continent of endless crises: coups, civil wars, child soldiers, refugees, epidemics.

Heineken became doubtful too. Until 1985, its African joint ventures were still selling more beer than its subsidiaries in

North and South America combined, but the Dutch brewer observed that it had become increasingly difficult 'to make money "legally" in Africa'.[60] Dividends and royalties were seldom paid, and the payment of fees for technical assistance and other services was becoming erratic. What Heineken needed to do was to concentrate on secondary sources of income. The commissions paid on delivery of raw materials and spare parts were lucrative, also because the price cuts the company could negotiate as a wholesaler were not passed on to the subsidiaries. This was called a 'veto'. And yes, 'massaging the authorities'—probably a euphemism for paying bribes—was sometimes necessary in order to obtain hard currency for paying on delivery; the company took this in its stride.[61]

The revenues that arrived in this fashion were 'very substantial' and had 'the potential for strong growth ... in the coming years'. There were worries too: more and more people inside and outside Heineken became involved in these controversial practices, and it was paramount that the Board of Directors should not get caught up in any possible controversy. This is where Ibecor came in, Interbra's successor. The Belgian partner had retired from the business in 1982, leaving the company as a full Heineken subsidiary, still run by Van Boxmeer's father-in-law Bodart.

Ibecor became 'a vehicle to close the gaps in the veto circuit' and 'a way to keep the Africa management activities at arm's length from the Board of Directors'.[62]

It is largely thanks to Ibecor that Heineken continued to make money in Africa, even in the difficult 1980s and '90s, when many of its partners and competitors made life much harder for the company. This was the case, for instance, in Angola, where in 1985 the government passed a law that brought all commodity purchases into government hands. For Heineken, this meant a substantial loss of income, and that the country stopped being profitable.[63] By the end of the 1980s, Ibecor was an important contributor to the millions of guilders that Heineken continued to take home from battered and bruised Africa.[64]

During a conversation at Head Office, Van Boxmeer recalls that European agricultural subsidies were also part of Heineken's revenues from Africa. 'We exported European barley malt to Africa and part of that subsidy went to us, the buyer.'[65]

In short, Heineken managed to keep its head above water, and the company continued to see bright spots on a continent where stories of doom multiplied. It kept a keen eye for the golden opportunity, and after a few failed attempts secured a stake in a brewery in Cameroon, one of Africa's great beer nations.[66] The year was 1984.

However, optimism was usually short-lived during this time, and at the end of the 1980s even the usually optimistic board members at Heineken did not know where the light at the end of the tunnel would be. 'Africa's prospects are frankly depressing: limitations on commodity transports, currency devaluations, shrinking purchasing power and Aids.'[67]

Rising Africa

It did get depressing. Nigeria fell prey to two military coups. Sierra Leone, Burundi and Congo-Brazzaville became the theatres of long and brutal civil wars. In Zaire, Mobutu was finally pushed from his throne in 1997 by Laurent-Désiré Kabila, triggering a war that continues today. And in Rwanda the conflict between Hutus and Tutsis led to the genocide, in which the Dutch beer brewer played an important role, as we shall see.

Even this catastrophe changed nothing about Heineken's determination. 'The Rwandan situation will not result in us withdrawing from the African continent,' according to its director at the time, Karel Vuursteen. 'We cannot simply close a brewery and withdraw from a country. The investments are much too high for that,' adds Jean Louis Homé, a former Africa director:

We don't just look at the financial aspects of the business. It's part of the Heineken culture not to give up too easily. Heineken is not an enterprise that is looking for quick money. We have a long term strategy and a long term commitment to the workers. This is Heineken's strength and the people in Africa know this.[68]

A dedicated salesman, in the best Dutch traditions—this is how the beer brewer likes to present himself.

In the end, the skies slowly cleared over the continent and suddenly 'rising Africa' was being universally acclaimed as 'the place to be' for future business. Heineken no longer saw Africa as 'the periphery of our business' (Van Boxmeer) but began to take the continent seriously; '1999 was the turning point for us,' a former manager says:

In the 1980s and '90s Africa was the place where you did not strictly have to play by the rules. You could do things 'the African way'. But that year was the moment we no longer considered Africa a backward region. Our approach became professional, with modern efficient breweries. Africa was in the game.

Homé recalls the ambitious programme Heineken developed to change mentality and management styles in Africa.

We brought 750 African managers to Amsterdam for intensive training. We wanted to be rid of the postcolonial approach, which you still see so often around Africa. We hadn't been immune either. We wanted them to carry their own responsibility and participate in forging the strategy.

Still, it remained trial and error in Africa; risks and investments were kept to a minimum.[69] In 2004, Heineken sold the shares it held in breweries in Chad and Angola and largely withdrew from its old bastion, Ghana. 'There were times that we wondered why we went through all this trouble,' one source recalls. 'The interest on savings was high at the time and money in the bank was more profitable than investing in Africa.'

Van Boxmeer's appointment as president of the Board of Directors in 2005 brought a man with a passion for Africa to the top of the company. He put the continent back on the map with a series of takeovers and expansions. Heineken set foot in Algeria, Tunisia, Ethiopia and Ivory Coast and invested hundreds of millions of dollars in Lubumbashi (Congo), Sedibeng (South Africa), Addis Ababa (Ethiopia) and Abidjan (Ivory Coast). Mozambique is likely to follow in 2019, and opportunities for growth are also being examined in Francophone West Africa.

For more than a century, Heineken has shown an impressive amount of perseverance and tenacity in the most difficult of times. The rewards have often been rich. At the same time, fraud and other controversial practices have played a significant role in that survival strategy. It is difficult if not impossible to ascertain whether these factors have been critical to the company's decision to remain active in Africa and whether or not they have made the difference for its competitors that abandoned the continent. This would require more historical research. But there is no doubt that history and the present would have looked quite different without the millions that Heineken—in its own words—pumped out of Africa.

NIGERIA

INTEGRATION, IN EVERY POSSIBLE WAY

In February 2017, Nico Vervelde gave an interview to the Dutch weekly *Elsevier*. The magazine has a regular feature, which consists of inviting someone from the business world to lunch and letting him or her talk about their life and work in a relaxed atmosphere. Vervelde, Heineken's managing director in Nigeria, was interviewed in the Lagos Radisson Blu; over a club sandwich with bacon and French fries, he talked freely about his life as an expat ('I love an international environment'), the phenomenal success of Heineken's subsidiary Nigerian Breweries and his love for golf and jogging. He had been living in the country for seven years and had no plans to move. 'I'm having a great time in Nigeria.'[1]

For Heineken, Nigeria is by far the most important African country: it delivers about half of the brewer's continent-wide turnover. It's the law of numbers here: Lagos, the economic capital, is the heart of a conurbation that 20 million people call home. Nigeria as a whole is about 200 million strong; no other African nation comes anywhere near. Since the turn of the century, it has stabilised somewhat and has become substantially more affluent, and this means Nigeria is turning into a potentially vast consumer market.

Heineken has been here since the late 1940s and controls two-thirds of the beer market. The recent drop in oil prices has meant that its profits have slumped a little, but in good times the gross margins are above 50 per cent; only Mexico is more profitable. In absolute terms, selling beer in Nigeria is more lucrative than in Great Britain, even though consumption in the latter is 2.5 times higher.[2]

Heineken is proud of its Nigerian empire that mainly thrives on the sale of local brands: Star, Goldberg and Gulder. The company has managed to become part of society, as was advocated as far back as the 1950s. 'We identify with Star, it's part of us,' confirms a local journalist who works for *This Day*. 'I admire them because they have always stayed, even in difficult times. Nigeria is not an easy country, and many foreign investors prefer going to Ghana—it's calmer there. Heineken has always believed in us.'

Madame Vervelde can arrange a contract

What the *Elsevier* story does not say is that, one month before the interview, Vervelde was interrogated at the headquarters of the federal police in Abuja. The questions he had to answer there were rather more challenging. The police wanted to know everything about a notorious corruption case in which his wife was the prime suspect and he a key witness.[3] The case made headlines in Nigeria and internationally but was never followed up.[4]

And then, unexpectedly, Vervelde resigns in the month of May and transfers to Singapore for a role that is yet to be specified. There is no successor, the papers say.[5] A former colleague is astonished: 'Nico wanted to finish his career in Nigeria. He knew that at his age the chances of moving up at Heineken were slim.' There is no mention of the corruption case. What is going on here?

Let's go back to 2013 and a jet-set party in Lagos, attended by oil trader Alhaji Amadu Sule. On that occasion, he is introduced to Clémentine, a woman he describes as 'not young but stunning'. She gives him a business card in the name of her company, Limitless Mind Africa, specialising in musical productions, conferences, artist management 'and more'.[6]

This is not an exaggeration. Clémentine does more, much more. Consultancies, for instance, and managing a network of excellent connections. Would Sule consider becoming the oil supplier for Nigerian Breweries? Coming from the Islamic north and remembering that his recently departed father had always forbidden him to do business with alcohol producers, he hesitates. But he is not that strict, and besides, it dawns on him that this is not a matter of a few barrels of diesel for some lorries. Most of the ten breweries run by this beer giant rely completely on generators that consume millions of litres every year. Of course he is interested!

But what about the open tender? As a listed company and part of a multinational with operations around the world, Nigerian Breweries has strict procedures for these kinds of contracts. Nothing to worry about, assures Clémentine. In exchange for the correct fee, she will arrange everything.

One of the things she arranges is a meeting with Nico Vervelde, on the Radisson Blu terrace, clearly a spot where the beer chief likes to relax. Sule is impressed by Clémentine's persistence, and he leaves the meeting feeling positive. It is only when he arrives home and puts the two business cards next to each other that he notices they carry the same surname. But he considers it impolite to enquire further.

Shortly thereafter, Sule is invited to the Vervelde home in upmarket Banana Island. Here, he also meets Jasper Hamaker, the man who runs the money side of things at Nigerian Breweries. Sule: 'The financial director saw opportunities for me.'

And indeed there were. In the autumn of 2013, TMDK Oil Traders, Sule's company, became the oil supplier for the Kaduna factory and Ama Brewery, near Enugu, Heineken's largest brewery on the continent. The contract was for three years. Sule claims that he had an unwritten agreement with Clémentine for another two years. Nigerian Breweries was expected to buy 3 million litres per month, making the entire deal worth some 60 million dollars. They agreed on a first payment: 200,000 dollars, in cash. 'I paid and she chucked out the previous supplier,' the businessman recalls.

But the honeymoon did not last. Irritation arose when Sule was accused of delivering sub-standard oil, which supposedly caused a fire in the Enugu mega-brewery. An internal inquiry concluded that there was nothing wrong with his product and rumours circulated that the fire may well have been the result of arson, an attempt to tarnish his name. Then followed a drastic reduction in the monthly orders, as the breweries made a partial change from oil to gas, a setback for Sule.

The oil trader says that this was in breach of the deal he had made with Clémentine, who also kept asking for more money. And that was not even the end of it. 'Everybody had to be bought off,' he says, 'also at the lower levels.'

A Dutch source confirms that suppliers routinely pay bribes. 'A guard charges you less than a dollar to let you in. At a slightly higher level you pay a few dollars and once you're at the level of the financial controller 10,000 dollars is the bare minimum if you expect to get paid. That's how it works here.'

But now Sule has had enough. His people, the Fulani, are proud and headstrong, and he comes from an influential family. They were messing with the wrong guy.

When the controller and a colleague demand another 20,000 dollars, he pays. But this time he does it through the bank, with proof of payment. He then confronts the top management of Nigerian Breweries and the auditing department. The company is forced to react: both employees are fired, another internal inquiry gets underway, leading to more dismissals. Amsterdam Head Office is also informed and starts its own investigation.[7]

But still Clémentine Vervelde—nicknamed 'Madame'—kept asking Sule for money. According to the businessman, the total amount was 878,000 dollars at the time he discovered that Nigerian Breweries was swapping his company for another. He claims to know that the company in question is Forte Oil, a long-standing Heineken supplier, but the beer brewer insists that it is a different supplier. In the end, he found himself deprived of the extra two years of contractual oil supply that had been promised and for which he says he paid 'Madame' an extra commission.

Next: an angry visit to the Vervelde residence, where Sule told the man of the house that his wife was playing games with him. He also intimated that he had proof she was taking money from Forte Oil. According to Sule, the reply amounted to a threat. Vervelde is supposed to have said: 'Don't you dare take on Nigerian Breweries. Nobody does that, we're too powerful. You had a three-year contract. That's over now. It's best you leave quietly.'

The Criminal Investigation and Intelligence Department

The Federal Police headquarters is located at the Louis Edet House in Abuja, named after the first Nigerian inspector general, who took over from the British in 1964. It is an imposing white edifice, standing in an area with many other public sector buildings. The president resides in the Aso Rock Presidential Villa, a few minutes' drive away; Parliament and the High Court are also nearby.

Louis Edet House—and more precisely the Criminal Investigation and Intelligence Department—is where Clémentine and

Nico Vervelde presented themselves on 23 January 2017. The department is a special elite unit of the Nigerian Police, which also works on the case of the Boko Haram terrorist organisation. Sule was suing Clémentine for fraud (see fig. 2). The case was taken seriously enough for her to be named as the suspect. Nico, some other board members and managers at Nigerian Breweries were heard as witnesses.

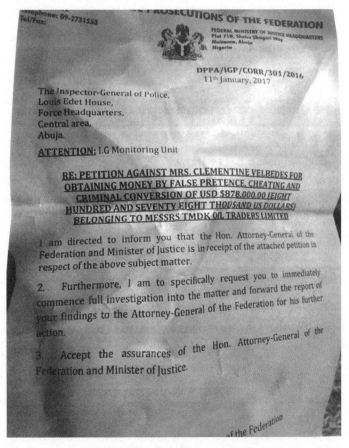

Fig 2: Petition against Clémentine Vervelde, Nigeria

The Nigerian Police motto is 'The police is your friend', but on this day in January that didn't apply to the Verveldes. The commissioner ignored telephone calls from influential compatriots, recruited by the beer brewer's top management (according to an internal source) to put pressure on the police to drop the case. Before the interrogation, Nigerian Breweries' lawyer had been issuing threats: 'This is a large company. Whatever it is you are planning to do, I'd be careful.' However, the police were not to be intimidated. Insiders think they were in possession of a very large body of evidence, partly because the phones of those directly involved had been tapped.

Nico had a hard time. 'After twelve hours of questioning he looked terrible, he had suddenly aged ten years,' one of those present remembers. With Clémentine, the impact was more difficult to ascertain, but she certainly suffered too. From the same source: 'The commissioner played a very smart game. He sat at his desk, behind a huge pile of papers. She could not handle the situation and just kept on talking. He was feeding her, waiting for the exact right moment to give her another morsel by asking the right question.'

At first, Clémentine denied everything, but in the end she admitted that she had taken money. For others, she added. The commissioner piled on: 'Well, in that case I would imagine that it's in your interest, too, that we pursue our investigation thoroughly.'

Relieved, Clémentine wanted to go home, but first someone had to be found who was willing to act as a guarantor for her bail; failing that, she would have to spend the night in a police cell. The commissioner commented: 'I'm afraid you will find the accommodation we offer here not up to the standards you are accustomed to.'

Various sources state that the guarantor was a very senior executive, Forte Oil's top manager and one of the richest businessmen in the country. Remarkably, Nico Vervelde had been part of the board of this supplier since December 2016, as a supervisor. The guarantee only partially worked: his wife, considered a flight risk, had to leave her passport behind.

The trial never took place. Sule agreed to a settlement of more than 2 million dollars, an amount largely in excess of what he had paid in commissions. Heineken decided to clean up its Nigerian subsidiary. Those directly or indirectly involved lost their jobs, were shunted aside and Nico Vervelde disappeared to South East Asia.[8]

Sources within the police say that the Heineken manager can count his blessings:

> Had this gone to trial, he would have been prosecuted for abuse of power. Why did Clémentine have an office paid for by Nigerian Breweries while the company did not employ her? Abuse of power is a form of corruption, which is punishable. The prison sentence depends on the evidence provided: it can be anything between three and seven years.

Moreover, and in relation to the case, the police also discovered that Nigerian Breweries was evading taxes. 'Each contract of this nature implies payment to the revenue authority. Nigerian Breweries had promised to pay 120 million naira in withholding tax on behalf of Sule, who later discovered that the company had only paid 19 million. So that is a 100 million naira fraud case.' The equivalent is more than half a million dollars, using historic conversion rates. Heineken denies that its subsidiary was involved in tax evasion.[9]

No incident, a system

'A good shopkeeper, a solid director, one that every company needs.' That is Nico Vervelde, as described by a former colleague:

But I did find him a little hesitant, slightly weak. And if your wife happens to be larger than life, you're being overshadowed. It was never clear who was in charge: Mr or Mrs Vervelde. That does not work in Nigeria. You must always be hyper alert and radiate authority.

The former colleague finds it strange that Vervelde still works for Heineken. 'This is not the first time his wife has been linked to controversial practices, and he has always maintained that he knew nothing of her activities. We found that questionable. I assume that in a marriage there is no Wall of China.' 'Nico must have known,' says a former manager who worked frequently with him. 'He comes across as someone with integrity and his reputation is good. At first, I really thought he didn't know, that he was naïve. But it's simply impossible. It's too big, it has too many tentacles. And he's the boss.'

Various sources within the company say that the TMDK Oil Traders affair is just the tip of the iceberg and that it is unfair to blame just Clémentine (and Nico) for everything. What emerges from a series of conversations with those directly involved is the image of senior managers, both Dutch and Nigerian, indulging in all kinds of controversial deals and shady business practices in order to enrich themselves. It infected the entire organisation. An insider speaks about a company 'rotten to the core, with fraud and corruption happening at every level'. He remembers the first clean-up. 'It was mainly cosmetic. The top echelon stayed in place and the system did not change. Almost everyone gets their share, so what you have is a tight and unbreakable chain.'

The system revolved around Clémentine. 'Everyone in the industry knew that she held all the power,' says a former Nigerian manager. 'If you wanted to get anything done at Nigerian Breweries, *go see Clémentine.*' Whether it was a house for a new expat or airline tickets for a business trip, everything went through her hands. With Limitless Mind Africa, her company, she frequently organised conferences for Nigerian Breweries, usually at the Eko Hotel on the luxurious Victoria Island in Lagos.

Clémentine was also involved in sponsoring contracts, from small cultural occasions to major television events, and again there are indications of odd things going on. One person involved says: 'You would go to such an event we were sponsoring to the tune of 250,000 dollars without any idea where the money had gone.'

After the settlement with Sule, many sponsoring contracts were abruptly ended. A prize for visual artists and a famous writers' workshop organised by best-selling author Chimamanda Ngozi Adichie did not survive. Heineken says these were austerity measures, but close associates believe that the real reason is that the managing director's wife was involved. This time, a real house-cleaning was needed.

There was yet another noteworthy deal, worth millions. This involved the throughput of barley malt, which would require the construction of two silos in Port Harcourt. Just a few days after 12 February 2015, when Nigerian Breweries and a Lebanese businessman signed the contract, the brewery changed its mind and decided that the silos were not needed after all. This triggered a cancellation provision that landed the businessman, who had spent relatively minor sums, more than 8 million dollars. Again, there is allegedly a role for Clémentine Vervelde here, internal sources claim, although in this case there are no eyewitnesses or direct evidence.

Clémentine Vervelde-Murekatete, which is her full name, was born in Rwanda where she maintains good relations and commercial interests. For instance, she mentioned to Sule that RwandAir, the national airline with daily flights from Lagos into Kigali, was another potential client.

In Rwanda itself, Clémentine runs a transport company, about which a former Heineken top manager has this story:

> She said that she'd be given a contract with our brewery to use those lorries but the director said: I don't know anything about that, we don't work that way. Next thing we saw was Ms Vervelde kicking up an almighty fuss, going all the way to the highest level in Amsterdam to get what she wanted. And again, Nico supposedly didn't know. This I find hard to believe: a woman is investing in lorries to deliver beer, her husband is a man from the beer business—and they wouldn't discuss these things?

Various inside sources say that, after the Executive Board intervened, Clémentine was allowed to distribute the crates of beer, which Heineken denies.[10]

Nico and Clémentine met in the early 1990s, after he had been appointed marketing director at the Heineken subsidiary in Rwanda. He succeeded none other than Jean-François van Boxmeer. Several sources who know the Vervelde couple confirm that they have had close ties with the chairman of Heineken's Executive Board for well over twenty years. One manager in Nigeria was struck by how quickly Clémentine knew about matters that had been relayed confidentially to Head Office. 'Without protection, Nico would no longer be working for Heineken,' says a former colleague. Those in the know are also astounded by the fact that Van Boxmeer allowed Nico Vervelde to take up the board position at Forte Oil, an important supplier. 'That smells very strongly of a conflict of interest. In the Netherlands, this would very likely not have been permitted,' a former director in Nigeria says.[11]

Has Heineken committed punishable offences in Nigeria? 'If this story is correct, then we're looking very likely at a classic case of corporate criminality, in this case bribery and private corruption,' says Wim Huisman, a professor in criminology at the Vrije Universiteit Amsterdam. 'Bribery is often linked with governments but that does not need to be the case. When companies do it, the law applies as well. Mind you, it is not illegal to award contracts to those close to you, but when bribes have been paid it's a different story.'

A former expat is outraged:

> To me, this represents everything Heineken does not stand for. Everywhere in Nigeria we write INTEGRITY in capital letters and we forbid our drivers to pay even the smallest bribe. We want to show that you can function in a climate where fraud pervades, that you don't have to participate. And now that it is supposedly happening at the highest level it should all be swept under the carpet? No way.

'One million here, one million there'

To the outside world, Heineken likes to project an image of integrity. In the 2016 annual report of Nigerian Breweries, which was published after the police interrogations, Vervelde is even credited with a Corporate Governance Award for transparency, honesty and the culture of good governance and ethics that supposedly permeates the company.[12] When the Dutch specialist recruitment firm Brunel left Nigeria in 2015 because it was unable to handle the rogue business practices it had to contend with, Heineken stated that it was not so apprehensive. 'We are putting corruption in Nigeria on the agenda in various settings,' a spokesman said. 'Perhaps we can do this more easily than other businesses because we are such a large player.'[13]

The company declared earlier that it was hedging by keeping large stocks in order to avoid depending on one cargo that the port is supposed to release. 'In such cases, they suddenly cannot locate the containers,' says Tom de Man, one of Heineken's former Africa directors. 'You must find a general manager who can resist threats and has access to a minister.'[14]

A top manager with connections—there was none better than Festus Odimegwu. In his nearly thirty years with Nigerian Breweries—he started as an apprentice beer brewer and ended in the top post—he became the key to the company's success.

It was on his watch that the sales figures went through the roof, much to the delight of the Amsterdam Head Office. It was he who secured permission to build the hyper-modern mega brewery near Enugu, Heineken's largest in Africa. 'He had the qualities to become the first African to join Heineken's Board of Directors in Amsterdam,' says a Dutch personnel manager who was close to him. 'If only he had stayed a bit further away from politics.'

I meet Odimegwu in a residential area of Abuja, the administrative capital. In his village, he is the traditional king (*eze*), and his city home is a sumptuous palace. The tinsel-filled interior reminds one of Donald Trump's Manhattan penthouse. A butler from Benin—in Nigeria, having staff from the French-speaking neighbour is considered chic—serves champagne.

Without holding back, Odimegwu talks about his excellent relationship with President Olusegun Obasanjo, whose time in office almost completely coincided with Odimegwu's reign at Nigerian Breweries (1999–2007). Odimegwu had seats in a variety of advisory councils to the president and was a regular visitor to the presidential villa at Ota, outside Lagos. 'Every time he had to make an important decision, he asked me for advice,' he says. This proved particularly useful when SABMiller wanted access to the Nigerian market, where Heineken and Guinness had a cosy and long-standing arrangement: Heineken dominated the lager market, while Guinness took care of the darker variety, stout.[15] The arrival of a new player would not only diminish profits; it also came at the time when Heineken had just opened the Ama Brewery, which meant it had to sell another 3 million hectolitres of beer. The top manager talked the government into thwarting SABMiller's arrival. 'They were confronted with all manner of administrative difficulties, for instance with the necessary permits. In some countries this would violate competition legislation, but we don't have that.'

Another thing the local top manager achieved was to reverse plans to increase a certain tax. 'The minister of finance wanted to double the excise duty, but I told her she should not do it. And so it did not happen. It's that simple,' Odimegwu explains.

One year, the company's record beer sales were threatening to cause a shortage of raw materials. Odimegwu says that he got government permission to use the strategic grain reserves the country usually maintains in the event of famine.

But what if there had been one? Odimegwu does not see the problem and assures me that no bribes were paid: his influence was sufficient. What he does admit is that the PR budget is being used liberally to grease the palms of politicians and other authorities with influence. 'You give 1 million naira [equivalent to around 6,000 dollars at the time] here, 2 million naira there. Otherwise you will not do business in Nigeria.'

Other problems were also addressed with great inventiveness. When northern states decided to introduce sharia law and limit the sale of alcohol, the beer trade moved to the military bases, where the federal government is in charge. Even today, these are the places where there are enormous drinking sprees. To keep the alcohol abuse off the streets, the company had 'waiting rooms' built for the drunkards. 'They would be kept there until they were sober, to prevent people from saying that beer is evil.'

In 2005, Odimegwu was unpleasantly surprised. The president was about to travel to the Netherlands without telling the beer brewer about it. To add insult to injury, he had planned a meeting with Shell and not Heineken. Van Boxmeer, already on the Executive Board but not yet its president, was upset. 'Call Festus,' he reportedly told his Africa director Tom de Man. Odimegwu: 'I got Obasanjo to talk with Heineken for two hours. He arrived at the Queen's residence an hour late because I had told him: "Baba, stay with my bosses."'

Odimegwu says that his Dutch superiors always knew about his actions. The company's Africa director had a seat on the

Nigerian Breweries board, where all decisions were discussed and approved. He reported to Heineken's CEO, Tony Ruys, and after 2005 Van Boxmeer. Odimegwu maintains: 'I did nothing in secret. Van Boxmeer and De Man were encouraging me: go see Obasanjo. Once I took De Man to the president's bedroom in Ota.' He says that the large bonuses and generous retirement scheme he enjoys are signs of an employer who is happy with the work he has done.

After his retirement, Odimegwu and Van Boxmeer fell out with one another. The former claims that Heineken had reneged on an agreement that gave him the right to the same medical facilities he had used when he was still working:

> They wanted to send me to India or South Africa for a major treatment. But I went to a private clinic in London and sent the bill to Heineken. I told them: you must be honest. If you don't pay within a week you will find out who I am. I can close down Nigerian Breweries tonight if I want to.

Heineken paid immediately. 'Amsterdam was scared of him,' says an insider.

Odimegwu could now concentrate fully on politics but did not get the governorship he had set his heart on. He led, briefly, an important commission under Obasanjo's successor, Goodluck Jonathan but two years later switched support to Jonathan's competitor Muhammadu Buhari, who won the next election. Odimegwu was part of the transition commission and was mentioned in connection with a possible ministerial post. 'I very quickly got a call from the Nigerian Breweries PR manager, who wanted to greet me. Van Boxmeer also wanted to talk with me again. When it looked as if I could be a minister they were all queuing up to see me.' Sadly, for Heineken at least, the ministerial bid failed.[16]

Of course they sleep with the clients

The conversation—mostly a monologue—with Odimegwu lasts four hours, but he continues to hold my attention effortlessly. Without hesitation, he relates how Heineken hired almost 2,500 young women to support and help launch a massive marketing and publicity campaign for a local brand. He explains that Guinness had begun a campaign for their own clear beer, Harp, thus violating the informal agreement with Heineken. Odimegwu: 'It was a declaration of war.'

Nigerian Breweries brewed its own dark beer, called Legend Extra Stout, but sold very little of it. That had to change. However, given his limited resources, Odimegwu would never be able to compete with an iconic brand that was hugely popular:

> We asked ourselves the question: Where does the brand meet the client? In the bar. And how do we reach the client in the most efficient way? First of all, via the barman. So it's him we pay for the bottle tops he hands to us. And then there's the prostitutes. In Nigeria, the upper and middle classes drink in clubs without prostitution but poor people go to bars where you pay 2,000 naira [around 10 dollars at the time] to sleep with a woman. You give her gonorrhoea and you get HIV in return. That's where our chances were.

The company took to organising training workshops for sex workers. 'There are prostitutes who work in hotels, the leaders who train new colleagues. We had a separate programme for them. Make sure that your client, your sex partner, drinks Legend instead of Guinness, because that gives more energy.'

And so it came to pass that the company designated 500 well-frequented bars as so-called hot spots, where young women had to promote the beer. When I ask if they were also encouraged to sleep with the clients, Odimegwu's eyes grow large as he looks at me. 'What kind of question is that? Of course! They are prostitutes. What do people do in your Amsterdam Red Light District?'

In this fashion, Legend profited handsomely from the existing and risqué Guinness campaigns that suggested that drinking stout would lead to better performances in bed. Many African drinkers, both inside and outside Nigeria, believe this. Odimegwu: 'It's nonsense of course but perception is reality. In scientific terms, alcohol is a depressant: it does not enhance your performance. But our clients are not scientific; otherwise our churches would not be full to overflowing.'

Someone who was directly involved confirms that the campaign was predicated on the link between beer and sexual success. 'We wanted to convince the revellers that our beer gave them more strength and masculinity than Guinness. You cannot spread such information on television, you'll get into trouble for that. But you can do this in the bars.'

The anniversary book *Sixty Years of Winning with Nigeria* (2007) describes the Hotspot Scheme as 'a bold initiative' that doubled sales figures within a year. According to Odimegwu, the end result was a fourfold increase in sales.[17]

Some insiders maintain that not all Hotspot Scheme promotion women were sex workers and that Odimegwu's figure of 2,500 is an exaggeration. But there is no doubt that in Nigeria Heineken has recently used the unique appeal of a large group of young and often vulnerable women in order to boost the sales of a non-performing brand, at very little cost to itself. The general manager was aware of the fact that in doing so he was contributing to the spread of sexually transmitted diseases.

'What could we do?' says a former expat who knew about the problems:

These girls are let loose in a bar and at the end of the evening the male clients think: they're part of this, we can take them home. So then you must ask yourself: How do we manage this? In the end, people were hired to bring them all home in minibuses.

The source points out that sex work is not a clearly defined profession in Nigeria and disagrees that Heineken has knowingly hired prostitutes:

It's different over there. It starts early. In Nigeria girls must sleep with their professors in order to get good marks. Terrible. I once got talking to a working girl. She had worked in a hair salon but had to sleep with her boss in order not to get fired. 'Well,' she thought, 'if I do this, I make as much in one night as I normally do in a month and I have to sleep with somebody anyway.' So it's hard to draw the line, really.

Ending the practice was not an option. 'Turnover would have dropped like a stone.'

4

SALES AND MARKETING

AFRICAN BEER WARS

There are many ways to sell beer in Africa. The continent is a paradise for slick salesmen and smooth talkers. Advertisers have little to fear from laws that govern marketing or officials supposed to enforce them. It is not that unusual for the authorities to look the other way.

Let's stay in Nigeria. I have an appointment with Ifedapo Adeleye, a marketing expert from the prestigious Lagos Business School. He is full of praise for Nigerian Breweries: 'Unbeatable'. He waxes lyrical about the television shows the company commissions; they are hugely popular, especially among the young. The 'Star' brand is the prop for a show featuring budding celebrities. Gulder, the robust beer marketed at men, has its own reality TV and adventure series, and the alcohol-free Maltina brand sits pretty on a dance show. Their logos are on everybody's television screens for hours on end, and of course the Heineken brand itself gets a mention. In football-mad Nigeria, many fans refer to the UEFA Champions League as the Heineken Champions League. Adeleye: 'When the game is on, the brand name stays on the screen. That's fantastic publicity for them! They're grateful for the fact that there's virtually no limit. Everything is possible here, the more outrageous the better.'

A near-absence of competition …

As we have seen, brewing beer in Africa is highly lucrative. The latest available figures show that the continent represents nearly 21 per cent of profits, while turnover and volume sold are just over 14 per cent.[1] So, profits on beer sales in Africa outstrip the global average by almost half. And it is not just Heineken: the competition also knows the continent to be a profit paradise.

One of the reasons for this is, indeed, the competition—or rather: its near-absence. Between them, the Big Four (AB InBev, Castel, Heineken and Diageo) own a whopping 93 per cent of the African market, and in fact it is only a Big Three if you take into account the cooperation between AB InBev and Castel. Worldwide, the picture is the same: a few players dominate the field, with the Top Three (AB InBev, Heineken and Carlsberg) owning about half of the global beer market.[2] But while the top dogs have to contend with powerful regional or national competitors on many of the world's markets, this is not the case in Africa, where many countries have monopolies or duopolies. A high-level source at Heineken puts it like this: 'When there's only two of you, you can work something out.' Profit margins start to taper off when you have three or four players on the same market.

As we have seen in Nigeria, Heineken and Diageo had a long-standing informal agreement to stay out of each other's territory. In 2011, Heineken got permission to acquire another five breweries, even though they had already cornered 60 per cent of the market. The main objective was to thwart SABMiller once again. 'It defied all logic. Had the Nigerian competition authority functioned as it should, it would have vetoed that deal,' an insider says. 'This could never have happened in Europe.'[3]

SALES AND MARKETING

When SAB and Diageo were both vying for East African beer markets at the beginning of this century, they came up with a very easy solution: Diageo got Kenya and SAB took a near-monopoly in Tanzania. The two companies took a minority stake in each other's breweries, and the only one losing out was the local beer drinker.[4] In Burundi and Rwanda, Heineken was able to keep the competition at bay for years, with the help of the authorities.

The near-absence of competition has a consequence: a beer in Africa will often cost you more than in Europe, not only measured by purchasing power but also in absolute terms. On my African travels, I have rarely seen the equivalent of a crate of 24 'premium' beers for as little as 10 or 12 dollars, as you can get in a Dutch supermarket.

Brewing companies justify their large profit margins by pointing out that investing in Africa carries great risks. 'Make no mistake,' says an inside source. 'Before the oil price dropped we were figuring out how we could quickly double volume in Nigeria. There were plans to expand, three or four breweries extra. Instead we had to close bottling lines. If we had made that investment, we would have lost a lot of money.'

But a former colleague takes a different view. 'More than 60 per cent of the population here is under twenty-four years old. So you can have a couple of bad years because of bad government policies or a weak currency, but the good times always come back.'

The McKinsey consultancy firm says that risks in Africa these days are hardly any worse than in developed countries, provided you spread them among several markets. A lot can go wrong in one country, but because economic and political ties among African nations generally are not that strong, chances of a major crisis breaking out are small.[5] Besides, returns on investment in Africa arrive faster than in Europe. An insider says:

The time-frame we are working with in countries like Congo, Rwanda, Burundi or Nigeria is three years. In Europe, you have to make that seven to ten years. Of course it's bad luck when a brewery is nationalised or gets destroyed in a civil war, but you'll find that even when such things happen investments have already royally paid themselves back.

... But vicious beer wars

It is a strange contradiction that despite this virtually non-existent competition, Africa has become enthralled by the battle of the beer giants. Have a look at the newspapers. 'Heineken Sparks Beer Wars with Nairobi Office', writes the Kenyan *Business Daily*. Or this one, from a website: 'Beer War in Nigeria, Who Wins?' And this from Ivory Coast: 'Earlier than Expected, Heineken Opens Hostilities against Castel'.[6] There are several such battles going on in South Africa, Ethiopia, Rwanda and Congo.

It is true that the media tend to blow these things out of all proportion and turn ordinary competition issues into all-out wars, but in this case the beer companies themselves fire the shots. It starts at the top, where the competition is called 'The Enemy' and managers call for more aggression and commitment from their staff. 'We have won a great number of battles, but not the war,' is the rallying cry at Bralima's marketing department.[7] Those who work in sales, distribution, customer service and are in direct contact with the customers are said to be 'The Frontline'. The in-house magazine *Leader* features pictures of the sales troops standing to attention, war drums at the ready, their right arms raised and ending in clenched fists. Attack!

In the absence of a governing body that can call the warring sides to order, as is often the case in Africa, the parties doing battle tend towards excess. Nowhere is this clearer than in Congo, where real wars have done immense damage. According to a Dutch intern at Heineken: 'The rivalry is really intense, and because this is basically a lawless country some really weird things have happened here.'[8]

We will see that in Kinshasa entire neighbourhoods are painted blue, the Primus brand colour, including a school bus and a police station. Another brand-related novelty has been 'exclusivity': bars that are only allowed to sell Bralima products and nothing else. Says a former director: 'We had the full product range. All you had to do was to give the operator a few plastic chairs and tables, a fridge and that would be it.' Bracongo, the rival company, did the same. The upshot was that you could have one brewer holding a contract with the proprietor while the other had a deal with the manager of the same establishment. 'In which case,' recalls the same source, 'there would be fist fights between salespeople and fans of the two different brands. Both sides would often call in policemen to join the fracas, customers would throw bottles at each other. It was really dangerous.'

A Heineken salesman from Lubumbashi has this to say about the sales tactics:

> They [the competition] have been here for much longer than us, so we're being told to be especially aggressive. We sabotage sales in their exclusive bars by selling our beers by the side door. When we have conquered a bar, we call our friends for a show of force. We provoke them; this is our turf now.

And yes, this can turn nasty too:

> When the competition has conquered a bar and is ready to re-paint the walls, that's when we strike. We throw out the paint and tear the posters off the walls. You must show them that you're no pushover. One of our colleagues got hurt when somebody hit him with a bottle. It's part of the game. We also strike when we find their bottles in our fridges. The first time we warn them, but if it happens again we flush it all away. Management does not want us to smash the place up, but other than that we can do pretty much what we want.

One of his colleagues adds this:

We must defend our bars. I have informants who keep an eye on everything. If our competitor moves on a bar we have a contract with, I quickly take my motorbike to alert my friends. It's not supposed to get physical in principle, but if that happens it's just a case of *force majeure*. Bralima understands that.

Live longer, drink beer

While the salesmen wage their wars around the bars, upper management are thinking about the big bucks. Their largest future profits will have to come from those millions of consumers who are currently sticking to their palm wine, their sorghum beer and other popular local thirst quenchers. They talk about these drinks in disparaging terms ('a brew that you and I would never touch'[9]), but they do consider them serious competition, not a relic of tradition. To corner this market, Heineken highlights the benefits of its own product: clear beer not only tastes better; it is also healthier and safer because of its consistent quality.

By contrast, the industry loves pointing out the dangers of illegal hooch like *chang'aa* in Kenya (commonly nicknamed 'kill me quick'), which—allegedly—can contain raw sewage, rats and cockroaches. These drinks kill scores of people every year or render them blind after consumption.

Heineken purports to stand for its clients' health. 'Since we're the biggest beer brewer we have a responsibility,' said Roland Pirmez in an interview shortly before he was appointed Heineken's director for Africa. 'We must invest in transport and storage to make sure that our beer reaches the people instead of the stronger and dangerous illegal stuff. Banning alcohol is not the solution. If you do that, people will fall back on those home-made brews.'[10]

The truth is that most of these home-made brews contain more vitamin B and C, more iron and more potassium than clear beer—and fewer calories, alcohol and salt.[11] Another plus is that, unlike industrial beer in Africa, these traditional drinks do not contain added sugar. The trick the beer brewers deliberately use is to equate concoctions like *chang'aa* with all traditional drinks and make it seem as if they are all poisonous and dangerous.

In 2014, Heineken decided to take its health claims to the next level. It organised the first Nigerian Beer and Health Symposium, attended by celebrities from the entertainment and business world. Location: one of Clémentine Vervelde's favourite spots, the Lagos Eko Hotel. Professor Tola Atinmo of Ibadan University delivered the keynote address. He presented his paper ('Beer as Part of a Healthy Lifestyle') with the requisite fervour. Did the audience know, for example, that their beloved Star beer protects them against cardiovascular disorders? Did they know that the consumption of beer, in moderation of course, contributed to the prevention of (among other things) diabetes, high blood pressure, brittle bones, arthritis and various cancers? And that beer drinkers, provided they consume in moderation, may live longer and with a sharper mind than others? Oh, and the beer belly, yet another myth. Beer has few calories in comparison with other alcoholic drinks.[12] He also pointed towards a World Health Organisation (WHO) paper that counselled the consumption of two-and-a-half bottles of beer per day; in Nigeria, with its standard 60cl bottles, this means a litre and a half. His source was in all probability Kari Poikolainen, a former WHO expert, who wrote *Perfect Drinking and Its Enemies* in which he claims that dangerous drinking only begins at thirteen units per day (i.e. more than one bottle of wine).[13]

On hand to support Professor Atinmo's claims was the writer Bankole Omotoso, 'not an expert but an enthusiastic consumer'. He also pointed out how beer consumption, moderate of course, could help prevent Parkinson's disease, dementia and kidney stones. What's more, the thinning of the blood caused by alcohol would prevent blood clots from forming in the vessels, thus reducing the risk of a heart attack.[14]

Nico Vervelde, the top manager at the time, also made a contribution. 'There's a negative stigma attached to beer abuse and that is hurting us. This negative perception has a severe impact on this fine product.' He managed to convince Bisi Abiola, the publisher of a health magazine: 'Until today I used to just enjoy my bottle of red wine but from now on, having heard this instructive lecture, I will have a glass of cold beer every night.'[15]

The press was ecstatic. *This Day* ran a headline: 'Experts Reveal Amazing Health Benefits Derivable from Moderate Beer Consumption'. The *Daily Independent* opined that, finally, facts were victorious over fiction.[16] Only one publication, *The Guardian*, was critical and invited a professor who pointed out that it was unethical for Nigerian Breweries to encourage people to drink more beer while alcohol was already contributing to many problems in Nigeria.[17]

To make sure that its message was reproduced in the media, Nigerian Breweries organised an intensive workshop a few months after the symposium and called it the Media Beer Academy. Journalists who attended the course would be able to put on their CV that they now had an 'MBA'.[18]

'We're here to sell as much beer as possible'—journalist

It is likely that the journalists who were present at the course got the red carpet treatment and were paid very well for the articles they wrote afterwards. Payment for coverage is the norm in many parts of Africa (and is getting more and more common elsewhere too), not just for companies but also for politicians and organisations that want to spread their information. There is hardly any discernible difference between a story that comes through the editorial process and a sponsored feature.

'For an exclusive story I'll get 300 to 600 dollars,' a journalist working for *This Day* in Lagos reveals. 'If the brewery wins an award in London, they will send an experienced journalist who can analyse things well. We don't make much money and the children must eat.'

In Africa, press conferences usually come with presents: gifts or cash. 'They pay us so we can write nice stories,' says Véron Kongo of the Congolese daily *Le Potentiel*. 'The newspaper gets 400 dollars for half a page and part of that goes to me. When I throw a party or get into trouble at home because there isn't enough beer, they give me coupons for a box or two. They're a humane company.'

La Prosperité director Marcel Ngoyi has a fixed contract with Bralima. 'We publish at least six stories per month about them. Usually they determine the subject, but we suggest stories as well. We regard ourselves as external advisors.'

But what if he, inadvertently, discovers something negative about the company? Ngoyi suddenly becomes defensive. 'We have freedom of the press here,' he gloats. 'They can't prevent me from doing anything. But my job is to never surprise Bralima. Suppose I hear something bad about them. What I will do is speak to them and write their version of the story. We are here to sell as much beer as possible, together.'

Fellow Congolese journalists are getting paid to copy press releases and re-publish them under their own name. The goal is to please your partner to the best of your abilities. Bralima's media department is the arbiter of the articles, and if it is unhappy, the unfortunate hack who wrote the offending piece will lose revenue and free beers. Here's one, writing for *Le Phare*:

> I am proud when Bralima tells me my article is the best. It is moral compensation. 'You have done very well' they will say, and I get a small stock of beer in return. If I find out something negative, I'll keep it to myself. Recently, for instance, I heard some employees

complain about a deterioration in working conditions, but journalists don't have to report everything.

'A company never likes criticism,' says Wolf Kimasa, Bralima's former marketing director. 'You have to guide the way the media report about you and this is very easy around here. Journalists make about 200 dollars a month. They need extra money to make ends meet.'

Given this background, it is the height of cynicism to see Heineken award a prize that is supposed to be promoting 'professionalism in journalism'. It is the Golden Pen Award in Nigeria, but you would be mistaken for thinking that someone will ever receive this award for presenting a revelation based on solid investigation. Journalists need to cover the innocuous themes Heineken dreams up, such as talent development or youth empowerment.[19]

The future belongs to the young

The young are not just a theme: beer brewers have their eyes trained on them all the time. Take one look at Africa's demographics and you will see why they are so upbeat about the future. Collectively, the West is growing old quickly, but in Africa hundreds of millions of children are growing up to become potential customers.

They need to be wooed, and this starts early. In Nigeria and Congo, Heineken paints its logo on the school buildings it rehabilitates with money from its charity programmes. The minute school children can read, they will know whom to thank. 'The alcohol industry grooms children.' That is Bill Sinkele's judgement; he runs a centre for addicts in Kenya. He discovered that young children choose a favourite brand long before they are of legal age to consume alcohol.[20]

The WHO found out that in eastern Nigeria it is quite common for adolescents to have a beer before they go to school. A girl called Alfa has integrated a beer into her morning ritual, while other children carry a bottle of Star on their way to the classroom. Esther, who is fourteen, regularly gets treated to a beer by her father when he comes home from work. 'It's good for keeping sickness away.'[21]

Research reveals that Africa's young people are the prime target of the brewing industry's marketing campaigns that latch on to and exploit their interests. Nigerian Breweries leads the way. It organises fashion shows at university campuses, free nights out in dance clubs and sponsors music and sports events. The earlier you rope in your new clients, the bigger your chance of securing their enduring loyalty.[22]

Nigerian Breweries also sponsors the national secondary school essay competition. During one such event, the company's top manager personally visited a school as a guest teacher. A reporter mentioned that he made a promise to continue sponsoring the competition for the next five years, while consuming a bottle of Gulder 'in a stylish fashion. The children will have come away with the impression that Gulder is good for you if you want to be successful.'[23]

Getting away from the publicity onslaught in the cities is impossible, and even in the rural areas it is becoming harder and harder, as I found out on my travels. Billboards, large plastic bottles embossed with names and logos, bars in the brand colours—they are everywhere. The beer brewers only match the cellphone companies when it comes to their fanatical devotion to publicity, even when there is no competition in sight.

The results are noticeable. Research in Europe and the United States tells us that publicity contributes to higher consumption levels, especially among new drinkers.[24] In Africa, this impact is probably more pronounced, because there are virtually no limits to how and where one can advertise. Besides, the target group's education levels are lower, which renders them more susceptible to such targeted campaigns.

Heineken sees nothing wrong with the way it works. 'Africans have their own mind and they must decide for themselves whether or not to buy a beer,' responds a former expat. 'We're simply using the fact that Africans like beer.' This source holds that Heineken adapts to local culture and points out that many of its campaigns have been developed by local marketing companies.

Heineken has its own advertising Code of Conduct, which puts limits on what it can do. For instance, marketing should not imply that choosing a particular brand of beer enhances someone's social status or increases success. Nor should it suggest that beer is beneficial for an individual's power, health or sexual performance. Heineken claims it does not target vulnerable groups.[25]

In practice, though, the company works extra hard to establish links between its brand names and positive values. Its Mützig brand is 'the taste of success', and we have already seen how Legend was associated with sex in Nigeria. The health symposium, meanwhile, is in clear breach of its own responsible marketing code, which forbids it from claiming beer can be beneficial to consumers' health. The company refrains from suggesting that customers should have a beer for this reason.[26]

Vulnerable groups, like the youth and underage children, are similarly targeted; they even get special treatment. Two researchers, David Jernigan and Isidore Obot, may overdramatise matters slightly but are essentially correct when they state: 'If the youth survive HIV, military conflicts, and the corruption endemic in many national economies, marketing strategies more sophisticated and ubiquitous than those allowed in developed nations will present alcohol—particularly beer—to them as an emblem of success, a symbol of virility, the embodiment of courage and heroism.'[27]

5

SIERRA LEONE

THE MYSTERIOUS GODFATHER

'Transparency is beautiful if you have nothing to hide.' This is the slogan Heineken uses to promote its products in Sierra Leone. When I saw it for the first time in the capital Freetown, it struck me as most remarkable. Transparency? Nothing to hide? Not the qualities I immediately associate with Heineken, but that might just be my professional instincts getting the better of me. There are more mysteries hidden in Sierra Leone. First off: What on earth is Heineken doing in this far-flung corner of the continent? This West African state is home to just over 7.5 million people, most of whom are Muslim. Average beer consumption per person is a paltry 2 litres, and that is not a lot, even by this continent's standards. Sierra Leone is extremely poor and still recovering from a civil war (1991–2002) that killed 200,000 and the vast Ebola epidemic of 2014. Heineken's local subsidiary, Sierra Leone Brewery, uses a run-down facility and never makes much money. You will find no expats here looking at the profit margins with a happy glint in their eyes. This is the place where people count the days until they are allowed to leave for their next posting. 'If you're ambitious, you should not be there for long,' says Tom de Man, former Africa director. 'And you'd better like fishing. A lot.'

'Everybody wins'

With the words *Di war don don*, spoken in the Krio language, Sierra Leone President Ahmad Tejan Kabbah marked an end to more than ten years of civil war. The president was hoping that Heineken could help his country. During the war, the brewery had served as a rebel base for a while—beer was boosting morale—but it was slowly getting back into business. Now, Sierra Leone's head of state was asking the beer brewer if it could stimulate agriculture by using local crops. Heineken thought this a good idea, and in 2005 it began a public–private partnership. The aid organisation EUCORD joined the project, and money came from a United Nations fund. It was decided to concentrate on sorghum, a millet variety known as 'the poor man's crop'. Heineken hails the project's success and has expanded the scheme to other African countries. Using local commodities has become a key part of its corporate social responsibility. I want to see for myself how this works and have chosen Sierra Leone, reasonably small and manageable, as the place where I can talk to farmers who are part of that scheme. And I want to do this on my own, which means: without interested third-party interference.

My Freetown contacts tell me to try my luck in Makeni, in the north. It seems the war has only just ended here. Multi-storey homes stand by the side of the road like skeletons, as if looting rebels left only moments ago. That President Ernest Bai Koroma is from here helps a little: it is said that the town receives more electricity than elsewhere and there is some investment going on.

Even here, Heineken's footprint is visible. The outside of my hotel is adorned with an old advertisement featuring a smiling waiter in conventional attire serving a glass of beer. The slogan is in Dutch: 'Heineken's bier, het meest getapt' (Heineken beer, the most sought-after draught).

Looking for the sorghum farmers, I'm told to go to Panlap, a short ride from Makeni on the back of a motorbike. Sadly, the traditional leader, always your obligatory first port of call when visiting a village, is away. Still, the local youth chairman is at hand, and together we visit a few village dignitaries, but no one knows about the project I am looking for. I'm being referred to the next village, Bombali-Bani. It looks like this is going to be a very long day.

We leave the main road and pass by a centre for amputees, the result of one of the rebels' trademark actions during the civil war: hacking off limbs. The road to the village becomes a narrow jungle path where we meet a young man with a machete who is harvesting fruit. We are going ever farther into what one might call deep traditional Africa with huts and scantily clad inhabitants. But then, all of a sudden, we come face to face with a cargo train, a few hundred metres long, thundering along a brand new railway. This is how iron ore is transported to the port, an echo of the colonial practices of yore. The local chiefs asked for a passenger service, in vain.

The only way you can get to Bombali-Bani is by taking a small motorbike or going on foot. The village is an open space surrounded by huts made of wood and mud. The chief is still asleep, and when he emerges a little while later he has no idea what to do with me. The motor taxi driver and I manage to convey the word 'sorghum' to the chief, and I point at a boy who happens to wear a Star T-shirt. The boy thinks he can make a deal: Would I buy his T-shirt? The chief motions that we stand a better chance in the next village, which is a little larger.

Binkolo is located on the main road to Guinea. It has two distribution points that sell Heineken and Star, and it is in this village that I find Chief Alimamy Dura III, at home, in a Western-style villa, his 'palace'. He knows about the sorghum project, but there are no farmers participating in the scheme around here. He also knows where I should go. And he happens to know the chief of that area, he'll call him immediately ... in Krio: 'Hello chief ... How di body? ... How di chiefdom?' I am more than welcome to visit, but there is just one problem: the chiefdom's location. It's on the other side of the country.

It is already late afternoon, and since we are not far from the equator it will soon be evening. I decide to return to Makeni. On the way back I pass more remote villages, playgrounds for a huge array of international aid organisations: UN Women and Cooperazione Italiana have built a little something here, War Child runs a youth centre there, the International Red Cross digs wells and Kuwait has paid for the mosque. The children yell *Opoto! Opoto!* (White man! White man!). They hold out their hands, anxious to find out what I brought with me.

Next day, I have more luck, but not after another ride that takes more time than anticipated. On the way, I see squirrel monkeys and one bright green snake slithering across the red earth road. The undulating landscape is breathtaking, dotted with huge boulders and large termite hills shaped like works of art. Bare-breasted young women are pounding grain in wooden bowls, and little boys use long bamboo sticks to get at the mangos high up in the trees.

In Mile 91, a small town 91 miles from Freetown, I finally find two sorghum farmers who send their produce to Heineken. They are sitting under a straw roof in an open structure made of wood, busy separating the light grains from the dark. The brewery only accepts light grains; the rest is for their own consumption. At times, the harvest yields them the right grains straight away; now it takes them ten hours to fill one bag. They often use children for this menial task.

SIERRA LEONE

Abdul Karim Kamara used to grow rice, but he has switched to sorghum and peanuts, crops you can grow on the same land in one year. The sorghum ripens after nine months, and he harvests the nuts three months later. This combination was recommended to him during a training session EUCORD had organised. It was held at the beer brewer's main office, and he is more than happy with the outcome: 'I have learned a lot, and my harvests have improved. I used to do extra work in construction, but now I concentrate all my attention on agriculture. I make more money than before, not much more but enough to continue.' He can send his children to school—and his son Saïdu can even attend university.

He shows me his contract. The company pays him just over twenty dollars for a 50 kg bag, and if he delivers 2,000 bags, his target, he gets a 10 per cent bonus. Unfortunately, he will not hit his target this year. 'Transport is costing me too much money; I haven't got enough funds left to buy seeds. I'd love to borrow more, but it's not possible.'

Karim employs forty people, and they get about two dollars per day. Not too bad for a place in Sierra Leone's interior. He has noticed sorghum's increased popularity. 'At first, there was just one customer, the brewery. They paid less. Now they make porridge out of it, and it's being used as food more often.' He calls it a 'scramble for sorghum'—surely some exaggeration. Karim is Muslim and does not drink beer, unlike many of his fellow believers. 'But I am proud that the brewery is using my crop to make Star.' When we say goodbye, the farmers tell me that I should not have needed to spend two days on the back of a motorbike in the baking sun: their colleague Samuel Kamara has an office in Makeni, a few minutes' walk from my hotel.

Samuel Kamara is a so-called nucleus farmer. His job is to collect the bags from his own harvest and all other participating farmers in the area and then take them to the brewery:

It's all very small scale. There are no tractors, and nothing has been mechanised. So you have farmers with small plots of land. They take a few bowls [of 3 kilos each] to a farmer with more land. For that, they get paid less than a dollar. Most farms send ten or twenty bags. If you take all that together, this project provides work and income to thousands of small-scale farmers and farm hands.

He speaks warmly about the many children who work alongside them in separating the grains—as I was told in Mile 91—and transport. But then he suddenly realises that the subject of working children touches a few raw nerves in my region of origin. He corrects himself: 'We never pay these children. We don't do child labour. It's true: we cannot follow what happens on each and every farm, but we only work with people who are eighteen or over.'

Kamara has done well out of the project. 'We nucleus farmers have received motorbikes, and this enables us to fetch two 50kg bags from a farmer during a single visit. And I have built a better house, with four rooms.' Kamara also says the farmers have gained confidence:

They want to work more because they know that there's money in it. They can send their children to school and buy zinc when the roof is leaking. The brewery pays on time. When we were still growing rice we sometimes had to wait a whole year for our money. With this, everybody wins.

Back in Freetown, I am meeting the project coordinator, Ivan Carrol, a former director of Sierra Leone Brewery. We meet at a bar on Lumley Beach, a sea and sand paradise for the country's elites. Sierra Leone wants to attract more tourists, and the potential is evidently there.

Carrol first talks about sorghum's former bad reputation:

It wasn't even sold on the market. If there really wasn't anything left to eat, that's when you started looking under the bed to see if some sorghum had been left there. Then we turned up and asked for thousands of bags of the stuff. At first, a lot of farmers just didn't believe us, but when we started paying the early adaptors—and we paid well, on delivery—others started showing interest too. We also taught them how to keep the area clean, about harvesting methods and we gave them 50kg bags. Many farmers had never worked with scales before so we had to explain that as well.

No profits but Heineken makes money

After a day's work, I relax in the Bliss Café, a Lebanese restaurant with all the modern conveniences one is used to in the West. Every major urban area in Africa has a few places like this, with good espresso and a reasonably fast wireless internet connection. Outside, the parking lot is always filled with four-wheel drives belonging to diplomats and employees of non-governmental organisations (NGOs). I order a Lebanese sandwich and a Star beer; the flavour is a little sweet, due to the sorghum. Almost everywhere in Africa the routine is to open the bottle in the presence of the customer; this way you can be sure that the bottle-top is being removed for the first time and no poison has been added. The waiter must put the top next to the bottle, but in this case he casually takes it away. When he thinks I am not looking, he checks the underside. His expression is unchanged; no prize for him today.

Star has started a raffle in a bid to increase sales. It is a tried-and-tested marketing trick, and it has worked as planned, according to insiders. Once the bottle top is off, you turn it and you'll see immediately whether or not you have won anything. All over town there are posters showing what you can win: a motorbike, a flat-screen TV, money, power generators, bags of rice and some happy-looking live goats. Even I strike it lucky and win a baseball cap with the Star logo.

But still Sierra Leone's results do not live up to expectations. One local newspaper says that between 2005 and 2015 the brewery has not made a single leone in profit.[1] Frank Tucker is a shareholder and worked as a company engineer for almost thirty years. He said that during all that time he has never received any dividend payment.

After he left the company, Tucker started his own bar on the busy Congo Town Main Road. Car horns blast from the street; the sound rebounds under the awning. We discuss why Heineken remains active in Sierra Leone after half a century, even when it has withdrawn from a promising place like Angola and largely turned its back on Ghana. 'Maybe it's for strategic reasons that they stay in this part of Africa, but I must say that the advantages aren't altogether clear to me either.'

He points out though that Heineken does make money in Sierra Leone, by delivering material and ingredients and by providing technical assistance.

> They charge the earth for raw materials and spare parts. You cannot negotiate, and you're not allowed to look elsewhere and compare prices. But we'd very much like to imagine that they just have a soft spot for us at Heineken. They seem to know that Sierra Leone is essentially a peaceful and hospitable country full of boisterous people who love their beer. There will be opportunities when purchasing power keeps rising. The conclusion me and my colleagues have drawn is that inside Heineken there is some mysterious godfather somewhere who protects us.

6

IMPACT

ARTISTIC ARITHMETIC

Happy farmers and cheaper supplies for Heineken. In Sierra Leone, the scheme had all the appearances of the much-loved win-win scenario, even though my sample was small. Heineken, buoyed by this success, decided to expand the programme to other countries and other crops: rice, cassava, maize and barley. The end product is a clear and perfectly drinkable beer, even though the taste may differ slightly from place to place. But how successful are these projects, and how much does Heineken contribute to the development of the countries where it works? More precisely: Is the economy in a host country performing better thanks to Heineken's presence? And what is the impact on employment?

Great PR stories

Big business has become part of the language of development. Decades of development aid have done nothing to reduce the wealth gap between Africa and the West; now the hope is that trade will succeed where aid failed in taking Africa to new levels of prosperity. Western governments still spend billions on traditional development aid, but they have also become ardent advocates of development through trade. Now the watchword is partnership between business, government and NGOs (public–private partnership), but each partner operates in its own particular way. The aid organisation carries out a project, a company integrates it in its commercial operations and government pays and facilitates.

Heineken's agriculture projects are an example of this approach. Government and NGOs hope that local farmers will prosper, the brewery wants to cut costs and be less dependent on commodities and their unpredictable price movements—or foreign currency availability in the host country. But most of all, local agriculture has become a key part of Heineken's corporate social responsibility policy. 'You can write great positive stories about these projects, and we at Public Relations will happily use them of course,' confirms spokesman John-Paul Schuirink.

And sure enough, as a theme, 'Heineken and the African farmer' is a media winner. Major newspapers in the Netherlands and abroad, including the *Financial Times*, have all written about it. The left-leaning Dutch website OneWorld came up with this headline: 'A Better World with Heineken'. Dutch national television spoke about the 'unique cooperation' between the company and the Dutch aid organisation ICCO. There was only one exception: an investigative news programme, which produced a critical report (based on my findings).[1]

Politicians of all stripes are also full of praise for Heineken's agricultural policy. Dutch Prime Minister Mark Rutte wove this glowing reference into his speech at a United Nations summit:

> What does private sector involvement look like in practice? It could look like the ambition Heineken has formulated for its breweries in Africa and the Middle East, to source 60 per cent of all its ingredients locally. The Netherlands is supporting this effort by offering

training for farmers. And it's working. In Burundi, for example, this partnership has already enabled 18,000 farmers to make a steady income by supplying this world-famous Dutch brewer.

Experts were taken aback. A prime minister singing the praises of a brewery from his own country on a major occasion in world politics? 'Rarely have I heard such blatant advertising. It's all a bit shameless, really,' said a UN specialist. Another added: 'I have heard mid-level government officials recommend their nation's businesses at the UN but never a minister, let alone the leader of a government.'[2]

The former Dutch minister for trade and development cooperation, Lilianne Ploumen, was equally keen to extol the beer brewer's virtues. When she visited Rwanda and Congo, she pointed out that Heineken had put tens of thousands of people in work. She also praised the expats and their involvement in solving local problems. In Ethiopia, she personally laid the first stone for a new brewery in Addis Ababa. And even Queen Máxima, who holds a symbolic position, couldn't stop herself from admiring Heineken when she was visiting Ethiopia. 'A fantastic example,' she commented.[3]

However, I found out there's much more to report than just success stories. Not only did I visit farmers in Sierra Leone, but also farmers in Burundi. In the north of that country, scores were sweet-talked into growing sorghum, as Heineken had promised to pay them a good price. But the final offer was so derisory that the farmers preferred to sell their harvest to a porridge producer in neighbouring Rwanda. In addition, a top manager at national level allowed the project—and all the work that had gone into it—to slide. The result was unsurprising: the planned output was 5,000 tonnes, but four years into the scheme Heineken has bought less than 5 per cent of that volume.[4]

Congo provides another example of the gap between reality and the image given to the outside world. 'We're now running the country's largest agriculture project. I guess that puts the aid organisations to shame,' boasted Hans van Mameren in an interview with a reporter for the Dutch daily *De Telegraaf.* The same reporter met a politician at the Bralima brewery: François Rubota Masumboka, who heaped praise on the company.[5] This stands to reason. Rubota is a member of parliament, an ally of President Joseph Kabila, and a major rice supplier for Heineken. In short, he is an influential politician who stands to do well from an agricultural project. Sustainable development or mutual benefits? Sometimes it is hard to draw the line.

Even Henk Knipscheer, a former project leader at EUCORD, points out the fragility of the first results. In an interview, he says:

> Importing commodities often works out cheaper, in spite of custom duties and the costs of transport. The quality of imported grains is excellent and it is always on time, while local crops are surrounded by uncertainty. Next, you'll have to hope and pray that your own financial people don't fiddle with the books, and to top it all you must make sure that local sourcing doesn't interfere with the incentives of your managers. If it means their bonuses take a cut, they prefer importing raw materials.

Child labour? Famine? 'We are not aware of any of this'

In its sustainability report for 2009, Heineken announced for the first time that it intended to source 60 per cent of raw materials for its African beers from local suppliers by 2020.[6] That sounds ambitious, but the company fails to mention its breweries were already buying 48 per cent of those supplies locally when the announcement was made.[7] Latest reports put the figure at 53 per cent, an increase of only 5 percentage points. Roughly one-third of that local content comes from the kind of large-scale farming enterprises you see around the world, including in South Africa, Egypt and Nigeria.

Incidentally, 'local' can mean quite a few things for Heineken. 'Continental production' would be more accurate: barley from Egypt, which it hauls across half a continent for use in its Rwandan brewery more than 5,000 kilometres away, is included. The company states that 12 per cent of the raw materials that are called 'local' are in fact imported from another African country, and even within the same country the distances can be enormous. Rice from Bumba in the north of Congo travels more than 1,000 kilometres before it disappears into the boilers at Heineken's Kinshasa brewery. The company does not know whether local production means more CO_2 emissions or less, compared with importation.

Conversations at the Amsterdam Head Office reveal the uncertainties that come with these projects. Not much thought seems to have gone into the possible negative side effects, such as water shortages or the impact of fertiliser usage on pristine African soils. There is also a lack of clarity about the effects on child labour and food security. Which is remarkable when you realise the name of the scheme: 'Increase Food Security and Improve Livelihoods of Sorghum and Rice Producers'.

'These are the questions we are asking now,' says Roland Pirmez, Heineken's director for Africa. 'What is the effect of our strong demand for barley in Ethiopia on prices for other crops? We'll find out before long.'[8]

Could this not have been done earlier? Heineken has been working on these agricultural projects since 2005. Pirmez replies that these are dilemmas that have recently emerged. 'We must refine this.'

A researcher who analysed some of these projects on the spot has a less charitable conclusion:

> Heineken is there for its own good. Potentially, that farmers' story is great, but Heineken has paid insufficient attention to the implications. They do not ask what the farmers need, payments arrive late,

seeds are not delivered on time. And they have no idea of the impact on food security. Sure, it is better for the farmers, but how about the others in the same area?

More than 2.5 billion dollars in profits … and corporate welfare

Heineken is the big winner in the African countryside. The extra return on investment goes to the company, while a big part of the costs are carried by other parties. According to the latest figures, annual profits have gone up to more than 2.5 billion dollars, but the company has managed to attract over 10 million dollars in taxpayers' money from a variety of countries for its rural projects: 7 million dollars from the Netherlands, 1.5 million dollars from the United States, and the rest from Germany, the UN Common Fund for Commodities and the World Bank.[9] African countries also make contributions. Burundi, virtually bankrupt, waives 80 per cent of the excise duty on Nyongera beer, which is composed entirely of local ingredients, bar the imported hops. The result is that the Burundian revenue authority gets more income from soft drinks than it does from sorghum-based beer.[10] So it is subsidised beer then? It sounds a lot like it.

Heineken has admitted that in the case of Ethiopia it would have made the same investments without the government lending a hand. In so doing, the company has violated a Dutch rule that says companies are only eligible for government support when it is indispensable.[11] However paying it back is out of the question. The donor, in this case the Dutch Ministry of Foreign Affairs, points out that its support was intended to benefit the farmers, increasing their know-how and boosting their income.

Heineken claims the cooperation with governments and NGOs helps to run the projects more efficiently. 'They force us to be committed,' says Van Boxmeer, before adding: 'Of course, we never say "no" to a government subsidy, just like you will never hear us campaign for tax increases.'

IMPACT

The Ministry of Foreign Affairs calls it 'a real win-win-win', even though a ministry official who is involved with the scheme attaches an important proviso: 'All eyes must be on the same prize.'[12] The time when business, government and NGOs regarded each other with a healthy dose of suspicion is long gone. The three are now partners, which implies equality and having common interests.[13] Government and NGOs in particular want to show that they understand the modern mindset and are able to think and act in line with the rules of the market.

In her doctoral research on public–private partnerships in the agricultural sector, Verena Bitzer concludes that corporate interests are front and centre. She studied dozens of these partnerships, attempts to render coffee, cocoa and cotton production chains more sustainable.[14] 'In practice,' she comments, 'attention is focused on corporate economic objectives. Farmers are best served by having their own organisation reinforced. That gives them a stronger position in negotiations and increases their chances of getting funds for new investments.'

Bitzer's point is that you cannot expect commercial enterprises to defend the interests of producers:

> These interests are likely to clash. NGOs, on the other hand, should have their eyes on the bigger picture. That requires a much longer time-frame. Often these partnerships exist for a period of two or three years. That is not enough to achieve structural changes and improve the farmers' organisational level. If partners leave, things fall apart.[15]

Indeed, in its partnerships, Heineken rules the roost. This does not mean there is no benefit for the farmers, but it is often the beer brewer who determines the price and who can decide, from one moment to the next, to discard a local supply chain. Heineken can leave a project to its own devices for a few years, or get a local politician profitably involved without any accountability to either the farmers or the public donors.

All parties seem to yearn for success in the complex world of development cooperation. They think they have finally found that magic bullet. Government regards collaboration with business as the best chance to save development cooperation—it is an institution that has been under heavy and sustained fire because there are doubts about how effective it really is, while many citizens think that the billions spent on aid are needed at home. The partnership is a form of aid that appears to be effective and, at the same time, beneficial to the domestic economy. Development organisations face similar problems, since they largely depend on government finance for their survival. Knipscheer, the former EUCORD project leader, says that, despite the weaknesses, he has never seen a scheme with a comparable impact in all of his forty years in the business of development. 'It was very rewarding.'

Famine in northern Nigeria

What is the risk of these new-fangled production chains collapsing again? The current movers and shakers talk about 'ground-breaking' and 'revolutionary' social experiments, but the truth is that agriculture has been on Heineken's agenda for more than fifty years.[16] When the company came to apartheid South Africa in the 1960s, the use of local sorghum to replace imported malt was discussed, and in the same period Nigeria was experimenting with local barley, a process that gathered speed in the 1980s because of an import ban.[17] Nigerian Breweries' very survival was at stake, and with technical assistance from the Netherlands, the company managed to create a supply chain that delivered sufficient maize and sorghum to continue brewing beer of acceptable taste and quality. In Burundi, also in the 1980s, Heineken started to source a proportion of its raw materials locally.[18] 'The beer tasted good and became cheaper,' recalls a former expat. 'We bought directly from local farmers and contributed to agricultural development. It made sense economically, but after I left they stopped the scheme. I don't know why.' In neighbouring Rwanda, there was a similar sorghum project, described internally as a success, but again discontinued for no apparent reason.[19]

Knipscheer says that most of the programmes now run independently, and he is confident about the future. But Head Office is deeply worried. After a recent devaluation of the Nigerian naira, Paul Stanger, the local sourcing director, discovered that the use of local crops is not always sufficient protection against currency fluctuations. When the naira plummeted, imported cereals became more expensive and local sorghum more attractive. Traders from neighbouring countries realised they could buy the local crop at knock-down prices. But this unexpected rise in demand, compounded by the negative effects of the Boko Haram insurgency on harvests in northern Nigeria, caused the price of sorghum to skyrocket, triggering the 2017 famine.

That put Heineken, the biggest buyer of sorghum in the country, in a difficult position. It needs 150,000 tonnes every year, about 2.5 per cent of national production.[20] The company stresses the importance of its 60 per cent local supply target and will continue to buy sorghum even though imported barley malt is cheaper. Very laudable, but what if Heineken pushes the already problematically high sorghum price up even further, when it can easily get its hands on the alternative, barley? 'When you are a big industrial buyer, you have influence but real percentages are small. The food market does not suffer,' assures Stanger. 'You must continue to support it, through thick and thin. But when the situation begins to differ so drastically from your previous expectations that it no longer makes any business sense, then you must stop fooling yourself.'

That moment may, according to Stanger, soon arrive in Nigeria if local prices stay as they are. This would then mean that the 60 per cent local sourcing target for raw materials disappears beyond the horizon, since Nigeria accounts for more than half of the beer brewer's Africa-wide consumption. 'Personally, I would hate it if that happens because this is one of my key performance indicators,' comments Stanger, who strikes me as a committed and passionate manager. But of course his first thought is whether he will qualify for a bonus, not the farmers and villages that have pinned their hopes for development on Heineken.

Just before this book went to press, Heineken confirmed it had begun to substitute local sorghum in Nigeria with imported barley on a large scale. As a result, the percentage of Africa-wide-produced raw materials dropped to 42 per cent for 2017. This means that after receiving millions of dollars of various government subsidies, Heineken currently uses a lower percentage of African raw materials than its initial total of 48 per cent almost a decade earlier, when the 60 per cent target was first announced.[21]

'Organised theft'

There are other complications. One well-informed staffer in Burundi lets rip: 'First, they are promoting local agriculture, and the next thing you know is that they've dropped it. Sometimes you hear that Heineken prefers importation because it wants to protect its own malted barley market.' Whether this last statement is true is difficult to ascertain, but what is very clear is this: Heineken is making very good money from its deliveries to Africa through its two full subsidiaries, both Belgian, Mouterij Albert and Ibecor. However, De Man claims that cost reductions and other advantages of local production far outweigh the revenue from Ibecor and the malting plant. 'A no-brainer,' the former Africa director concludes.

Ibecor. Sounds familiar? It should: the name has appeared earlier in this book. The International Beverages Corporation, its full name, maintains an office in southern Brussels, on a tree-lined lane in a calm and prosperous neighbourhood adorned with embassies, a golf club and a racecourse. The contrast with the instantly recognisable Heineken offices in Amsterdam is stagger-ing. Ibecor resides on the fourth floor of an anonymous office block. No sign, no neon lights, no advertising. You pass it by, even on foot, without noticing.

The outside world is blissfully unaware of the existence of this Brussels-based company. The Belgian subsidiary never gets a mention in interviews or press releases. Searches in the data-bases of newspapers or magazines returned no results until I started writing about them. In a recent book that relates the history of the company in more than 600 pages, Ibecor is not mentioned a single time; since 2013, the Belgian subsidiary has completely disappeared from Heineken's annual reports.

The only time the company's existence was acknowledged hap-pened more than thirty years ago, when it was said to play 'a very important role in Heineken's Africa activities' and considered 'a buffer between Head Office and the African breweries'.[22]

Nowadays, Ibecor is said to be a necessity because of the excep-tional circumstances prevailing on the continent. According to Heineken, the Belgian subsidiary is responsible for procurement and logistics for the African region. Says De Man: 'In the Netherlands, we lack the knowledge to locate spare parts for near-obsolete equipment or how to find the right local transporter in, say, Mombasa. Only the Belgians can do that sort of thing.'

And yet it is noteworthy that no other similarly challenging region benefits from the specialised services of a company such as Ibecor. Would it really be so much more difficult to trans-port machines or barley from Germany or Belgium to relatively nearby and reasonably developed North African countries like Algeria or Tunisia, compared with breweries in Haiti, Papua New Guinea or the Solomon Islands? Or the deep interiors of India, Laos or Mongolia?

Expats and local staff share their incomprehension and even indignation about what Ibecor was up to. A former employee in Algeria says:

> Before Heineken took over our brewery in 2008, we were dealing directly with Krones, a German company, for maintenance and spare parts. Heineken then told us that we should be using a central procurement centre that was supposed to negotiate better prices. But in fact they are a lot more expensive and they inflate invoices to gain even more.

'We always needed lots of sugar, for our soft drinks and our beers,' recalls a former director in Congo:

> I used to purchase from a local wholesaler, 8 to 9 per cent cheaper than Ibecor. Quality was good, and we always had reserves. So I wanted to increase those purchases to cut more costs and promote local commerce, but Heineken refused. I had to continue to order from Ibecor.

A former deputy warehouse manager in Rwanda does not hide his anger when remembering Ibecor:

> I know exactly what we received and what we paid: raw materials, publicity stuff, stationery, cars, equipment. If you converted their prices into Rwandese francs you'd fall off your chair. It was theft, organised theft. If you needed a simple spare part, you could have it made locally but that wasn't allowed. Ibecor over-invoiced us tenfold. It is very unfavourable for our company and Rwanda's economy.

A former Dutch staffer was equally astonished:

> They often did not have the requisite specialised knowledge, their raison d'être. We found it much better to deal with a supplier directly. And they were expensive. We wanted to get Ibecor involved in buying tablet computers, but we found a Dutch website that was 20 per cent cheaper.

Adding to the discontent of the local breweries is Ibecor's frequent insistence on a monopoly position. If you need malt, you must go through Ibecor and get it from the Albert malting plant. Something similar was happening with transport. For a very long time, the contracts automatically went to SDV, part of the French Bolloré conglomerate and today called Bolloré Logistics. CEO Vincent Bolloré, a good friend of former president Nicolas Sarkozy and well connected to current President Emmanuel Macron, is known to be a key player within La Françafrique, an opaque political and business network that France has carefully kept in place in order to safeguard its interests. It was only after a long period of intense lobbying that Nigerian Breweries finally managed to get SDV out the door and replaced with GMT, a Nigerian company that according to an insider is better, faster, cheaper and contributes to increased profitability.

A cover for shady business

'Give them parliament and keep the banks.' When the Europeans realised that their reign was coming to an end, they kept this maxim in mind.[23] Power was going to be lost on paper, but in practice the former colonial masters kept the reins after independence, with businesses often acting as bastions of influence.

Heineken was certainly not planning to give up its African goldmine without a fight. The company was actively thwarting the fledgling governments of newly independent states by evading taxes and 'pumping' as much money as it could away from local economies. Heineken, a pioneering enterprise in many African nations, appears not to have *adapted* its business practices to the culture of fraud, corruption and self-interest—it appears to have had an active hand in *creating* it.

Heineken has never stopped selling its African host nations short. Foreign exchange evaporates, and massively inflated commissions reduce local profits, which means less revenue for the local tax authorities. It is likely that the beer company's actions

violate the guidelines of the Organisation for Economic Cooperation and Development: the OECD considers transfer pricing (i.e.
deals among the various units that make up a single multinational conglomerate) 'an extremely important subject regarding
good citizenship for enterprises'. The OECD recommends working according to the so-called 'arm's length principle'. This
means that companies within a conglomerate should trade with
each other at existing market rates so as not to depress profits
and thus reduce tax payments. Heineken does not appear to be
an adherent to that principle, but identifying fraud and verifica-
tion in general can be difficult since these are, as the OECD puts
it, 'not exact sciences'.[24]

There are other disadvantaged parties: the partners and private
shareholders of Nigerian Breweries and Bralirwa of Rwanda,
Heineken's two listed subsidiaries in Africa. As local profits are
kept low, they receive less in dividends.

In Belgium, a beer nation like no other, Ibecor has become the
seventh-largest company in the brewery business, ahead of well-
established names like Palm, Chimay and Westmalle. Expenses are
extremely low: with a turnover of around 70 million dollars, the
company makes more than 65 million dollars in profit, equivalent
to 9 per cent of Heineken's overall African profits.[25]

A high-level source in the company says that part of the
amounts Ibecor puts on its invoices comes back to Brussels and
that another part ends up in Amsterdam. 'Nobody understands
the nuts and bolts of this, and everybody I ever contacted about
Ibecor was thinking: What's the reason? Why only in Africa?' In
1989, a former Ibecor employee threatened to release confidential
information, which he clearly considered high value: he wanted
1 million Dutch guilders (the equivalent of almost one million
dollars today) in hush money. No publicly available information
from the archives tells us how this affair ended.[26]

One former staff member who has had many dealings with the
Belgian subsidiary recalls: 'I was always struck by the amount of

secrecy that surrounded payments to Ibecor. Never should a written record be made, absolutely no paper trail.' The ex-staffer continues:

> When Heineken took full control of Ibecor, it would have been logical to move its activities to Amsterdam or to the company procurement office in Zoetermeer. The reason this was never done is simple: Ibecor is a cover for the kind of business Heineken wants no public association with, to safeguard its good name.

Heineken emphasises that its subsidiary operates fully within Belgian law, publishes an annual report and that its audits have never uncovered malpractice. 'But we have come to realise recently that its commissions were a bit on the high side. We have reduced these,' says De Man. Heineken chooses not to release accounts or other financial data to back up its assertions.

Unreliable figures

Ibecor's commissions have an adverse effect on local economies, while the agricultural projects may have a positive impact, if they don't disappear. Can an overall picture be drawn of Heineken's economic influence in the countries where it operates? In other words: Are the African host nations better off with or without Heineken's investments?

During a debate at the University of Amsterdam, CEO Van Boxmeer gave an interesting response to that last question. After heaving a deep sigh, he said: 'We tend to think: yes, they're better off with Heineken. But we are a drop in the ocean. You must see yourself as one such drop. Don't exaggerate the role one single company can play in any country anywhere.'[27]

That is a remarkable assessment. In the main, Heineken does not suffer from such modesty. On the contrary: the company claims it adds billions of euros to African economies and creates hundreds of thousands of jobs. The company's top management makes these claims based on impact studies by Steward Redqueen, a consultancy firm. Bralirwa's former top manager Door Plantenga says the findings are 'extremely helpful for a good assessment of our company's positive influence in Rwanda'. She adds that these arguments are also highly useful 'in our discussions with stakeholders, particularly the government'.[28]

A former director in Burundi recalls: 'We took that report to the Ministries of Economy, Finance and Agriculture and we said: "Look! That's how things are! Don't kill the goose that lays the golden eggs."' And it worked. The reports made the government call off tax increases on several occasions. They also agreed to decrease the excise duties on beer that contained local raw material. The same source continues: 'We put serious pressure on Parliament.' A director in Nigeria has also used the reports to stop more stringent tax measures being imposed. 'We brandished these reports when we were crossing swords with government representatives about how much we could demand in royalty payments for the use of our brand names. Very useful.'

All well and good, but can they be relied on? Steward Redqueen does not do field observations or on-the-spot verifications; instead, it uses a so-called input/output model. The model begins by ascertaining the size of the national economy, average productivity of various sectors and the financial transactions among those sectors. Based on these data, the consultancy firm then estimates Heineken's added value to the economy and the number of jobs that 'are somehow related to (but not entirely dependent on) Heineken'.[29] It is basic arithmetic, adding the direct jobs, on average a few hundred per country, and the indirect jobs, mostly in agriculture and distribution.

The result is a guesstimate. Using this model, Steward Redqueen arrived at the conclusion that in 2009 Heineken was 'supporting' some 600,000 jobs in Nigeria. Two years later, this figure had been reduced to less than half that, and today's figure is 213,000 jobs (see fig. 3).[30]

IMPACT

Serving the planet, Serving Nigeria

The socio-economic impact of
Nigerian Breweries

Final Draft

The Hague, May 2009

TRIPLE VALUE

The socio-economic impact of Nigerian
Breweries in 2013

1 May 2014, Final report

steward redqueen

In the entire economy, 637 thousand jobs are somehow related to (although not entirely dependent on) the presence of Nigerian Breweries. In the value chain, approximately 415 thousand jobs are present, the bulk of which are in agriculture and trade (97 and 268 thousand respectively). The large amount of jobs in agriculture is related to Nigerian Breweries' substantial Sorghum procurement (60,000 tons, 0.5% of Nigeria's total production) and the inefficiency of agricultural production. The quality of these jobs is therefore low, as indicated by a per job value added of NGN 32 thousand (about 20% of the per capita GDP). In trade the large amount of jobs is attributed to the extensive distribution network needed and the labour intensiveness of retail. The regional distribution of the jobs is uneven. The jobs in agriculture are located in the North of the country whereas the jobs in the trade and transport sectors follow the regional differences in beer consumption, which are determined by population density and religion. Manufacturing is concentrated mostly in Lagos.

This socio-economic impact assessment (SEIA) captures the ripple effects NB has on the wider Nigerian economy. In 2013, NB:
- Supported NGN 292 billion value added (0.4% of GDP), of which NGN 98 billion directly (0.1% of GDP);
- Supported NGN 110 billion tax payments (4.6% of non-oil tax revenues), of which NGN 58 billion directly;
- Supported 279,000 jobs (0.3% of total labour force);
- Employed a skilled and productive workforce of 3,200 employees.

Figs. 3.1–4: Two impact studies on Heineken in Nigeria, 2009 and 2013

But curiously, the consultancy firm claims that Heineken's impact has not diminished. How is this possible? Steward Redqueen director René Kim explains in a Skype conversation that these big differences are the result of fluctuations in local data, for instance the increase of Nigeria's gross domestic product by 89 per cent in 2014. 'As a result, productivity per employee increases strongly while the total numbers of jobs in our model decreases,' he says, adding: 'There is no place where figures are less reliable than in Africa. This is why we made the conscious decision to opt for the most uncomplicated model we could find. The downside is that the uncertainty margins are very large.'

Another limitation, says Kim, is that this model assumes that the productivity of Heineken's suppliers is equal to the sector average, while you may assume that multinational companies work with suppliers that perform above average. If this proves to be correct, then the true number of jobs supported by the beer brewer will be even lower.

Kim makes the point that he urges his clients to be cautious, not to reduce the findings to a few abstract figures, and above all provide context. 'Be modest when you communicate this type of data. We dissuade them to use the term job multiplier, as in: every job in our company generates sixty or seventy jobs elsewhere in the economy.' Kim thinks Heineken listens closely to these suggestions.

Not Heineken's achievement

Let's take a look at the beer brewer's website. Under the heading 'Creating a Real Impact on Local Economies and Communities', the company claims it supports more than 1.6 million jobs in Africa and adds more than 3 billion dollars to local economies. There is nothing about the limitations of the research. And the job multiplier is there in all its shameless glory: 'One position at Heineken supports 108 jobs in our Africa and Middle East region.'[31]

Steward Redqueen considers these figures outdated, but the consultancy firm says it is unable to make new estimates. Kim also refuses to cite country-specific figures. 'Updates are being carried out in the major markets as we speak. We are waiting for those.' That is all he wants to say. Taking into account the drastic adjustments in Nigeria, one can imagine the new figure to be perhaps just one-third of the 1.6 million cited on the website. And given the unreliability of the data, it could even be fewer.

Moreover, the vast majority of the jobs 'somehow related to Heineken' are not jobs, maintains Kim. 'This is work in the informal sector, often without a real salary. It's like the sorghum farmers who earn just enough to get by.' Kim does not mention them, but there are others who belong in this category. The children in Sierra Leone, for example, separating the light sorghum grains from the dark. Or the children you encounter across the continent, carrying a crate of beer from one village to another.

Kim: 'Most of that employment hardly adds any value. And it's not Heineken's achievement either. Having 50,000 farmers in your production chain is not necessarily a sign of your company's strength. It's more likely an indicator of the huge unproductiveness of the economy where you operate.'

Heineken does not mention this and moreover ignores the new—lower—figures. When in 2014 Van Boxmeer was a guest at the World Economic Forum in the Nigerian capital Abuja, Heineken proudly proclaimed that it had managed to create 632,000 indirect jobs nationwide, and this was after this figure had already been halved.

Moreover, Heineken talked about 'created' jobs, not 'supported' ones. By doing so, the company suggested that this work would not exist without Heineken, which is incorrect. In passing, and for unknown reasons, Heineken also quadrupled the number of direct jobs: in 2014, the company directly employed 4,000 people (today it is 3,000), not the 16,000 it claimed.[32]

In an interview in 2013, Africa director Siep Hiemstra pulled an even larger number out of his hat: 681,000 Nigerian jobs. Based on what? Nobody knows: the last available Steward Redqueen study at the time mentioned just over half that number, 348,000.[33]

Can they get away with it? Heineken orders impact studies in order to impress local authorities. What they get in return is tax exemptions and a good reputation. It's only later that these figures are revealed to be gross exaggerations, but by then the advantages have already been pocketed. Should you not then eat humble pie and admit that your contribution is less than you made out? Kim takes a charitable view. 'It's always with hindsight. I still find those old figures justifiable. Economics is not an exact science.'

Like governments and NGOs, impact researchers see themselves as Heineken's partners. They are external parties, that much is true, but their interest dovetails fairly neatly with that of the beer company. If they can show sufficient positive impact, new research may well be commissioned, and other companies may start showing an interest too.

Kim does not want to divulge how much Heineken contributes to his annual sales. 'Less than 10 per cent,' he says. 'Heineken is a good client and we appreciate the long-standing relationship that gives us strength and stability.' He claims he does not tell his clients what they want to hear. That the employment figures have been revised sharply downwards is enough proof, he thinks.[34]

However, impact studies have no room for critical questions. For instance, what is the economic impact on traditional beer brewers when industrial beer starts flooding the market? 'Perversely, economists and politicians calculate the conquest by industrial breweries as economic growth while the value of small-scale traditional brewing goes uncounted,' writes Chris

IMPACT

O'Brien, author of *Fermenting Revolution: How to Drink Beer and Save the World.*[35]

In a 2002 report about alcohol in developing countries, the WHO reached the interesting conclusion that at the end of the day the beer industry hardly creates any jobs at all in Africa. The arrival of automated breweries and the fact that traditional brewers lose market share under the onslaught of the newcomers means the very opposite: the destruction of work. Women, usually the ones involved in the production and sale of traditional African brews, are hardest hit by this because their influence on the household income recedes, while they tend to spend money more wisely than their husbands.[36] Whereas Heineken and its competitors seek to take the largest possible chunk of their revenue back to Europe, local production and sales benefit society at large.

The second issue the impact studies studiously neglect is connected to the economic and social impact of the huge amounts of alcohol Heineken releases into communities. How does this affect modern Africa? We'll go to South Africa to find out.

7

SOUTH AFRICA

THE FIGHT FOR POWER IN THE TOWNSHIPS

Call it progress if you like. More than a century ago, South Africa was rocked by two destructive Boer Wars; today, the country is in thrall to the Beer Wars. No blood gets spilled, but the competition is intense. 'The press loves it,' says Anne Mager, a historian at Cape Town University. She wrote a book about South African Breweries (SAB) and sees parallels between the two conflicts.[1] The Boers were colonists of mainly Dutch descent, fighting against the British; in the current battle for the beer market, it is 'Brit versus Boer' all over again. Heineken is unmistakably Dutch, SAB had long established connections with Great Britain. Following a series of mergers and acquisitions, SAB, the jewel in the crown of South African industry, has become part of world market leader AB InBev.

There is much at stake in South Africa. Here, the dimensions of the local beer market are completely different from the rest of the continent. The country may have been overtaken by Nigeria—which is three times more populous—as Africa's largest economy, but South Africans still have much more spending power, and they love their beer. Of every three beers sold on the continent, one goes across the counter in South Africa. The annual consumption rate here is 60 litres, almost on a par with some of Europe's thirstiest beer nations, like the Netherlands or Belgium or Slovakia.[2]

'The home market is so profitable for SAB that it has given them enough cash to conquer the rest of Africa,' says Tom de Man, the former Africa director. 'Direct competition was an important motive for us to go there.'

The first major contest between the two giants was the battle for the Amstel brand. During the apartheid years, Heineken had granted SAB a brewing licence with no time limit. A series of successful publicity campaigns turned Amstel into a premium brand with a big market share. But then the Dutch returned to South Africa in 2004, and they wanted their Amstel brand back. SAB said no, and Heineken went to the International Court of Arbitration at the International Chamber of Commerce. Heineken felt its demand was justified: a merger between SAB and the US brewer Miller had changed the ownership structure.

Against all expectations, the court agreed, but the euphoria was short-lived. SAB immediately halted the production of Amstel, and the beer was unavailable for several months. The South Africans used that window to launch, in quick succession, a series of new beers to take Amstel's place. The brand never recovered, and sales remain far below the records that were set when SAB owned it.

Nobody had said life was going to be easy in the lion's den.

150,000 illegal bars

One Sunday morning, I visit the great battleground of the Beer Wars: the popular neighbourhoods of the big cities, called townships. Taxi driver Thomas is my guide. We take the motorway from Johannesburg to the South Western Townships, much better known as Soweto. On our way, we pass the undulating hills and the elongated rock formations of the Witwatersrand.

Soweto has more than 1 million inhabitants. It is a vast area with dozens of neighbourhoods. Most people live in single small housing units. Commerce is everywhere, from a few caged chickens by the side of the road to massive shopping malls. There are more affluent neighbourhoods too. This is where the larger homes are, complete with security systems and 'armed response' warnings, just like the predominantly white neighbourhoods in other parts of Johannesburg.

In the early 1980s, South Africa's black population consumed 80 per cent of all beer sold countrywide. Up to date statistics are unavailable, but it is safe to assume that this percentage has gone up, the result of sheer numbers: there are more black people as a percentage of the overall population, and they generally have more money to spend.[3] For Heineken and Amstel, considered high-end market brands, the black neighbourhoods are key to their success. The townships are arenas where the choice of a beer brand determines your social status and class, more than anywhere else in South Africa. For this reason, consumers are prepared to spend more than they can afford.[4] Market analyst Chris Gilmour has a sobering perspective:

> The upcoming black middle classes have, on average, not a huge amount of readily available cash. Premium beer is one of the cheapest ways of signalling: hey guys—I'm doing well. One SAB marketing director told me once that some 30 per cent of the premium beer drinkers can't actually afford it. But still they buy—it's an aspirational product.

In today's Soweto, bars come in all shapes and sizes, from lounges with swimming pools to undecorated watering holes. Many living rooms also double as bars and very few have a licence. They are called *shebeens* and date back to the days of apartheid. For their owners, mostly women, this was a way to make some money. The white authorities wanted to close them down but all their efforts were in vain.

The arrival of democracy in 1994 did not put an end to the *shebeen* phenomenon. On the contrary, their numbers expanded fivefold, from 30,000 to 150,000.[5] Mager explains:

> This expansion has come about because of high unemployment, which fuels both supply and demand. For someone without work, a small bar is one of the best ways to make some money. And customers do come, because even the poorest households have some income thanks to small pensions, child allowances and other benefits from the new welfare state. The current government also fights against these illegal bars but ends up realising that very little has changed. You close a *shebeen* one day, it will be back on the next. This sector has always thrived on resistance.

Soweto's shareholders

Just after 11 a.m., I arrive at Fikile's place in the Diepkloof area, a classic home-based *shebeen*. The atmosphere is out of the 1970s. The doors to the living room and bedroom are open, both are just a few square metres in size. Fikile and her son welcome me in their small cluttered kitchen. Standing at the cooking stove, she is preparing a meal in two big pots. This is for her family, not for the customers. They sit on crates in the courtyard, under a roof, separated from the owners by iron railings. There are no chairs or tables. The mood is tense; most of the customers are not having conversations, they are exchanging sporadic shouts. A woman walks in with an empty bottle. There's a deposit on empties; after paying for the contents, she leaves with a full one.

'We don't see these customers as acquaintances or friends,' says Fikile's son:

> We see them as people we must protect ourselves against. That's why we don't sell strong stuff: you only get fights. And we often find that

beer has been stolen, when we forget to close the gate. My mother's house has also been attacked once, by seven armed guys. They took everything: money, the stereo, television, the freezer.

He says that many of the folks around here are unhappy and carry scars from the past:

They don't eat, they just drink. They start early in the morning. Not to have fun but to forget their problems and their stress. It's a big issue in our society. We open at 10 a.m., when they have often been standing outside for a long time already. We used to be open day and night. There were always customers but the neighbours complained. I can't blame them, really: at night our customers often start fights.

Indeed, the drinkers in the courtyard show tell-tale signs of having fallen on hard times or having lived hard lives, even though most of them cannot be older than their early twenties. Their faces look haggard, their clothes threadbare, and despite the early hour they have a dazed look in their eyes. At one point, someone starts a song, but when nobody joins in the silence returns. The biggest worry appears to be the next drink, and most of the time it's an SAB product. 'But', says the proprietor, 'Heineken's not doing badly either.'

One of the more approachable customers is Thando Ngobe, an unemployed young woman. Her monthly income is around 300 dollars, half of which she thinks she spends on beer. 'It's hard to calculate. I always spend too much. I'm looking for a job, but they're almost impossible to find.'

She started drinking at 8 a.m. 'Immediately after I woke up and since then I haven't stopped.' Every Sunday, she drinks together with her friend Penolope Gumade, a young woman with a tired face who works at the customer services department of Woolworth's, a supermarket chain. They say they take in two crates of beer on average. 'When the money is finished, we sleep. But fortunately we have lots of friends. So we always find a way to have another beer.'

Both women, it turns out, love Dutch beer, even though Gumade has switched to cider this weekend because she says she wants to stop drinking. Ngobe: 'Heineken is our favourite. I used to always drink Amstel but it made me unhappy. Heineken is better for me. You see: it doesn't make me fat.' They have an instruction for me: 'Tell the people in Holland that they must never stop selling this beer.'

Thomas and I continue our trip. We traverse Orlando West, where Nelson Mandela and Archbishop Desmond Tutu used to live. Vilakazi Street is now a tourist hub, with Western-style restaurants, bistros and souvenir shops. Organised Soweto trips are a hit among tourists; they include visits to iconic *shebeens*.

In Orlando East, we arrive at Mavi's place, a red brick house. Nothing on the outside suggests the presence of a *shebeen* inside. Mavi does not need iron bars. I'm given a seat among the customers in the living room, on a large plastic-covered armchair. The owner talks about her mother, who also ran a *shebeen* from this very house, half a century ago:

> She had to hide the drinks when the police came. Where the customers are seated now there was a big tree with a thick trunk. That's where we hid the stock. We mostly sold strong stuff: gin, brandy and *skokiaan*. It was easier to hide. In the eighties, the economy was doing fine and we had plenty work. My mother earned enough so she could close the *shebeen*. But when I lost my job I decided to open it again.

Like many of the *shebeen* owners, she does not serve the youth:

> They don't have respect and they're nothing but trouble. I like my customers and they like me. I can go to the toilet and never have to worry about my things. Many of my customers are on benefits. If the money runs out, they just come to watch television. They're most welcome.

As the day wears on, more and more beer drinkers appear in the street. Among the houses, plumes of smoke begin to rise from the many barbecues (*braais*). The taxi driver becomes a bit more hesitant. 'You shouldn't really be here after lunch. They become more dangerous once they're drunk.' But I want to see a proprietor who does serve alcohol to young people, and I find one in Zenzele House Shop, Mofolo. The driver will not go inside with me. He parks his car, ready for a quick escape.

Inside, I find Phumlani, who addresses his customers from behind a door with iron bars, telling them to be calm. Yes, I can come in. Why did he start a bar? He talks about his conviction: fifteen years for armed robbery. Before I can ask myself whether I am on the right side of these iron railings, he tells me that they let him out after twelve years on account of good behaviour. He has renounced his previous life. Alright then.

Phumlani says: 'I'm open from six in the morning to half past seven at night. The money is good, especially at the weekends. I don't have too many problems because I close early. There are too many rascals around at night.' He shows me the empty drinking room, in use when the weather is bad. Right now, his customers are hanging around in the street. The room is tiny and bare, maybe 6 square metres, and like his office it has a steel door. It looks as if he is imitating his former prison cell: the only decoration is a large advertisement featuring a sultry model.

Thomas, my taxi driver, is relieved to see me emerge from the bar in one piece. The atmosphere at our last stop, Mum Tozi's Tavern in the Zola neighbourhood, is a lot better. In contrast with many of her fellow *shebeen* owners, she has made a real effort to make her bar cosy. There is a jukebox in the corner and there are bar stools. Mum Tozi is also concerned with her customers' health: a condom machine has been put in a prominent place. Her daughter says that it's a busy weekend. 'Many of our neighbours were paid yesterday, they can drink whatever they want. Some of them spend almost all their money. Even if they're hungry they end up spending their last few rands on another beer.' Sometimes she refuses to serve, not selling beer to drunk-ards, children or to women she knows are drinking the house-hold budget. She is under no illusions that it really helps. 'They just go to another bar around the corner, there is always someone who will serve them. At least I have done what I could. And maybe someone will go home.'

Despite the growing competition, Mum Tozi is doing a roar-ing trade. 'As soon as someone starts a rival business we organise a special offer and everyone is back straight away.' And what are the best-selling brands, I want to know. 'SAB's,' she says without hesitation. 'Carling Black Label, Castle and Hansa are the favou-rites. Amstel used to be popular but that's over.'

Mum Tozi has an extra motivation to sell SAB's beers. 'We became shareholders five years ago, and now we're getting paid a dividend twice a year. That's a nice little extra. I have also been to workshops where you learn how to keep your temper when things get out of hand. We really feel connected to SAB.'

There is a project, called Zenzele, which means 'creating some-thing out of nothing' in the Xhosa language. Mum Tozi is a par-ticipant, together with 40,000 other black South African bar and bottle store proprietors and many SAB employees. It is SAB's way of fleshing out Black Economic Empowerment (BEE), a series of—partially successful—measures put in place by the ANC gov-ernment since 2003 aimed at reducing inequality. Employees get SAB shares for free, while the bar and store owners pay a small fee. When the company makes a profit, they get their share.[6]

'They started this in 2009, shortly before Heineken opened its brewery,' says analyst Gilmour:

> Of course this is no coincidence. They wanted to make sure the owners stayed loyal to them. You offer your clients a packet of shares, almost for free, and say: look, it's in your best interests that the value increases. If there's a better way to create loyalty among your dis-tributors, I'd like to hear about it ...

SOUTH AFRICA

The Ruud Gullit trap

The trip around the Soweto bars reveals that SAB brands hold all the power, the number of Heineken fans is growing and Amstel is having difficulties holding its ground. Before SAB lost Amstel, the brand was growing at the rate of 30 per cent per year. Heineken had set itself a target, over time, of a 20 per cent market share in terms of volume.[7] Today, its share has dipped under the 5 per cent mark.

Heineken claims that the disappointing results are due to whispering campaigns in the townships. De Man says: 'Internationally, we are used to stiff competition, but it is remarkable that a company with their pedigree should lower itself to employing such base methods.' 'For instance, they have started whispering campaigns in the townships. It is said that the water used to make Amstel is no longer the same and as a result the taste is different.'[8]

Gilmour says that Heineken is missing the point here. The company has made a major strategic error. It got itself into a battle it could not win. What did the South Africans do? They turned Carling Black Label into a slightly more upmarket brand, a little chic, semi-premium. They chose not to increase the price and invited Ruud Gullit to take part in the publicity campaign. Black South Africans have never forgotten that the Dutchman dedicated his 1987 Ballon d'Or award for the best European footballer of the year to Nelson Mandela, languishing in a South African jail at the time. One year later, Gullit was featured in a song by the reggae band Revelation Time, singing about repression in apartheid South Africa.

Gilmour: 'So this was the backhanded plan of trapping Heineken: "Come on in, boys!" And that's precisely what happened. Heineken reduced the price of its Amstel brand and got itself into a fight with Carling Black Label. They downgraded their brand, a rookie mistake.'

The South Africans have declared themselves the winners of the Beer War.[9] Gilmour thinks this is a bit premature:

> The brewery has been built. Heineken is here for the long haul. Maybe they are looking at South Africa as a starting point for distribution to other Southern African nations. The brand Heineken is doing well; you can see that for yourself in the townships. But the question is: Are they ready for another full-bore confrontation with SAB? Another full frontal attack? That will take a lot of money, time and energy.

Shortly after my visit, Heineken opted once again for an attack and launched the Amstel Light brand. The logo bore a striking resemblance to Castle Light, so much so that SAB lodged an indignant complaint with the advertising commission. The initial ruling was in its favour, but then Heineken appealed and won.[10] South Africans will enjoy the spectacle of the Beer War for some time to come.

8

CORPORATE SOCIAL RESPONSIBILITY

ALCOHOL AND CHARITY

Development and the up-and-coming middle classes—this is one way of looking at Africa's future. But if these positive developments arrive in tandem with the kind of drinking sprees I witnessed in South Africa's townships, the continent will be in for a rough ride. The WHO has pronounced Africa to be 'the next battlefield', and this time the war is not between competing beer brands. 'It's difficult for us,' says Dag Rekve of the United Nations World Health Organisation. 'We want more equality between men and women in Africa, and more wealth. But we also know that this usually leads to a strong increase in the use of alcohol. We are worried about that.'

The beer industry, with Heineken in the lead, says it is equally worried. Spreading the 'drink in moderation' or 'drink responsibly' message is an important pillar of the company's corporate social responsibility policy, on a par with its African agriculture projects. How does Heineken carry out this policy, and is it working? And what other actions does it undertake to show the world that it is serious about its corporate citizenship?

HEINEKEN IN AFRICA

Heineken writes Nigeria's alcohol policy

Let us first go to the question those impact researchers whose work is commissioned by Heineken never ask: What price does society pay for beer in Africa? In the West, it is known that alcohol consumption comes with heavy costs in terms of healthcare, safety and social care. In the Netherlands, hangovers leading to sick leave and lower productivity cost the country more than 2 billion dollars a year.[1] Add to this the alcohol-related accidents that keep police and the justice system occupied and costly prevention campaigns. Frequently, alcohol plays a role in crime, violence and the spread of sexually transmitted diseases. In France, the total damage that can be attributed to alcohol amounts to 1.7 per cent of gross domestic product, in the United States it is 2.7 per cent and in South Korea no less than 3.3 per cent.[2]

Such data are thin on the ground in Africa. In terms of public services (social and healthcare), these are likely to be relatively low, since these services are often absent or weak. Someone with drink- or drug-related problems may rely on religious figures or traditional healers, who will try to exorcise the devil or evil spirits that have taken hold of the drinker. Prevention programmes are only in their early stages.

Nevertheless, African countries pay a heavy price for alcohol problems, probably more so than the West in relative terms. Researchers are convinced that alcohol abuse is an impediment to economic development and emancipation.[3] Problem drinkers are fatalistic and less ambitious. Alcohol abuse lowers life expectancy and engenders a culture of poverty, in which a salary does not serve to improve life but is squandered on beer. A South African spends roughly 13 per cent of his income on alcohol and tobacco; a Burundian 17 per cent. Clothing and healthcare merit just 1 per cent of a Burundi salary, education 0.5 per cent.[4] Why would you work hard for success when the beer industry has persuaded you that beer means status, masculinity and heroism?

South Africa is the only country that has done research into the costs and benefits of the alcohol industry, and the findings have been alarming: negative economic effects are an estimated 10 to 12 per cent of national revenue; by contrast, the industry's own research estimates a 4.4 per cent benefit.[5]

To prevent damage, the WHO advised African governments to adopt protective alcohol policies. This was in 2005—but there is little or no incentive for these measures because selling drinks equals tax revenue, and political elites have shares in the industry. Cameroon's authoritarian President Paul Biya is a shareholder in the largest beer company in the country, in which Heineken also has a minority stake. Nigeria is another country where prominent politicians invest in beer brewers.[6]

When policymakers do want to take action, by increasing duties for instance, beer companies respond by warning that sales will drop, lowering government revenue. They rely on their impact studies to tell governments how many jobs are supposedly at stake and how much economic value is involved. Their message: getting customers to drink in moderation—that's our job. We'll take care of that.

In some countries, the brewers went proactive. A manager at SABMiller wrote the draft alcohol policies of Botswana, Lesotho, Malawi and Uganda, stressing the role of the industry in future decision-making:

> The Government will encourage active participation by all levels of the beverage alcohol industry as a key partner in the policy formulation and implementation process. The beverage alcohol industry has a vested interest in ensuring that alcohol misuse is substantially reduced, and has a unique capacity to access those responsible for promoting and selling alcohol as well as to those who consume their products.[7]

Market leader Heineken did the same in Nigeria. As one insider said: 'It makes a minister happy. After all, it's not the kind of work they like to do. If you do it yourself, things remain more or less respectable, but if you let your attention slip you may be in for a nasty surprise.' The scary spectre for the industry is the stringent anti-tobacco legislation that was gradually passed in most of the West, leading to dramatic decreases in the number of smokers and the damage they do to themselves and society.[8]

One of the industry's priorities is redirecting responsibility for problematic drinking behaviour to the end user: the product is harmless, but unfortunately some people use it in the wrong way. 'You don't control everything in your life—but you can control how much you drink,' is a Heineken slogan.[9] The brewer talks about a 'targeted approach at the individual level'. Choice quote: 'We don't believe that restrictive measures such as extra duties or a publicity ban affecting the entire population will necessarily lead to less alcohol abuse.'[10]

What we do know is that individual awareness has virtually no bearing at all on consumption levels. Coincidence? The self-regulating beer industry generally seems to prefer measures that do not have any proven effect. What does reduce alcohol abuse, according to research, is a raft of measures including higher prices, rigorous alcohol checks on the road and limiting availability by reducing the number of outlets, introducing a strict licensing regime and forcing shorter opening hours. Limiting advertising options is another possibility, especially in Africa, where people with the least resistance are being exposed to the most ingenious novelties advertisers can devise.[11]

Heineken teaches alcohol in Rwandan schools

So Heineken advocates moderation—but how? Western governments usually prescribe two glasses per day for men and one for women. Heineken writes:

CORPORATE SOCIAL RESPONSIBILITY

> We do not think it a good idea to define 'responsible' in terms of
> alcohol units only. We believe that there is one rule that guarantees
> success for all consumers, men and women, large or small. And that
> rule is: drink in moderation, at the right moment, the right place
> and for the right reasons.[12]

Communication professionals call this 'strategic ambiguity'. It
is used to appease the critics while never losing sight of the
actual objective: to sell as much beer as possible. The same ambiguity underpins campaigns like 'Dance more, drink slow', featuring the Dutch DJ and global star Armin van Buuren. The campaign exhorts drinkers to go easy on the beers—so they can
party all night. Heineken considers it self-sacrifice: the brand is
used for a moral message that runs counter to its own best interests. But critics speak of underhand marketing, since viewers will
remember the brand name and the great party atmosphere, not
so much the message that you should not drink to excess.
Presented in this way, alcohol doesn't seem dangerous but
socially accepted and harmless.[13]

Emeka Dumbili, a researcher, points out that the juxtaposi-
tion of the words 'drink' and 'responsibly' serves to instil the idea
that drinking is responsible behaviour, especially in Africa, where
English is rarely the first language spoken, and people use a
simpler language of communication like Pidgin. The slogan does
not come across as a warning. Instead, it is an encouragement:
drinking is part of a successful and responsible life.[14]

Worse, the 'drink responsibly' message is used to get children
acquainted with beer. In Rwanda, Heineken ordered 20,000 flyers
printed in the corporate colours of its Bralirwa subsidiary. These
were then distributed in schools, ostensibly to teach children not
to drink. When the campaign was launched, a banner prominently
showed the company's name.[15] Public awareness or publicity?

Former Africa director Jean Louis Homé writes that when he
was in doubt about any of his decisions he would always wonder

how a similar issue would be handled in Europe.[16] Well, how would European parents respond if their child came home from school and cheerily told them that there was this very nice lady or gentleman from this Heineken company telling them about the consumption of alcohol? This is not even a purely hypothetical question. It happened in 2005 in Spain, the Czech Republic and the United Kingdom. If successful, the programme would have been rolled out elsewhere, but nothing has been heard of it since 2006.[17]

Outside the beer sector, there is virtually no doubt: self-regulation does not work, not in the West and certainly not in Africa. You do not ask a bird to clip its own wings.[18]

The importance of heavy drinkers

'We prefer ten people all having one beer to one person drinking ten,' says spokesman John-Paul Schuirink during a conversation at Heineken Head Office. The message: our company is really serious about this, and fortunately most of our customers do drink responsibly.

'But Heineken would not be so big if everyone were to drink in moderation.' During a public debate, Heineken CEO Van Boxmeer was asked to comment on this statement. He was visibly annoyed. 'You are not going to tell me that we have to thank the world's alcoholics for most of our profits. Nobody is going to believe that.'[19]

Research, however, points in precisely that direction. A relatively small number of drinkers equals a large chunk of turnover. In the United States, 10 per cent of alcohol consumers take in half of what the nation drinks. In Britain, risky drinkers (those who exceed the guidelines of 14 units of alcohol a week for women and 21 for men) represent 38 per cent of all sales. Another quarter goes to so-called harmful drinkers: men who drink at least 50 units a week and women who consume more than 35 units.[20] Take out those groups and the industry would see its sales dwindle.

For Africa, this kind of research is not available, but the indications are that reliance on the heavy drinker is even more pronounced. One South African study, carried out in the Pretoria area, found that 10 per cent of all adults consume 70 per cent of all the alcohol.[21]

Available statistics suggest that in Africa sales of alcoholic beverages depend heavily on a small group of big consumers. Africa is home to an impressive number of abstainers, of which many are Muslim or Protestant. Nearly 70 per cent of Africans over the age of fifteen don't drink, which is proportionally almost twice as many as Europeans. Still, Africa consumes as much alcohol as the rest of the world on average, and Nigeria, Uganda and Burundi, to name a few, are drinking nations on a par with the world's biggest consumers in Europe.[22] In short, those who do drink in Africa do so with a passion.

Beer brewers put in their best efforts to increase the intake of an individual drinker. Have a look at the standard bottle, which contains at least 600 ml in almost every African country. In Congo, Rwanda and Burundi, ordering one beer gets you 720 ml and in South Africa 750 ml, that is the same amount of liquid as an entire bottle of wine or just under a pint and a half in an English pub. When I visited Sierra Leone, the standard bottle was a modest 330 ml but that went up to 600 ml shortly afterwards. The brewers like to explain this away by saying that Africans like to share their beers. There's more than a whiff of the old paternalistic attitude towards the happy socialising African;[23] reality shows us that almost everywhere the refrain is 'One Man One Bottle'.

Tastes have also been adapted to facilitate steady demand, explains Hans van Mameren in Congo. 'You know, Primus is just a blond beer, half malt, 30 per cent rice and 20 per cent sugar. It tastes a little less bitter so you can wash down loads of the stuff.'[24]

Huge risks

When in 2016, Heineken decided to start sponsoring the Formula One Championship, the corporate social responsibility department immediately sensed it had a problem. They had just issued a bulky sustainability report featuring windmills, solar panels and the quiet crystal clear waters of a countryside stream, and here they were suddenly sponsoring a circus of screaming gas guzzling race cars. Moreover: How on earth were they going to reconcile drinking with a bunch of daredevils trying their best to avoid crashing their cars?

'When it was announced, I was disappointed,' recalls Willem de Jonge, director for sustainable development at Heineken. 'But then I realised we could turn this on its head. We are using the sponsoring in order to say: when you drive, never drink. And then I thought: how clever. How unexpected.'

Heineken made an ad with Jackie Stewart, the Scottish motorsport legend. In the film, you see him repeatedly refuse a beer to reinforce the message. At Head Office, I heard: 'This is an ad to make people aware, not to sell more beers.'

It made me recall the conversation I had had in Kinshasa with Chantal Mabunda, director for public relations in Congo. She worked very hard to present Bralima, arguably the most controversial Heineken subsidiary (more on that soon), as some kind of a development organisation with a mission to promote nature conservation and the well-being and economic advancement of the Congolese. Her message appeared to be that if there were profits to be made with all those good works, so much the better.

She talked with great passion about the sustainability programme called 'Brewing a Better Future', which was supposed to have heralded a veritable revolution in the country's rural areas. To illustrate her point, she gave me a brochure highlighting the beer brewer as the 'growth sower' that was placing people 'at the heart of the economy'. Thanks to Bralima, people would now be able to 'develop their talent and potential'. Mabunda: 'We build schools and hospitals. We teach the population to read and write, we give away free computers and we do our very best for the orphans.'

It was all a bit over the top, but it illustrates the importance multinational corporations attach to corporate social responsibility. Modern companies are 'modern citizens', with a human face and a sense of community. A responsible enterprise not only wants to make profits. Instead, it uses a triple bottom line, which consists of a balance between social, ecological and financial achievements, also known as 'the three Ps': people, planet and profit.

This is even more true for multinationals in developing countries, as they risk getting their hands dirty and may suffer damage to their image as a result. They must justify their existence and have a good story to tell to shareholders, critical consumers and society's watchdogs.

Heineken faces huge risks, not only because it sells a harmful product but also because the name of the company and its signature brand are identical. If AB InBev gets caught up in a scandal, it is unlikely to lead to consumers leaving their Stella Artois or abandoning their Budweiser. Heineken is more vulnerable in that respect.

A responsible company treats its staff well, pays its taxes, adds jobs and value to the local economy and doesn't get involved in human rights abuses or other bad practices. At the same time, corporate philanthropy is also gaining ground for many companies, Heineken included.

Knowledge is power

I am in the heart of Nigeria, not far from Enugu and the giant Ama brewery, negotiating small sandy roads that take me through the deepest jungle to the village of Awhum and the Ugwuokwusinoke community primary school.

The construction of the brewery was overseen by Festus Odimegwu (we met him earlier), but its arrival has led to very little local employment. 'Everything has been automated to the highest possible degree,' manager Bernard Eloy told a Dutch daily in 2009. 'To keep the brewery operational we need just 400 staff, management included.'[25] Those living near the plant rarely qualify for a position there because their level of education is too low. The best they can hope for is a job as a security guard or a driver. As a gesture of goodwill to the local community, Heineken dug a well (not working when I visited), built a community centre and a few schools.

'Knowledge is power', says the sign outside the school at Awhum. Heineken constructed and equipped the building, painting it in the colours of its subsidiary and including the company logo. When I enter the schoolyard, two girls are crouching in the grass and look at me shamefacedly. Their teachers are gesticulating to me: don't pay them any attention. They think I am another do-gooder from overseas. Sweating profusely in the heat, they tell me how grateful they are.

When I tell them that I am on my own and want to know what works and what doesn't at the school, they show me the basic furniture and equipment. The classrooms are full to overflowing. 'The toilet has no water tank so the children must go into the bush, where there are snakes,' says one. Another says she regrets that Nigerian Breweries only provided the building and some benches. 'There are no books. And no material for a school band.' She illustrates this by making dance moves.

I have also been to a few schools in the popular Kinshasa neighbourhood of N'Djili. A member of staff at one of them, Groupe Scolaire Luango, tells me that there is capacity for 1,000 pupils, ranging in age from four to twenty years old. He shows me a few miniscule classrooms. 'Most important are these solid benches. Now everybody can sit down. We never count on the local authorities or the Ministry of Education for anything. I'm so grateful I only drink Bralima products now.'

When I ask for the rest of the story, he tells me that electricity was promised and that the roof, which is leaking, was supposed to have been repaired. None of this has happened. 'When it rains, we put all the kids in the annex. No lessons, impossible.'

In the centre of Kinshasa, I report my findings to a former Bralima director, who explodes in indignation: 'They do everything to exploit charity. I have always said that there should not be any company logo anywhere in those schools. Keep children away from that!'

Amsterdam is divided on the issue. Blanca Juti, the internal affairs director, says that she called Nigeria immediately to put an end to the business of painting company logos on schools.

'So you told them to re-paint?' I ask.

No, that's not the way things work at Heineken. This is a process that takes more time.

Africa director Pirmez does not see the problem anyway. 'The company logo is reasonably neutral,' he says, 'we don't turn this into a high-profile thing, it's just mutual recognition. We're proud that we are sponsoring this school, and they are proud that it's us sponsoring them.' Research reveals that the alcohol industry's charity projects serve as a sales tactic, especially in 'emerging markets with a large youthful population'.[26]

'I cannot tell you with a straight face that the two are unrelated,' a former director confesses. 'We believe in charity, but we also think: hold on a second, we're also a company. We don't do these things entirely for free. There must be a clear signature.'

Same story with the hospitals. An internal source at Bralima tells me that the company got into a row with the famous 2018 Nobel Peace Prize-winner Doctor Denis Mukwege. In his Bukavu clinic in eastern Congo, the doctor treats hundreds of women who have been raped and mutilated.[27] The source continues:

> We repaired a children's ward there. A Dutch specialist was sent, staff were trained, equipment arrived. When the opening ceremony came we got the media involved, as we always do. It was necessary to have our name in clear view but the doctor said no. He did not want any publicity at his clinic and certainly no beer ads. So we had a problem. We ended up putting HAF on the building, Heineken Africa Foundation, with the Heineken name in small print.

The aid industry: treacherous ground

Shortly before he retired, former director Homé bluntly admitted that Heineken's charity in Africa should not be taken too seriously:

> Community projects are more a PR thing; they are undertaken to be able to say, 'Look, we are good and beautiful.' Community projects are not fundamental. If you carry out community projects you cross the border between a development organisation and a company. We do things in terms of charity, but we never disclose them because we do not want to use this image of helping poor people.

Homé also held the view that multinationals should not take on tasks that belong in the public sector. 'We shouldn't enter that domain. We draw the line at providing healthcare for our own workers and their families. [...] Many times we have been asked to build primary schools. I have always replied that I cannot explain such expenses to my shareholders.'[28]

Well, that was in 2002, and there have been a few changes since. Clearly, a public-sector task like building a school is no longer taboo; nor is the image that Heineken is helping poor people. At the 2018 World Economic Forum, Heineken even announced a partnership with the Global Fund, a multi-billion dollar foundation supported by the Bill and Melinda Gates Foundation, which fights against Aids, tuberculosis and malaria.

The company was going to help distribute medicines in Africa and issued a press statement saying that, just like the Global Fund, its aim was to eradicate these epidemics. But very soon the company and the foundation found themselves under fire, with heavy criticism coming from the healthcare sector. Some 2,000 organisations signed an open letter claiming that Heineken contributes to the spread of those diseases and that they suspected this was just another ploy the brewer was using to influence the host countries' alcohol policies.[29]

Moreover, the company has its own charity, the Heineken Africa Foundation, with an ambitious target: to reduce the gap between the haves and the have-nots on the continent. To achieve this, the foundation has an annual budget of just over 1 million dollars available for health initiatives. Dr Mukwege's hospital was one of these projects. Partnerships with local authorities and NGOs are common, a model we saw earlier with the agricultural sector. An ambulance was acquired in Freetown. In Nigeria, there is a programme to combat yellow fever. In Rwanda, mosquito nets have been distributed to protect against malaria.[30]

The foundation's aim is to set up projects and ensure they can function independently after an initial stimulus. This is far from easy. In a poor region of Burundi, for instance, a clinic was built that gave free medicines to children, an initiative the company internally hailed as a success. But when the foundation ends its support, everything collapses. The project is unable to maintain itself because the people it serves are too poor. What is to be done?[31]

'You are entitled to your scepticism regarding these projects, and of course it's never more than a drop in the ocean, but what do you want us to do ... nothing?,' asks Katinka van Cranenburgh, who led the foundation for five years:

> Van Boxmeer has once said that we should not seek publicity with the Africa Foundation because compared to the amounts of money

we take out of these countries it amounts to nothing. That is a realistic point of view, I think. It is short term but at least we're doing something. It would be ideal if we could work for stronger democratic institutions but here at Heineken we lack the capacity to do that.

Here is another dilemma: the level of involvement of your local directors. Can you ask a top manager to immerse himself in charity work? And if so, should he be rewarded, through extra bonuses? And if you do that, are you then not defeating your original goal—doing good? The demand to make sure that administrative expenditure does not exceed 5 per cent of the budget, that is, just over 50,000 dollars per year, adds more headaches. How do you measure the impact of a project, and who should do the measuring? If you are serious about this, costs will rise well beyond that self-imposed ceiling.[32]

The development sector has known about these thorny issues for decades. With the creation of its Africa Foundation, Heineken has entered the treacherous ground of the aid industry, which is ironic in and of itself. Public confidence in development aid is waning, NGOs and governments are embracing the rules of the market, business is seen as the ideal catalyst for sustainable development; this is the spirit of the age. And now commercial companies are getting themselves involved in aid work. Just as the media are busy rebranding Africa from aid project to promising consumer market, watch the business world skillfully reintroduce well-meaning paternalism ...

By getting involved in public sector work, multinationals are facilitating corruption and bad governance in the same way the donor organisations used to do. Governments no longer see the necessity of putting their house in order when they know that third parties will do this for them. Another consequence is that the good works are unevenly spread, increasing inequality. Heineken cannot possibly repair every school near one of its breweries: So, which one gets lucky and which one does not? The selection process in Kinshasa, as one source who saw this first-hand told me, is tainted by what he calls 'Mafia practices', which means most of the money disappears along the way.

If Heineken is really serious about development, why not simply donate one million dollars a year to a reputable aid organisation? After all, the company says that all it wants to do is 'give something back to the societies where we operate' and not 'sell more products'.[33]

One possible answer is that charity, despite the misgivings about how effective it can be, is still looked upon favourably by the public and, crucially, stakeholders. Having your name attached to some projects, no matter how insignificant, makes you look good. In short, then, the Heineken Africa Foundation is primarily a PR instrument. There is no need to feature this work in yet another advert, but you can name-drop it in a presentation about Africa, on your website and when engaged in tricky negotiations with the authorities. As Homé put it: 'Look, we are good and beautiful.'

9

BURUNDI

DICTATORS COME AND GO, HEINEKEN STAYS

Burundi has no need for charity-related PR. It was, after all, Dutch Prime Minister Mark Rutte himself who praised Heineken to the heavens at a United Nations summit as an example of what this 'world-famous Dutch brewer' and its socially conscious entrepreneurship could achieve. The choice to highlight Burundi was, shall we say, a trifle unfortunate. Not everyone is happy with the role Heineken plays in a country that worships beer and refers to it as 'sacred froth'.

Between 1993 and 2005, Burundi was devastated by a civil war that killed an estimated 300,000 men, women and children. The war, similar to the genocide in its northern neighbour, Rwanda, was fought largely along ethnic lines: Hutu (about 85 per cent of the population) versus Tutsi (about 15 per cent). Since independence, Burundi has seen two major mass killings that have been called genocides. Ten years into its independence, in 1972, the Tutsi government brutally repressed a Hutu revolt, killing between 100,000 and 200,000 people. In 1993, the reverse occurred, resulting in 25,000 dead.[1]

In 2000, the warring parties signed a peace treaty, and in 2005 elections were held that brought the former Hutu rebel leader Pierre Nkurunziza to power. Things were looking better for a short while. 'There was jubilation in 2005 and 2006,' a Heineken expat remembers. In contrast to Rwanda, where the official rule-book ordains that ethnicity is socially irrelevant, Burundi instituted ethnic quotas for roles in politics and government. Initial results were encouraging.

The next elections in 2010 revealed the fragility of this success. Most of the opposition boycotted what it called a charade, and Nkurunziza was re-elected with 91 per cent of the vote. Intimidation and murder ensued, mostly targeting members of the opposition. Burundi slid into a dictatorship, and life was becoming increasingly dangerous for critical journalists, human rights activists and even ordinary citizens.

High-ranking judge works for Heineken

Burundi's Constitution states that after fulfilling two terms of office the president must go. For Nkurunziza, that moment came in 2015, but he had other ideas. When I visited Burundi for the first time, in 2012, one of his closest advisors, Willy Nyamitwe, told me that the government had been working on a ruse to stay in power. The argument ran that the president had first gained power through a parliamentary vote, as per the peace agreement, and not through direct suffrage. That was the loophole: now he would have the chance to get re-elected again but this time by the people.

Easier said than done, even for an autocrat like Nkurunziza. First, he tried to change the Constitution, but he failed to get the required majority in Parliament to push that through, and he was nearly toppled in a military coup. In the end, he put his fate in the hands of the Constitutional Court, which examines whether or not laws comply with the country's most fundamental piece of legislation.

Enter stage right: Heineken.[2] The Dutch work hand in glove with the government. They own 59 per cent of Brarudi, the local brewery; the state owns the rest. This gives the president the right to appoint non-executive members to the Board of Directors, including the chairperson.

President Nkurunziza gratefully exercised that right: on 8 April 2015, he appointed the president of the Constitutional Court, Charles Ndagijimana, as non-executive member of the board at Brarudi. On 5 May, the court almost unanimously approved the president's bid for a third term, and five months later Nkurunziza signed a decree promoting the judge to the position of chairman of the board (see fig. 4). To Stef Vandeginste, a specialist in Burundian politics at Antwerp University, this looks like mutual backscratching: 'It gives the distinct impression that prior to the court's decision they wanted to encourage the judge very strongly to take the preferred political decision, for which he was then rewarded.'

Nkurunziza kept his job, despite the protestation of the United Nations, the African Union and the European Union. Opponents remarked in jest that there was just one judge in the country: the president himself.[3]

Heineken in Burundi thus came to be formally directed by arguably the most important judge in the country. 'A *fait accompli*,' responds Africa director Pirmez at Head Office. 'They have the right to appoint him. We shared our reservations with them but that is all we could do.'

Since the president's re-election, the violence has increased, and there are fears of another civil war. Paramilitary actions and police brutality threaten not only critics of the regime but also ordinary citizens. Hundreds have been killed, many thousands are missing and up to a quarter million Burundians have fled the

REPUBLIQUE DU BURUNDI

CABINET DU PRESIDENT

DECRET N° 100/ 4 4 DU 10 OCTOBRE 2015 PORTANT NOMINATION DE CERTAINS ADMINISTRATEURS REPRESENTANT L'ETAT DU BURUNDI AU CONSEIL D'ADMINISTRATION DE LA SOCIETE « BRASSERIES ET LIMONADERIES DU BURUNDI « BRARUDI »

LE PRESIDENT DE LA REPUBLIQUE,

Vu la Constitution de la République du Burundi ;

Vu la Loi n° 1/09 du 30 mai 2011 portant Code des Sociétés Privées et à Participation Publique ;

Vu le Décret n° 100/253 du 03 octobre 2011 portant Réorganisation du Ministère du Commerce, de l'Industrie, des Postes et du Tourisme ;

Vu le Décret n°100/29 du 18 septembre 2015 portant Révision du Décret n° 100/125 du 19 avril 2012 portant Structure, Fonctionnement et Missions du Gouvernement de la République du Burundi ;

Vu le Statut de la Société « Brasseries et Limonaderies du Burundi, BRARUDI » ;

Sur proposition du Ministre du Commerce, de l'Industrie et du Tourisme ;

DECRETE :

Article 1 : Sont nommés Administrateurs Représentant l'Etat du Burundi au Conseil d'Administration de la Société « Brasseries et Limonaderies du Burundi, BRARUDI » :

· **Monsieur Charles NDAGIJIMANA,** en remplacement de Monsieur Aloys NTAKIRUTIMANA ;

Fig. 4: Presidential decree appointing Judge Ndagijimana chairman of Heineken in Burundi

nation of 10 million. Although ethnicity did not play a role in the initial stages of this particular conflict, the (Hutu) president has been ramping up ethnic tensions to such a degree that the United Nations fears another ethnic conflict.

In mid-2017, UN rapporteurs documented crimes against humanity committed by the regime: murder, rape and torture. 'We were struck by the scale and the brutality of the violations,' they wrote. Burundi then became the first country in the world to withdraw from the Rome Statute, making it impossible for the International Criminal Court to deal with crimes committed after October 2017. The regime may still be held accountable for crimes committed before that date.[4]

Ethnic lists

I am meeting Sylvère Nimpagaritse in the town of Wavre, not far from Brussels. He was the vice president of Burundi's Constitutional Court when the issue of the third term was addressed. He sits on a bench in the modest and slightly run-down station hall, waiting for me. He looks younger than I thought, and his clothes are nondescript. This man, once an esteemed high-level judge in his own country, is now a seemingly anonymous passenger in Europe.

Nimpagaritse was forced into exile because he was the one judge who resisted rubber-stamping the new presidential mandate. 'The powers that be attempted to buy our conscience,' he tells me as we sit on an outside terrace opposite an old church, despite the rather unforgiving autumn weather. I am allowed to quote him with his full name, but he wants to avoid anyone listening in:

> All judges suddenly got extra money, to be collected in person from the president. That bonus already equalled a monthly salary. Then there were promises of representation expenses, more than double

that amount. Brarudi started delivering crates of soft drinks to the court. That had never happened before and nobody had asked for it. These were all presents that carried the message: the president is thinking about you.[5]

Still, during the deliberations it emerged that four of the seven judges, him included, were in disagreement with the third term. 'The president of the court instructed us to consider the interests of the country. I was offered a whole range of sinecures, including a nice job at the revenue authority. In the end they asked me to name a price for my vote.'

Nimpagaritse ended up being the only dissenting voice, as he was convinced that a renewed presidential mandate would lead to more violence. He was forced to leave the country, pursued by paramilitary forces. His more flexible former colleagues have made impressive career advances. One has become the minister of justice, another a presidential advisor.

And the president of the court got himself that job at Heineken. In practice, being the chairman of the board does not amount to much. There are only four meetings per year, mostly brainstorming sessions about long-term developments. For attending these, he gets a payment equivalent to several times his government salary. Insiders think that when times are good the accumulation of a monthly stipend, payments in kind (crates of drinks) and a share of the profits can reach more than 30,000 dollars, an absolute fortune in Burundi. Heineken, which does not give specific details, says it is less than 25,000 dollars.

It seems that the principal imprint Ndagijimana wishes to make is ethnic. He is lobbying for an inquiry that will force employees to indicate whether they are Hutu or Tutsi. Burundi's Senate embarked on that exercise, ostensibly with the objective of confirming that the ethnic quotas are respected in the public sector. But in a country that has seen cycles of extreme violence and where tensions among various groups have been mounting again, such exercises provoke enormous suspicion. Brarudi does not work with quotas. The state holds a stake in the enterprise, but it is to all intents and purposes a private business. Unsurprisingly, employees and the company's trade union have resisted participating in the inquiry, which would have required every individual to put his or her name on a list. The directors are in full support: they want to hire people based on competence, not ethnicity.

However, sources close to the company say that Heineken is complying. Tutsis, considered to be overrepresented, are gradually being replaced with Hutus. Brarudi has very little wriggle room, owing to the scarcity of foreign exchange. If it wants to continue to operate, the company will need the best possible relations with the government.

'Heineken can save Burundi'

A prominent judge sitting on one of your subsidiary's Board of Directors—doesn't that look like a conflict of interests? Head Office does not want to answer this question.

Heineken tries to avoid rubbing Nkurunziza the wrong way. For his part, the autocrat is aware of the extent to which he relies on the beer brewer's money tap. As a shareholder, the government receives its portion of the profits, but it also gets a good chunk of its tax revenue from Brarudi. In 2015, it was 30 per cent, mostly duties, a percentage that has probably risen even further, since the economy has started to contract and many donors and aid organisations have stopped sending money.

Finance Minister Tabu Abdallah Manirakiza confirms to me that the monthly cheque Brarudi writes as payment for its duties on alcohol is spent on paying the civil service. This means that Heineken pays the salaries of the police officers, soldiers and security services.

This is not the only way the company helps out. Whenever the regime has been short of cash, Heineken can always be relied on to lend a hand by disbursing advances on future dividends or tax payments. Former finance minister Charles Nihangaza puts it bluntly: 'Brarudi is our cash cow. Our entire economy is based on that company.'

Heineken is also making friends by sending crates of drinks to influential people. For free. Here is an internal source: 'Until 2006, the list of addressees included the president, the vice president, the chairs of the National Assembly and the Senate and the minister of trade and industry. But then they also added the minister of justice and the minister of good governance. Good governance! This is pure corruption.'

And Heineken also plays a tactical game with the allocation of the more than 100 lucrative sales depots it possesses. Managing one of these usually demands a hefty investment, but high-ranking officials have access to favourable credit arrangements. 'If you have a governor or a minister with you, you avoid problems,' says someone with intimate knowledge. 'It is even smarter to enlist an influential senior civil servant or someone from the military. They stay; politicians come and go. That's the way we buy peace and security.'

When I briefly interviewed the president in 2012, I was struck by his praise for Brarudi, even though he presents himself as someone who stays away from alcohol. He told me: 'This company contributes tremendously to the development of our country because they pay a lot of taxes, they ensure employment and they increase the people's spending power.' (Shortly before the interview, an advisor called me and made it clear that I was not to ask questions about politics or human rights.)

Unfortunately, my time with the president was so limited that I could not ask him about the Fund to Support Good Initiatives. The sale of one bottle of Primus sends five francs into that fund, making Brarudi its principal donor. Every year, the fund has around 1 million dollars at its disposal. 'It's a presidential private account,' says journalist Bob Rugurika. 'There is no oversight. He gives the money to voters in a bid to gain popularity. He hands out 10,000 francs notes [6 dollars] to school children.' A former top manager at Heineken refers to it as 'presidential play money', while another journalist, Esdras Ndikumana, bluntly calls it 'a racket'.

'Yes, that fund plays an important role in corruption,' recognises Léonidas Hatungimana, a former presidential spokesman. 'Imagine it paying for a school, worth 10,000 dollars. What happens is that 14,000 dollars are awarded and 4,000 dollars goes to the presidential party. The fund is an important source of income.'

Hatungimana was one of the first big shots in the ruling party who disagreed with his boss's third-term plans. He fled to Belgium, where I meet him in a bar full of Burundian dissidents, not far from Antwerp Central Station. For eight years, he also sat on Brarudi's Board of Directors to top up his salary. 'When I started working for the president my salary shrank while I had a car and a house to pay off,' he says. 'To compensate for all that I was given a position at Brarudi. They help the regime with political and social issues. For us, Heineken is a female breast that gives milk to the children.'

Hatungimana is convinced that Heineken could save the country today by pulling the plug on the operation:

Financially, they are complicit. We know that politically speaking Heineken is not in favour of the president but they help him out. They and the government are completely intertwined. If Heineken takes the courageous decision to depart I am certain that within three months the regime will be history. If they block accounts and put an end to the supply of bottles and raw materials the state will be in no position to offset that.

Should that happen, Hatungimana thinks there will be two options: either the president accepts real peace negotiations that will allow him to leave office with his head held high or the defence and security forces go through a 'patriotic reawakening' that will result in the president's forced removal. 'I pray the Good Lord that this will happen. Heineken can save Burundi.'

The brewery as presidential morgue

Heineken has previously been implicated in political crimes and serious human rights abuses in Burundi. In the 1990s, the beer brewer got caught in the crossfire, and the question was raised of whether its prolonged presence could be justified. It seems as if history is repeating itself.

In 1993, there was cause for optimism when Melchior Ndadaye, a Hutu, was elected president in the country's first ever democratic election. Yet just a few months later he was dead, murdered by a mutinous group of Tutsi soldiers.

The phone rang in the Amsterdam office of Homé, director for Africa. On the line, Brarudi's top manager, Jean-Paul van Hollebeke. 'Jean Lou, I have an officer in my office here. He is asking for permission to use the cold room where we keep the concentrate for our soft drinks.'

Homé said nothing.

Van Hollebeke: 'It's to put the body of the late president there.'

'I don't consider that to be a good idea,' replied an astonished director, who had met the president not too long ago and had retained a good impression of him. Homé wanted to avoid associating the brewery 'any more than necessary' with this situation.

'He has a Kalashnikov,' the other side reported.

'You don't argue with a Kalashnikov. But try to make him agree that the funeral march does not start at the brewery.'[6]

The assassination did not mark a Tutsi power grab, but it was the start of a twelve-year civil war. As is the case in the current crisis, Heineken played an important role as it continued to bankroll the police and army. Back then, the authorities also resented what they perceived as the overrepresentation of Tutsis within Brarudi.

In late 1993, a chilling event took place at the Gitega brewery that would link the company directly to the ongoing slaughter. A menacing crowd of Hutus, armed with machetes and other weapons, had gathered at the gate. Their targets were the Tutsis working for the company. One of them, unable to reach safety, had been murdered immediately. Thirty others had gone missing. Towards the end of the afternoon, the army intervened and dispersed the crowd using a tank. And now, Homé recalls, the Hutus were the ones who felt threatened. Fifty of them took shelter in a building on the premises, where they would remain holed up for more than a month.[7]

Employees and neighbouring residents in Gitega filed a complaint and sent it to management. In it, they detailed six assassinations of company employees and claimed to know exactly who was responsible. Brarudi's deputy director, also the manager at Gitega, was named as the mastermind behind the killings, but Homé insisted that this was impossible: the man had apparently been elsewhere at the time of the events. Heineken decided to keep the murders of its own employees under a shroud of silence—after all, the brewery had expressed the wish not to be associated with the conflict 'any more than necessary'.[8]

The war got worse when Cyprien Ntaryamira died. He was the successor of the murdered Ndadaye and a member of the same party. Ntaryamira was sharing an aeroplane with his Rwandan colleague Juvénal Habyarimana when it was shot out of the Kigali sky on 6 April 1994, the event that triggered the Rwandan genocide. In Bujumbura, a macabre tradition seemed to be established, because once again, the mortal remains of a president were kept in the cold room at the brewery.[9]

Heineken ignores the embargo

Two years later, Burundi was rocked by another coup, staged this time by Pierre Buyoya, a Tutsi. Supported by the UN Security Council, the neighbouring countries announced a trade embargo in protest.[10] Heineken was exposed. 'If it weren't for us, this government would have been bankrupt,' admitted director Georges Hanin. 'Strange,' reflected a Nairobi-based UN staffer. 'If the Dutch shut the Brarudi beer tap, the Tutsi elite will not survive very long, given the size of the Hutu majority.' The German press agency DPA drew a harsh conclusion: 'Without beer, this Burundi war would have ended ages ago.'[11]

The entire national economy had ground to a halt with the exception of the breweries. And—as in the current conflict—the donors decided to suspend their aid, thus increasing Burundi's reliance on Heineken even more. The brewery in the capital became a fortress, 'quite possibly the most tightly guarded building in Bujumbura,' surrounded with barbed wire and a permanent military security presence.[12] Ordinarily, the folks who stage a *coup d'état* target the presidential palace, radio and television headquarters and the airport, but in Burundi you will have made serious progress once you have the Bujumbura brewery under your control.

The brewery had to be kept going at all cost: after an attack that knocked out power supplies, the company changed to generators, and when militias paralysed bus transport, Heineken put its own personnel buses into service. The brewery also kept exceptionally large supplies in store. 'We managed to keep working for eight days in January while all of Bujumbura was without electricity and water,' boasted Hanin. 'Since my arrival in 1994, production has not halted even once. That's a record in Bujumbura.'[13]

In those days, the safest way to travel around the country was probably on board a lorry with Primus Beer, which reached every corner of the country. A journalist for *The Guardian* witnessed soldiers start the day with their ration of three large bottles of Primus. Critical observers allege that this contributed to their excessive use of violence.[14] 'The country was on its knees, but the lorries laden with Primus just kept on going as if nothing was happening,' recalls Ndikumana:

> In rebel-held territory, they had to give money or a few crates to get past the control posts. Beer is one of those products that just keeps selling. Some people had lost everything, but all of a sudden police, army and rebels were rolling in money. Everyone needed a beer more than at any other time I can remember, just to forget the day's events.

Externally, Heineken assured everyone it was respecting the embargo; internally, that was never the intention.[15] In 1997, when the brewery was faced with dwindling stocks, Heineken claims the Burundian government imported malt from Rwanda to be used in the local breweries. Heineken said it received 'veiled threats' to resume production. 'We have made a choice, for the sake of our employees' safety,' a spokesman commented.[16]

But in the book in which he extensively describes the conflict, Homé mentions no threatening authorities. Instead, he writes that 'we' (i.e. Heineken) succeeded in getting the delivery from Kigali to Bujumbura. The company also concealed the fact that it had found an ingenious back route, out of Durban in South Africa to the north of Zambia. There, on the southern tip of Lake Tanganyika, lies the normally sleepy little port town of Mpulungu. The place probably had the busiest few months of its entire existence, thanks to Brarudi. Mpulungu was the point of departure for the 600-kilometre northbound route across the lake—to Bujumbura.[17]

A former Brarudi director confirms this:

> The raw materials kept coming in, although they used back routes. But it is simple. The state wants beer, the army wants beer, the rebels want beer and the people want beer. What do you want us to

do? Beer is what we produce. The army got a daily beer ration, and the rebels had more meat because it was easier for them to steal cows. So sometimes they swapped: beer for meat. And then they started shooting at each other again.

In March 1997, Heineken dropped all pretence that it was respecting the embargo, even though the company kept mentioning threats to justify its decision. Frodebu, the Hutu party, considered this a scandal. 'Heineken is becoming an accomplice to genocide,' was the judgement of a party spokesperson. In this case, use of that particular term is without doubt a wild exaggeration, but there were certainly large-scale ethnically motivated killings going on.[18]

In the Netherlands, Frodebu's view that Heineken should leave because it was supporting a military regime engaged in a bloody civil war found support: FNV, the largest trade union federation in the country, and the Netherlands Burundi Committee agreed with its position. To increase pressure further and frame Heineken as the protector of a war criminal, Frodebu decided to reveal the Gitega murders three years after the fact and alleged that the company had failed to discipline the deputy director allegedly responsible.[19]

Heineken's defence was amateurish. Homé blames the short deadline provided by the Dutch *NRC* newspaper. First, the company said that there had been twenty-three dead at Gitega; a few days later, this figure had been reduced to one dead and five missing.[20]

This rank clumsiness handed Frodebu more ammunition. Only six months earlier, Heineken had been forced to beat a humiliating retreat from Myanmar, following growing international outrage about its collaboration with the country's dictatorship. Now the Hutus hoped to achieve the same in Burundi. The FNV stoked the flames some more by stating that employee safety had been compromised as a result of Heineken ignoring the embargo. 'The much more active role Heineken will be playing now may result in Hutu reprisals later.'[21] A taste of its own medicine, surely: the brewer's main concern was for its own workforce, right?

Clearly, the company had been caught in a web of lies and half-truths of its own making. Just like today, the only thing Heineken wanted to do was sell beer, irrespective of the consequences. The last thing it wanted to do was to turn its back on a beer-crazy country where it had been active for forty years. The conviction was that every civil war would come to an end and even this country would rise again.

The solution was to hold the line, and gradually the situation did indeed calm down. Homé declared himself the winner of the media battle, especially when the same Dutch newspaper (*NRC*) published an article arguing that both sides had a point under the headline 'Heineken in Africa, Peace Bringer or Collaborator?' Ahmedou Ould-Abdallah, the UN's special representative in Burundi and a friend of Homé's, said that if Heineken were to withdraw, he feared the worst:

> The government will do everything it can to keep the breweries open, and it will not hesitate to use forced labour, smuggling routes and other illicit practices. Should the government shut the breweries down, the economy will backslide even further, leading to a sharpening of the ethnic political conflicts in the country.[22]

History did not prove him right. The one party doing well out of all this was Heineken, as life in Burundi got steadily worse; it is currently the world's second poorest nation. One may well wonder what fifty years of economic dominance by Heineken has brought the people, apart from a phenomenal thirst ...

'What do you think would have happened if Heineken had decided to leave Burundi?' Homé asked this question when reflecting on the situation in the 1990s: 'We would have condemned the country to death, our 1,200 employees would have been made redundant and the country would have been in a terrible state.'[23]

10

WORKING FOR HEINEKEN

THOSE WOMEN WERE RAPED

There was something Homé forgot to say when he presented Heineken as the great protector of 1,200 jobs in Burundi, namely that shortly after the war had ended Heineken fired hundreds of people. There were 1,350 employees in 1997. Four years later, about half of them remained.[1] In its Code of Conduct, Heineken calls its workers 'our greatest assets', but in Burundi they served as its alibi, a screen to hold up and justify a difficult decision: Heineken stays in Burundi because it cares for its people, even when its presence supports a dictatorship.[2] This leads us to our next theme: working for Heineken—what is it like?

Training and perks

Not bad, at first sight. Across the continent, I have met former employees who look back with pride on their careers—no matter whether they were carrying crates or running the brewery. In their homes, photos and trophies from those days are prominently on display in the living room, and the old company glasses and beer mats grace the cupboards. Former managers in Kinshasa, Lagos and Freetown hold fond memories of their visits to Amsterdam, Rotterdam and other Dutch cities and wax nostalgic about seeing the country's largest brewery in Zoeterwoude near The Hague or the soft drinks factory in Bunnik, close to Utrecht. Some recall having met the legendary CEO Freddy Heineken, others remember a young and impulsive Van Boxmeer. Almost everyone still feels they are part of the Heineken family.

The brewer's approach is smart. Most of its staff members are on relatively low salaries, also in local terms, but Heineken compensates for this by being an attentive and encouraging employer. Remunerations rise in tandem with increased responsibilities, professionalism and performance. For many African employers, the dream to start at a low level and finish their careers as managers has become reality. 'As a simple operator you don't earn much,' says a former Rwandan manager whose first job was as a maintenance engineer. 'But supervisors and higher staff are well paid, and when I started out there were many more managerial roles available, compared to other companies. If you do your work well, you get recognised and promoted.'

Heineken endears itself to its personnel with incentives in different shapes and sizes. When salespeople reach their targets, they can double their modest fees or get even more. And then there are the perks that increase someone's status; these are very popular. Employees are proud to have a company car, motorbike or phone for free or given out under lenient repayment conditions, so everyone can see that they are doing well. In more and more countries, salesmen get tablet computers to keep track of their performance. And if the device is still working after two years, they can keep it.

For most of Heineken's Africa staff, there is no pension scheme, but at the end of their careers they are often entitled to a good severance package. Some of the more energetic ones use the money to start their own company. I found former employees who had started a fish farm, a consultancy business or a bakery. Still others stayed faithful to their old line of work and started a bar.

Employees also appreciate the wide range of training courses, available at all levels. New knowledge and skills facilitate promotion or a move to another company, for the benefit of the economy and society at large. The in-house courses have existed for as long as Heineken has been brewing beer on the continent. In the early days, staff learned production and sales techniques or simply to read and write.[3] Training became more intensive in the 1960s and '70s when Heineken answered the call for Africanisation. At first, Africans were readied for higher-level roles in the Netherlands and the United Kingdom, but later on the company built training centres in Nigeria and Congo.[4] 'The local school system is hopeless but you need engineers,' reflects a former manager in Nigeria:

> So the company trains more than 100 engineers, all expenses paid, and puts them to work in the breweries. It worked so well that Shell and other oil companies came head-hunting here, but that was not the idea. I went to Shell and told them: listen, it's fine if you want to join in but keep your hands off our people.

A little paradise on earth

One group of employees gets fussed over more than most: expats. True, the number of African managers has risen across the entire continent, but in most countries whites remain at the top of the pecking order.[5] Heineken takes extremely good care of them and always has. The records say that entry-level employees at Nigerian Breweries get a little over 2,000 dollars per year, while the company spends the same amount *every day* on a Dutch director—not counting the bonuses. The average wage is thirty-five times lower than that of the top manager.[6]

Very often, the company maintains luxury villas on or near the premises, for expatriate staff. They do not pay rent. The documentary *Een Hollands biertje in Afrika* (A Dutch beer in Africa) shows us around the Kinshasa homes of marketing director Dolf van den Brink and the brewery's manager, Remco Rijsenbrij, and their families. 'A little paradise on earth' and 'an oasis of tranquillity'—that is how Van den Brink's wife Sylvia describes the villa with a luxuriant garden, swimming pool and a staff of five. But she also feels part of Congolese life. 'If you step out of the gate, you are immediately surrounded by the madness.'[7]

At times, there is some resentment between expats and local staff. Often the Dutch are not terribly impressed with local know-how. One director says: 'Here in Congo-Brazzaville you must explain everything down to the tiniest detail. Assertiveness just isn't their style.' She qualifies the Congolese as 'nice, happy, opportunistic and disorganised. They don't plan ahead, but they always find a last-minute solution.'[8]

In the neighbouring Democratic Republic of Congo, Dutch expats complain about the local population: 'They don't have the aptitude for refined work, because very few have that dexterity. It's the result of bad education. A lot of them have never learnt how to punch little holes or colour inside the lines,' says former manager Hans van Mameren, who claims he knows the people inside out.[9]

Africans do not always feel appreciated, and sometimes the clash in attitudes causes resentment. That was the case in Algeria, where local employees were not impressed with the ostentatious culture among the expats with their luxury cars and all manner of finery, while their own requests for a modest raise were categorically refused. I also spoke to a former brewery manager, an African, who claimed he was paid half the salary of the man who reported to him, a European. Worse, the expat got more business class flights.

Expats who stay in Africa face risks and problems. One veteran remembers how he was sent to Angola in the 1980s, quite inexperienced. 'I got a crash course in Portuguese, but it would have been better if they had prepared me for the exceptional circumstances of the place.' Angola was embroiled in a furious civil war at the time. These days, expats are much better informed: they are briefed about current affairs in the host country and the kind of society they enter. The security situation is explained to them by the Protection & Security Company, or Proseco, a subsidiary created by Freddy Heineken after his headline-grabbing abduction in November 1983. Several former staff have told me that Proseco has on-the-ground knowledge of what is going on and whether or not a dangerous situation is developing. 'They're better informed than the Dutch embassy,' was the word in Congo and Burundi.

Partners of the expats, mostly women, tend to resign from their jobs and have difficulty finding something useful to do, far away from friends and family. Paul Kemp, an old Africa hand, says:

> In a place like Congo there is literally nothing to do for your wife. There is always someone doing the cooking, your house gets cleaned, you have a driver and a gardener. Basically, my wife is confined to the beautiful golf course in Brazzaville and the other options are tennis and going swimming.[10]

Expat families live in tiny cocoons. High points are the matches of the Dutch national football team, broadcast via satellite. The documentary mentioned earlier tells us that one of the partners finds Kinshasa far too hot; her routines have become even more mundane than they were in the Netherlands. The other admits in so many words that back home, she would never seek the company of the people who have now become her best friends. To add some purpose to their presence in Congo, the two women and a third expat wife have decided to deal with 'this whole poverty business'. With some money from the brewery and some fundraising of their own, they have rehabilitated a few schools and hand out pieces of bread.

Becoming an expat is not the exclusive preserve of Europeans. The best managers in Africa have these opportunities too and enjoy the same premiums and bonuses, although they are cheaper for the company because their basic salaries are lower. The Nigerian Oladele Ajayi made it to the post of director for Heineken in Hungary, not known for its tolerance towards non-Western foreigners. As for Eugène Ubalijoro, a Rwandese manager whom we shall meet later in the book, he became the export manager for North and South America, based in Miami.

Company clinics and antiretrovirals

Following independence, many African governments had ambitious plans for their healthcare systems, but political turbulence, mismanagement and lack of money put paid to most of that. Hospitals became 'autonomous', which meant that patients had to bring their own medicines and pay in cash for treatment. As an employer, Heineken had to budget for these costs.[11]

In 1989, the company decided to take matters into its own hands. Henk Rijckborst, who headed Heineken's medical service at the time, says:

> It was irritating to say the least that we were paying good money without getting anything in return, and we knew that if you ran your own clinics service would be cheaper and better. But that was not the main reason. It was emotion. Are those 8,000 staff in Africa other people? They are also Heineken. Those clinics were cheap to run.

His successor Stefaan van der Borght adds: 'It was humanism to a certain extent, but most of all it had to do with a sense of righteousness. Heineken was still a truly Dutch company with a Dutch ethos. Being Belgian, I noticed that. The default position was: this is how we do things at Heineken.' However, after the turn of the century, Van der Borght and other insiders watched that attitude quickly disappear.

Yet the old way of doing things still prevailed when towards the end of the 1980s the first alarming reports arrived from Africa about Aids. Rijckborst: 'We proposed to set up a prevention programme, immediately, which frightened the marketing boys. Like baby food, beer is a hyper-sensitive consumer good. Nothing should tarnish it.' So that programme never materialised.

Freddy Heineken's first worry was the pension scheme: this epidemic was likely to cost heaps of money:

> If the Aids disease develops worldwide in the way as is currently expected in medical circles a much higher mortality may well follow, also among a population that is still young. For the scheme this may mean that the obligatory payments to widows and orphans will rise strongly and unexpectedly.[12]

In the late 1990s, when the disease become the principal cause of sick leave and death among the African workforce, the company was implored to hand out antiretrovirals. There were sporadic prevention-related activities, but the beer brewer was not going to pay for medication that was costing more than 10,000 dollars per year at the time. That attitude changed after an Aids conference in Durban (2000), where Professor Joep Lange, a clinical researcher specialising in HIV therapy, called on companies to stop looking the other way. Lange was the founder of PharmAccess, a foundation that lobbied for cheaper antiretrovirals. He told Van der Borght that in the near future therapy would be available for a few dollars per day. 'You can afford this,' he said. 'Why shouldn't you do it?'[13]

In fact, there was a whole raft of reasons for saying no. Costs would be higher than benefits. Local subsidiaries would be swamped with seropositive job applicants. The treatments would link Heineken directly to Aids and would therefore lead to reputational damage. And it was thought that African employees did not have sufficient willpower to take daily treatment. Nevertheless, in the summer of 2001 the Board of Directors gave the green light, even when many other companies were unwilling to take the risk. HIV-positive Heineken workers in Africa and their immediate families were offered therapy for life, which would continue after retirement or redundancy. All objections were waved away, and the mortality rate at the breweries fell rapidly. Therapy always came with counselling, free condoms and HIV tests.[14]

The caseload turned out to be much smaller than expected. In all, Heineken gave antiretrovirals to no more than 500 people. Rijckborst comments: 'The high costs of paying for hospitals and funerals were gone. The best thing of all was that people could continue working, which meant that our training efforts were not wasted. It was beyond what we had expected.'

Van der Borght thinks the project was never set up to make the company look good:

> On the contrary: we were not allowed to publicise its existence because there was a fear that this could lead to criticism along the lines of 'Yes but you and your alcohol are responsible for those infections, it's like you are buying clemency.' This is not the kind of discussion you want to have.

Heineken eventually decided to come out once it became clear how much goodwill the project was generating. Rijckborst recalls: 'I was introduced to Bill Clinton and Ban Ki-moon. I have given lectures all around the world. At UNAIDS they told me that they only drank one brand: Heineken. The whole world was looking at us.' To this day, Heineken's Aids policy remains the company's showpiece.

Workplace deaths, especially in Africa

Heineken took a risk and was rewarded with satisfied workers, reduced costs and an improved reputation. One can imagine a

Board of Directors thinking wistfully: if only it could always be like this. Unfortunately, such behaviour is not always in evidence. Take, for instance, the issue of workplace safety. A constant headache.

According to the company's own statistics, 150 people—personnel or subcontractors—died in work-related incidents between 2005 and 2016, and the real figure, Heineken says, may well be higher. Each and every year, corporate communication relays the message that this is an issue 'of permanent attention and concern', but the trend is up rather than down. Incomplete information reveals that Africa is strongly overrepresented. If deaths occur at Heineken, it is mostly on this continent. People fall from scaffolding, are crushed under a fence, are killed in an explosion or burned alive. Also every year, many acquire permanent disabilities as a result of amputations, burns and other incidents.[15]

A former expat recalls seeing shocking scenes all over the continent. Handling chemicals and the palletiser carry the biggest risks:

> In a brewery, caustic soda is used as a cleaning agent. They come in flakes and you have to dissolve these in water. If you do it the wrong way, you will release a lot of heat and the tank will overflow. And if it's you standing next to the tank—it's basically goodbye. Happens on average once every year somewhere. I have pointed out internally that there's a solution for this, which requires a small investment, but it's not a priority issue.

The other problem is the palletiser, the machine that loads empty pallets with crates of beer and unloads the full ones. 'It's mostly maintenance engineers that get caught,' says the same expat. 'They are working on the machine, but the colleague at the controls doesn't know this. There are ways to organise this properly, but you'll have to spend some extra money on it.'

According to this expat, there is not a great deal of willingness in Africa to address the issue. Frequently, he saw people placing heavy bottles into beer crates all day long, or carrying 50 kg bags of malt. This is literally backbreaking work and unthinkable in the West but considered perfectly normal in Africa. There are stories of employees whose eyes were perforated by exploding glass and someone drowning in the water basin while having a beer at night without anyone noticing. 'That's their own fault. But these things wouldn't happen if you put a fence up. In Europe, these risks are kept at a minimum.'

But another insider thinks that Heineken is doing its best to bring safety standards on a par with the rest of the world. 'It's more than a fence here or there,' he says:

> Mostly it's behaviour. Africans arrive here from a totally unsafe environment. Just look at the traffic, or domestic amenities: everything outside the company gate is different, and when they come in they must behave in an entirely new way. We keep ramming the message home again and again and a lot has improved. But it's still a problem.

Staff and temps—two different worlds

Burundi and Ethiopia were not the only countries where hundreds of jobs disappeared. Hundreds, if not thousands, were made redundant in Congo, Nigeria, Algeria and Egypt, often carelessly. This is not just the result of modernisation and more efficiency; the other factor is subcontracting. The goodbye is rarely pleasant: Heineken sheds its workers as cheaply as possible, and it often takes legal action to force decent severance payoffs from the company. A former expat observed tartly: 'It's "squeeze them until they're dry".'

Subcontractors and zero-hour workers are increasingly used, and as a result Africa witnesses a now familiar division: on the one hand, employees with a contract, and on the other temporary workers and day labourers. Conditions of work for the latter groups are much worse, and often they do not know whether or not they will be needed the next day. They are no longer just doing jobs that are generally outsourced (security, cleaning, catering) but now also perform roles that are at the heart of the brewing process: bottling, warehouse jobs, administrative roles.

In 2017, a group of almost 300 South African temporary workers objected to their treatment and lodged a complaint against the company at the Commission for Conciliation, Mediation and Arbitration, a labour tribunal. They allege that Heineken is breaking a law that says that on-call workers must work under the same conditions as their permanent colleagues and that they have the right to a contract after three months of temping. They are also systematically underpaid. Worse, some of the temping agencies do not pay by the hour but only for the work done. On a slow day, workers may end up with no more than 24 rand (around 2 dollars), barely enough to cover travel expenses. 'It's simply the same old system of cheap black labour we had under apartheid—but in a different way.'[16]

In many countries, the income of a day labourer or a temporary worker does not amount to the 'decent standard of living' that the company says is its goal. A cleaner in Congo cannot survive on a monthly salary of 40–50 dollars, and even a security guard who makes three times as much will find it hard to make ends meet in this expensive country. Moreover, external workers have no rights to medical aid or other services. In theory, it is the agencies that must ensure these, but failure to do so does not stop Heineken from working with them. A former employee in Bukavu remembers that he had to work for nothing in the first month and for half a salary during the next few months.

In Lubumbashi, also in Congo, I meet a sales assistant who is working for Bralima but as a kind of freelancer. 'One week I get two crates as compensation, the next week I get nothing,' he says:

I hope that this leads to a real job. I make money by burning DVDs and sometimes I work as a DJ, just enough to cover my travel and phone expenses. I go to the brewery nearly every day and I visit the bars that do not order enough or where there are problems. It's a full-time job.

His boss, who does get paid, confirms the story. He gets four crates of beer per month, which he redistributes to maintain relations and keep customers. 'Sometimes I give away more and pay for it myself. Bralima feels that you must invest in order to show that your heart is in the business.'

In Lubumbashi, a temporary worker cannot take a break. 'When the directors leave for lunch, the staff just keeps working,' one of them says:

> They have to ask colleagues to get them a sandwich. We were sup-
> posed to get a canteen but the budget for that has been cut. They
> don't have the whip like they used to in colonial times, but the pres-
> sure of work is too much and bears no relation to our salaries. For
> instance, they want you to use and clean machines at the same time!

He says he laughs out loud at the slogan of the Fondation Bralima, Heineken's local charity: 'Committed to the well-being of the Congolese.' And concludes: 'Let them start with the well-being of their own workers.'

Research shows that they were raped

If there is one group to whom the temp's last words should apply, it's the 'beer promotion girls', young women who must use their charms in order to improve the sale of beer in the bars. In South East Asia, this has led to controversy on numerous occasions; in Africa, the practice occurs as well, albeit largely under the radar.

In 2000, a group of aid organisations in Cambodia sounded the alarm about these women. They spoke of 'indirect sex workers' who earned very little and ran great risks of being harassed and infected with HIV.[17] Heineken wanted to tackle the problem in South East Asia immediately. An internal working group was formed, which turned out to be a paper tiger.

More action came when an important shareholder lodged a complaint. 'Internally, we appealed to morality and the rights of women, but we saw that an angry letter from an investor yielded better results,' says Van Cranenburgh, the former Heineken for Africa director, who took responsibility for the issue within HR. She drew on her experiences to research and write a thesis entitled 'Money or Ethics'.[18]

Heineken issued a series of guidelines entitled 'Promotion Girls Policy: Selling Beer Safely'. Henceforth, the young women would receive training, and the company promised to try to ensure better working conditions. 'It was difficult because these girls were not directly employed by us and turnover was large,' recalls HR manager Hans Wesseling. 'We started off on the wrong foot by mistaking this for a medical problem instead of a social issue. Heineken was going to tell these girls how to have safe sex when research showed that they were raped.'

As early as 2003, Heineken became aware that similar problems were occurring in Africa.[19] A spokesman at the time commented in a Dutch daily: 'It's nothing special. It's like the girls you used to see walking on the streets in the Netherlands, giving away free magazines of a private broadcaster wearing a dress with its logo.'[20]

Wesseling:

We had promotion girls in Africa. We knew this, in spite of internal denials. It was extra problematic because we had been running a very successful Aids policy in Africa. We had won the admiration of many, including the American Congress, where black representatives and senators were pleasantly surprised at what we did in Africa. It gave our people in the United States a great story. So nobody was going to kill that image with African promotion girls having to sell our beer under the direst of circumstances. Better to frame that as a local custom: 'That's how they do things over there.'

In 2007, a large-scale internal inquiry showed that Heineken was using about 15,000 promotion women, mostly in non-Western countries. In some places, it was customary for a client to order his beer with one of the girls (not the bartender) and elsewhere they were cast in the role of hostess. No fewer than seventy markets were considered risky because the work involved or could lead to sexual abuse, low pay, being forced to drink or wearing provocative uniforms. Sixteen of those markets were in Africa: circumstances were least favourable there, and Heineken was said to use almost 2,000 promotion women. Only one African market was problem-free; in four others, those involved refused to fill in the questionnaire.[21]

Heineken chose Diego Centurion, a twenty-one-year-old intern at the time, to conduct the research, lending credence to the notion that the brewer did not consider this a subject of great importance. 'I was a little taken aback that they asked me for such a delicate and important subject,' he says. 'I considered it a sign of trust, and I was hoping I could do something meaningful for the women.'

Further research in Congo, the country where the most abuse was reported, revealed that unwanted advances not only came from customers but also from Heineken staff. Often, the girls, who earned less than half the income of a cleaner, had to sleep with managers if they wanted to keep their job. They regarded sexual acts as part of their job. But when it came to covering healthcare costs they had to sort everything out for themselves, spending most of their money at gynaecologists or (often illegal and dangerous) abortion clinics. They also had to drink five to ten standard 720 ml bottles of beer every working day, in order to persuade customers to consume more (see fig. 5). What did Bralima get out of this in terms of extra sales? The research says that this is unknown.

'I don't think they were that valuable,' says a former director for Congo:

Heineken
International

visit report

Health Affairs

visit to
Kinshasa & Matadi
period
16-21 October 2007

Heineken
International

The main issues in DRC are:

1. **Employment status:** PW have no contract although they can work for Bralima for several years. PW are hired via the company of "Zeng" but in fact Bralima is totally in control of all issues related to PW. The enormous uncertainty of keeping a job combined with the absence of employee rights or legal status makes PW vulnerable for misuse from several stakeholders.

2. **Organization of work:** PW application and supervision structure is depending on the decisions of individuals within the sales organization of Bralima and "Zeng". PW have little career chances, the "Zeng" company is not able to offer different jobs to PW when they finish working for Bralima. Employability is low and not being improved by the company.

3. **Transport:** PW are not transported back home by company bus but depend on public transport. The safety and security risk is mainly between approximately 22.00 – 23.00 hrs. Transport fee is fixed, 3 US$ per week

4. **Training and Information:** PW are not trained or informed on the health and safety risks they face at work.

5. **Harassment:** PW are pressured by supervisors to remain in their function. They have to deliver "love" or sexual services to Bralima employees within the sales organization in order to keep their jobs. Although a difference should be made in "love relations" and "appointment for sexual services", both are related to career perspectives of the PW and are therefore in conflict of interest. Sexual harassment by consumers is accepted as a normal occupational matter. Harassment by the outlet owner is experienced in the form of having to do work that is outside the scope of their jobs.

6. **Safety:** PW face occupational risks in the form of being exposed to fighting customers causing glass cuts, fighting with PW (Amazon) of BraCongo and by being drugged by having drugs being placed in glasses of PW

7. **Alcohol:** PW drink more than the advised daily units of beer (stated by PWs to be 5 to 10 bottles of beer on a daily basis). This is encouraged by the salesmen and seems to be necessary to convince the consumer to buy more beer.

Fig 5: Heineken internal report on issues regarding promotion women, Congo, 2007

It was a mess. When this thing was going on in Cambodia, we also got rules but they did not change a great deal. For a while, management hired taxis to get the girls home at night, but eventually they decided that this was too expensive. Those girls were getting less than the minimum wage, and they were used by Bralima personnel. Very often these were girls with problems, very vulnerable. Given that we paid them so very little, they were virtually forced to go home with a man.

Van der Borght of the medical service says that at one point Heineken tried promotion boys:

We wanted to take away the association with sex but it didn't work. Another problem was that we used subcontractors, for reasons of flexibility. Sometimes you needed a lot of girls, for parties, and at other times it was calm. So you were burdening these subcontractors with the workload and the social obligations while Heineken was held accountable.

The medical department lobbied hard at the top to address the problem, but the issue was not a priority. In 2008, eight years after the alarm was first sounded, the Dutch daily *De Telegraaf* wrote that more than half of Heineken's promotion girls in Cambodia were sexually harassed, 90 per cent were sexually intimidated and 20 per cent were HIV-positive. The basis for the story was unpublished research carried out by the humanitarian organisation CARE. The report stated that customers were touching the girls under their skirts and fondling their breasts. This was considered normal. Almost half of the women had at one point been threatened with a pistol and three-quarters were forced to drink on the job. One girl said: 'When I refused, he fired two shots into the ground to scare me. I was so afraid, I wet myself. The bar owners begged the customer for forgiveness and said that I was new; I did not know how to serve in an appropriate manner.'[22]

Note that this was the situation in Cambodia, a market that had been the centre of attention for years and where Heineken had been seeking to improve the girls' working conditions. Nobody was concerned about the fate of the girls elsewhere, like in Africa. Virtually no coherent and centrally coordinated measures were taken.

Van Cranenburgh:

> The internal 2007 research has not been followed up. There may have been some improvement in a few countries, but Head Office has adopted a *laissez faire* attitude and is no longer following these cases. I was struck by the fact that we do not put these guidelines online any more, together with the other policies. It's as if it is no longer an issue.

Sexual assault is part of the job

And so the promotion girls in Congo and Nigeria continue to work under the most dreadful conditions. The dividing line between promotion activities, prostitution and sexual abuse remains unclear.

'Every evening I am touched against my will. It doesn't matter whether I work in an expensive café or a popular bar,' says Peace, a promotion girl in Lagos. Sylvia, her colleague, adds: 'We learn how to handle this. During the instruction, they tell us that there will be annoying men. But you have to tolerate them because you are trying to increase sales and make the brand stronger.'

Peace: 'We learn that we should not respond aggressively or say "stop". By walking away, you let them know that it's not appreciated.'

But what if someone continues? Is there someone there, from the agency that is hiring the girls, someone they can talk to? Peace says:

> Yes there is, sometimes, but often not. It is a public space so there will be no rapes. That can only happen when the girls go with the customers. But that is a choice. Our employer thinks: if you don't like being fondled you must look for other work. I don't even notice it any more. I anticipate it.

The girls' incomes differ from one agency to another and on average they earn about 8 dollars per day at the time of this research. In expensive city like Lagos, this is not much, but it tallies with other forms of unskilled work.

A lot of girls take the risk of sleeping with the customers. Peace and Sylvia think that at least half of their colleagues are doing this. Peace: 'These girls can't support themselves and they are desperate. This is the way they earn much more money.'

And what do the employers think? Are they trying to prevent it?

Sylvia: 'No, definitely not. They like it when you act like this because it helps sales.'

Peace: 'They keep girls like that because they bring many customers.'

Both promotion girls say that many of their colleagues are in fact sex workers first and regard the promotion side of things as secondary. Sylvia: 'Our work is a very good way to meet potential clients.' This begins to look suspiciously like the Hot Spot scheme referred to above and managed by Odimegwu in the early 2000s.

The team leaders at the agencies and the sales representatives at Nigerian Breweries also pressure the girls into sleeping with them. 'Most girls are not hired because they are good at what they do but because they are prepared to have sex with their supervisor,' says Mary, a girl who works exclusively in the upmarket bars.

In Lagos alone, the estimate is that hundreds and quite possibly thousands of promotion girls are used to sell Heineken brands. Elsewhere in the country, the promotion girls' services are equally in demand.[23]

The situation in Nigeria is not exceptional. According to a well-connected source, there are at least 100 girls active in Kinshasa and an unknown number in the other Congolese cities. In the capital, they must survive on 120 dollars a month, which is by no means easy.

'Of course these girls are harassed, they are *filles à tout faire* [girls you can do anything with]. It's part of the profession.' That is the view of a Kinshasa salesman who used to work with the girls and clearly does not think much of them. He calls them 'whores' before continuing:

> Sometimes Bralima uses real prostitutes because they know how to seduce a customer and that's advantageous. But others are stricter and draw a line the customer must not cross. They have a difficult time because if you work in a bar you are considered a public girl. The brewery doesn't care about them.

In response, Heineken states that it is currently using some 9,000 promotion girls in Asia and about 200 in Africa, exclusively in the two Congos. The beer brewer does not know (or denies) that they are also working in Nigeria. The normal tendency for Heineken is to exaggerate the number of jobs it creates, but this time the company chooses to play down the number of women employed in this way.

#HeinekenToo

Even at Head Office, being a woman is not always easy. According to insiders, the mood there was not unlike a student society, with late night drinking, boasting about female conquests and 'testosterone in the air'. This is changing, thanks to increasing internationalisation. The appointment in 2015 of Laurence Debroux to the post of chief financial officer means that for the first time a woman sits on the two-member Executive Board.[24]

It is a different story in Africa. 'When it comes to the relationship between the sexes, we are forty, fifty years behind Europe,' says an influential former female member of staff. 'Our societies consist of transactions. Sex is one of them, and yes, it happens at Heineken too.'

Across the continent, ambitious women must get intimate with the HR manager, usually a local member of staff, to get a job or secure a promotion. Expats at management level know this (or at the very least know the rumours) but do not consider it their priority to bring the issue to attention.

Wesseling says:

> We knew that things were happening in Congo—former Zaire—that were beyond the pale. We had a very powerful HR manager who maintained a selection procedure that would not be accepted here. Women had to provide sexual services to get a job. Jean-François van Boxmeer knew about this, he has excellent knowledge of the country, after all. But he did not act when he was general manager there.

Heineken does not deny this.

One local source confirms: 'Everybody knew this was going on; the manager has slept with dozens of women. I know about two of them who fought with him in his office, when they resisted. His nickname was "the sniper".'

Expats themselves do not always set a good example. Whether or not a European has an African lover is a private matter, but you can certainly question the power relations that are the foundation of such a relationship, certainly in the light of the #MeToo debate.

And what happens when the boss's sweetheart gets perks that the company is paying for? We have seen how Clémentine Vervelde benefited from her privileged position. The Rwandan girlfriend of a top manager in Congo became the fuel supplier for one of their breweries even though the previous one was cheaper and more reliable, according to those in the know. In Nigeria, an expat director gave secretarial jobs to two of his conquests, for which they were entirely unqualified, according to colleagues.

And one national director used his position of power in a truly remarkable fashion. Female staff whom he wanted for himself were first sent to the medical department.

To have an Aids test.

11

CONGO

IF YOU CAN MAKE IT THERE, YOU CAN MAKE IT ANYWHERE

Bukavu is set against one of the most beautiful places on earth, close to the Rwandan border, overlooking a bay that is part of a much vaster expanse: Lake Kivu. We are in the east of the Democratic Republic of Congo. This town, nestled amid green and fertile hills, was once considered the pearl of the Belgian colonial empire and prospered while Mobutu was in power. Today, after twenty years of war and humanitarian catastrophe, Bukavu is a shadow of its former self. The small provincial town had swelled to an urban sprawl of more than a million people, most of whom live without basic amenities or infrastructure. Much of the city's economic life depends on aid NGOs and the UN whose staff whiz across town in their shiny SUVs.

And then there is Heineken, which for half a century has been running a lakeside brewery here. It is part of Bralima, the Congolese subsidiary that has legendary status within the conglomerate.[1] A couple of years in Congo is considered to be the best possible education for the rest of your career. Here are a few

Congo alumni: current CEO Van Boxmeer, his former right-hand man René Hooft Graafland, Van den Brink (currently director in Mexico, Heineken's biggest market in the world) and Marc Bolland (a former CEO at Marks & Spencer Group). The line 'If you can make it there, you can make it anywhere' is of course inextricably linked to New York, but seen from a Heineken perspective it more readily applies to Kinshasa, the Congolese capital.

Few know better than Heineken that you can do excellent business in Congo, as long as you do not reflect too long on how you do it, or contemplate the consequences. To take one example, part of the beer brewer's profits disappear into the pockets of former rebel leader Jean-Pierre Bemba, initially convicted for war crimes and crimes against humanity at the International Criminal Court in 2016, until the same court overturned his conviction in June 2018, to widespread incredulity. His family owns 5 per cent of Bralima's capital, has voting rights and the capacity to influence the Board of Directors. Heineken is the only other Bralima shareholder. You could say that Bemba is a business partner, but the Dutch brewer calls this qualification 'entirely unjustified'.

When I asked Van Boxmeer about his time in Congo (1990–6), the longest he has spent anywhere as an expat, he became irritated and wanted to change the subject. 'Congo is one of the eighty-six markets where we operate locally. My attention is not constantly focused on that country. Let's discuss our new brewery in Ivory Coast.'

David vs Goliath

Guillaume Matabaro's modest living room in Bukavu is an unlikely headquarters. But it is from this tiny place that a group of Congolese ex-employees is fighting their employer, a multinational with an annual turnover of 25 billion dollars[2] in a fight that resembles the tropical version of David versus Goliath. To get to Matabaro's house, you leave the main road and pass through a gloomy market hall with traders who look as if they have just walked out of an early Van Gogh painting. They are not that old, but their faces have a withered look about them, as they sit behind small stacks of coal, their only merchandise. Next, you walk alongside an open sewer and through narrow streets that go downhill and become treacherously muddy after a tropical rainstorm. Another steep slope and you find yourself in a courtyard with an impressive view of the poorer neighbourhoods built in the valley below and against the opposite hillside.

Former brewer Matabaro, former engineer John Namegabe and their colleague Godefroid Bayongwa (who is absent today) represent a 168-strong collective of workers who lost their jobs between 1999 and 2003, when their town was occupied by a violent rebel movement.[3] They greet me warmly, as if I am an old friend. Ever since I started reporting on their case in *Le Monde* and the Dutch daily *NRC*, they have discovered that—finally—somebody takes them seriously.

They talk enthusiastically about the negotiations with their former employer, at the Dutch embassies in Kampala and Paris. 'We very nearly would have stayed in France. The police thought that we would get no permission to travel through Rwanda,' recalls Namegabe. Laughing, he continues: 'Most of the time Africans find it very difficult to enter Europe, but we weren't allowed to leave ...'

Have I heard about that letter they received from Hans van Mameren? The former Heineken director in Congo spoke about the files being considered 'closed' and advised the claimants to stop wasting their time (see fig. 6). Namegabe says:

> For years, they tried everything to delay our case. Always playing for time and then saying: it is such a long time ago, there's no point any more. We had become used to it. So now you understand why this

PIĒCE 38a

Kinshasa, le 26 avril 2010

N° 013/CJ/TwT/NG/2010

A Monsieur NAMEGABE BUKABO John
à BUKAVU
SUD - KIVU

Monsieur,

CONCERNE : VOS LETTRES ELECTRONIQUES DU 02.09 ET DU 30.10.2009

Nous avons bien reçu vos lettres référencées en exergue, adressées respectivement à Madame Esther PALSGRAAF, Integrity & Compliance Manager du Groupe HEINEKEN au Pays-Bas et Madame Yvonne TSHILEMB, Directeur des Ressources Humaines de la BRALIMA-SARL à Kinshasa, lesquelles ont retenu notre meilleure attention.

Nous osons croire que les précisions détaillées ci-dessus vous édifieront utilement, afin de vous épargner à ne pas perdre votre temps en cherchant à revenir et sans qualité sur les dossiers déjà clôturés en bonne et due forme.

Recevez, Monsieur, nos meilleures salutations.

«BRALIMA - S.A.R.L.»

Administrateur Délégué

J.H. Van MAMEREN.

Fig. 6: Letter from Heineken to laid off workers in Congo

time we brought a 10kg pile of documents, to make sure that Heineken could not say that something was missing.

Peals of laughter fill the room.

Self-reliance is a national sport in Congo. Matabaro and Namegabe are not the kind to be discouraged when bad luck strikes. But things are different for Marceline, one of the most heart-breaking cases in this story. She lost her husband, Buhendwa Musole, during the war, and she cannot pay for her children's education.

We ask to meet her in the Muhungu neighbourhood, high up in the hills. Taking motor taxis, we follow the dirt roads into this densely populated area. Chickens scatter as local residents look at us in bewilderment: there's a white man and he's not locked in a four-wheel drive ... what's he doing here?

Marceline lives in a small tidy house. A portrait of her husband adorns the living room wall. 'I lost him because of Heineken,' she says. She shows me his company pass and puts old photographs on the table. 'This is how he looked when times were better. And here he lies dying. He never gave up hope he could be cured.'

For sixteen years, Buhendwa worked diligently for Bralima, until 2002 when he was struck with kidney failure. He could have been treated in Kenya, but the company doctor refused to cooperate— the medical budget was apparently exhausted. Buhendwa's contract was rescinded because he was unable to work:

> In November 2002, he requested all the money he was entitled to. He was trying to make arrangements by himself, but he was never paid. When he died, in January 2003, I could come and get his final settlement, a measly 6,000 dollars and a few crates of beer. I wanted to refuse, but they said that the money would go to the labour inspection authority if I didn't take it.

Collaboration and maximising revenue

To understand the struggle of the former employees, we need to return to 1998, when Bukavu was among the first places to be conquered by the Rassemblement Congolais pour la Démocratie (RCD), the Congolese Rally for Democracy. This blood-thirsty rebel movement occupied a large swathe of north-eastern Congo before splitting into two factions: RCD-Goma and RCD-Kisangani. The rebellion marked the beginning of the Second Congo War, which claimed between 3 and 5 million lives and was the bloodiest conflict since the Second World War.[4] The warring parties signed a peace treaty in 2003, but the conflict rumbles on and continues to take lives. Bukavu and Kisangani suffered extensive looting, but the Heineken breweries in both places were spared. A manager who was there at the time recalls: 'The rebels knew that the beer had to keep flowing. They wanted to show that normal life was continuing and beer is part of that.' A popular saying in Congo is that you can bomb a hospital, but not a brewery. That would get you into serious trouble.

Heineken's response was pragmatic. It treated the rebels as the new legitimate administration, while Human Rights Watch accused them of mass murder and rape.[5] The company continued to pay taxes and used the war as an excuse to carry out extensive austerity measures, even though the sales figures remained excellent, according to insiders. The beer brewer requested and obtained permission for mass layoffs, which happened between 1999 and 2002.

There were workers who immediately contested the dismissals and tried to force the company into paying correct severance packages, but most were unsuccessful. Matabaro and Namegabe did not give up. In 2015, they lodged a complaint with the National Contact Point (NCP) for OECD Guidelines in The Hague. Every member state of the OECD has such a contact point, where citizens and organisations can go if they think that multinational enterprises have acted in breach of these guidelines. Heineken repeated that the group of former employees was entitled to nothing, but the NCP considered the complaint sufficiently serious to start a review process and offer mediation.

The ex-employees say that Heineken remained unaccommodating. A company delegation, including regional director Pirmez, visited Congolese Prime Minister Augustin Matata Ponyo in April 2016.[6] On that occasion, the company reportedly attempted to persuade the Congolese government to support its position and put pressure on the ex-employees. The prime minister refused. On the contrary: he is said to have called Matabaro in person, wishing him and his colleagues good luck.[7]

Salvation finally came in the summer of 2017. Heineken admitted its mistakes and promised to pay up. Every complainant received individual compensation; the settlements ranged from 500 to 36,500 dollars and averaged 8,000 dollars per person. They celebrated: in a country where a median annual salary is just over 500 dollars, this was 'manna from heaven'.

If it had been up to the company, the payments would have been kept secret. Following publication of the first edition of my book in Dutch, Heineken pledged more transparency in its African operations, but in this case the beer brewer insisted on confidentiality: it did not want to set a precedent.

Why did Heineken pay, after all these years? Obbe Siderius, the so-called global director of business conduct, handled the case for the company; he admits that the publicity has had an impact. I learnt indirectly that my articles in the French and Dutch press had nudged the Board of Directors towards agreeing to a settlement. Siderius is full of praise for the NCP's mediation, which instilled confidence in the company that the outcome would be positive for all parties. According to Siderius, Heineken decided to give in because it was 'reasonable and fair'.

It is not a bad deal, says an insider, and not only because the amount involved is small beer for the multinational. The settlement would probably have been much higher, had the complainants been assisted by the best lawyers. Heineken's delegation consisted of three legal experts, while the Congolese had only one young lawyer accompanying them, who was not allowed to speak during the negotiations. Moreover, the company profited from a depreciation of the Congolese franc, the currency used for the settlement, as a result of which the final amount fell from 1.3 to 1.1 million dollars. Heineken denies this.

For Heineken, the more important aspect of the deal is that the former employees will no longer seek legal action. This means that another part of the original complaint, regarding the company's possible complicity with alleged crimes against humanity, will not be examined.

Heineken insists that this was nothing more than a labour dispute that had escalated: no law had been contravened, no contract breached and the allegation of complicity in crimes against humanity by rebels could not be further from the truth. Siderius reflects: 'It was a very delicate situation but RCD-Goma happened to be the authority we were dealing with in Bukavu at the time. During our own research, we have not found anything that would hint at collaboration.' Human rights lawyer Channa Samkalden, who represented the complainants at the initial stage, thinks it stands to reason that Heineken was, at least partially, motivated by fear of a court case. 'The damage to their reputation would have been considerable. Furthermore, it could have forced Heineken into opening files it wants to close for good.'

However, the complainants remain convinced that Bralima and its parent company were partners in crime with the rebels. This is a very serious accusation for which evidence is hard to find, but there are spoken testimonies and written documents that point in this direction. These include a letter, written by the director of the Bukavu brewery, in which he requests permission for a round of forced redundancies and mentions the *'franche collaboration'* (genuine cooperation) between the company and the rebels. I was given a copy of an official agreement between Bralima and RCD-Kisangani, in which the Heineken subsidiary declared itself committed to 'maximising revenue' for the rebel movement (see fig. 7, Article 2). This agreement was for the

REPUBLIQUE DEMOCRATIQUE DU CONGO
Rassemblement Congolais pour la Démocratie
R.C.D.

PROTOCOLE D'ACCORD

ENTRE , D'UNE PART,

Le Comité Exécutif du Rassemblement Congolais pour la Démocratie, ici représenté par :

- Le Département des Finances, Budget et Portefeuille ;
- Le Département de l'Economie , Plan, Industrie et Commerce ;
- Le Département de la Fonction Publique, Travail et Prévoyance sociale ;

ET D'AUTRE PART,

La Société BRALIMA, Siège de Kisangani, ici représentée par :

IL EST CONVENU CE QUI SUIT :

Article 1er :

La BRALIMA s'engage , en fonction des réductions des coûts à obtenir à travers les articles 2 et 3 du présent protocole d'accord, à :
a) Maintenir une activité minimale de production de sa Brasserie de Kisangani ;
b) Appliquer les prix de base hors – taxes de 8,51$ US et 5,82 $ US respectivement pour le casier de la bière Primus et pour le casier de boissons gazeuses tels que fixés aux annexes n° 1 et n°2 du présent protocole ;
c) Faciliter la maximisation des recettes de l'Etat et les verser dans le délai imparti ;
d) Apurer les engagements financiers qu'elle détient vis à vis de l'Etat suivant l'échéancier à convenir, sur place à Kisangani, avec chaque service public concerné.

Article 2 :
Dans le souci d'aider au maintien d'une activité minimale de production de la Brasserie de Kisangani, le Département ayant le Travail et la Prévoyance sociale dans ses attributions, recevra la demande de la Bralima / Kisangani sur le dossier de la réduction des effectifs du personnel afin de le résoudre conformément aux dispositions légales et contractuelles en la matière.

Fig. 7: Agreement between Heineken and rebels (tax collection in exchange for acquiescing in large-scale redundancies)

Kisangani brewery, but the source assures me that the same situation prevailed in Bukavu.[8]

'Our cooperation was excellent,' confirms Ernest Mundyo, who served as the RCD-Goma's vice governor of South Kivu in the provincial capital, Bukavu. 'Local production is very important to us, and we did all we could to provide the brewery with adequate water and electricity. They were the biggest company we had, and consequently very important for our revenues.'

Toll collection, the Kalashnikov way

This is not the first time Heineken has been allegedly implicated in serious human rights abuses in eastern Congo, a region where armed men continue to terrorise local communities with murder, rape and pillage.[9] One of the scarce products that still circulate throughout the region is beer. Bralima has an ingenious distribution network that ensures its Primus brand can be sold in the remotest areas. For many armed groups, a road block is the easiest and fastest way to get their hands on money: you put a tree across the road, a 'toll officer' next to it—with a Kalashnikov—and watch the cash roll in.

Victorine Lusamba Mwamba knows perfectly well how this works. She is a transporter for Bralima and takes beer from the town of Uvira on Lake Tanganyika to Misisi in the interior, where she runs a depot. She often joins the supply run personally, just to keep an eye on things, almost standard practice in Congo. In the not-too-distant past, this 200-kilometre trip would easily take two or three days, sometimes five. But the road has improved, she says; if you leave early, you can arrive before sunset. She ships around 700 crates on each trip and also takes a few dozen passengers with their own merchandise. They sit on top of the crates.

When I ask her about the kinds of obstacles she meets en route, 'Mama Lusamba' sits upright. 'Alright, how much time do you have?' An average trip gets her into contact first with FONER, the national road maintenance service. They demand a legal 5 dollar tax. Policemen are next. They have a habit of emerging when you enter or leave a village. There's no fixed rate, and on every journey you hand them between 30 and 50 dollars.

If she is unlucky, Lusamba will then have to deal with armed gangs and bandits. Right now, these are the Mai-Mai, a group of young and ultraviolent fighters, but there are also times when she gets harassed by Hutu militias who crossed the Rwandan border into Congo after the 1994 genocide and never returned. The Mai-Mai are unpredictable. 'Most of the time they demand 300 to 500 dollars but they can also take everything you carry. Or half of everything. They can also kidnap or kill you, but thankfully that hasn't happened to me yet.' She says the Hutus are less greedy: they will be fine with a few beers or some pocket money.

She makes the trip back and forth three times per month:

> I have been lucky this year. I've only been robbed three or four times by armed groups, and the last time it happened the Mai-Mai were happy with half of my load. Think about how things were previously! In 2010, I took this trip only once a month and every time I had to thank the Lord nothing had happened to me. I was taking care of a load worth 3,000 dollars, but I lost about one third of that paying everybody off.

In spite of that, Lusamba was making more money back then. No one else was brave enough to make that journey, so when her crates arrived safely they were worth at least double the price.

In Goma, the former ideologue of the (now defunct) M23 movement tells me the other side of the story. On a previous occasion, I had met a spokesperson of a violent armed movement who turned up dressed in a T-shirt sporting the logo of a mobile phone company; he ordered strawberry wine. Today, I am once again struck by the difference between expectation and reality: my interlocutor is dressed impeccably in a blue shirt, drinks mango juice and presents himself as a human rights activist and investigative journalist.

In 2012, M23 briefly ruled Goma; for a year and a half it also controlled an area north of the city and the only access road. 'You have to understand us,' he says. 'This zone is different from those held by other groups. There are no raw materials here, there is no fertile soil. One group grows cannabis, another is involved in mining. For us, the only way to make money was the road.' The road blocks brought in 85 per cent of all revenue; most of it came from consignments of beer. 'Bralima was our largest individual source of income.'

What did M23 do with this money? The ex-rebel sums up:

> We already had guns and uniforms. A small portion was for buying ammunition, but we stole most of that from the army anyway. By far the biggest part went on food and medical care for our troops, and because of that we were actually better organised than the army. Without taxing transport, we would not have held out as long as we did.

Obviously, controlling a main road means you can levy 'taxes', but it is not the only way to profit from the beer trade. The most remote villages, where lorries and even motorbikes cannot go, get their supplies thanks to carriers, mostly women. Carrying two crates on their heads, their journey often takes at least one day, for which they get paid a few dollars. They travel in groups, sometimes with children who carry one crate. Like everyone else, they risk being held up by militias or armed gangs and forced to hand over money or a costly bottle of beer. But that is not the only danger.

'This is a very vulnerable group,' says Lane Hartill of Human Rights Watch. In South Kivu, he met small groups of teenage girls who were carrying beer to a village 20 kilometres away:

> There were dangerous militias active in that area but those girls had no protection and were badly paid. I found that inexcusable.

We visited a hospital that treated many women who had been raped. 'We don't force them,' the company will say, but do they have any understanding of the day-to-day situation? Any idea of the risks these girls run?

My sources tell me that various armed groups were—or remain—dependent on these informal beer transport taxes. They include M23, a group calling itself Allied Democratic Forces in the north and the Mai-Mai of General Yakutumba. The American magazine *Foreign Policy* calculated M23's annual income from Bralima's beer transports and arrived at a minimum of 1 million dollars. A high-level source inside Bralima admits that the amounts involved are very high for local standards but does not think they went beyond a few hundred thousand dollars, because part of the transport had been diverted via Uganda and Rwanda.

Foreign Policy confronted Heineken with the issue of financing rebel groups. The brewer responded by condemning these practices and announcing that it was suspending all payments to the distributors in the area.[10] 'Head Office has indeed impressed upon us not to pay anything to the rebels and to avoid dangerous areas if and when necessary,' says another insider one year later. 'We passed this message on to our distributors. But you cannot monitor everything. So yes: it's still happening.'

Heineken is not the only multinational that indirectly finances rebels. Bracongo, its competitor and part of the French Groupe Castel, does the same, as do mining companies, timber transporters and even aid organisations. Nobody working in eastern Congo can escape it, and the organisations regard the payments as a kind of taxation.

Josaphat Musamba, who has researched the financing methods of militias, thinks this behaviour is indefensible:

You should never look at that money as if it were taxation. Our government institutions are far from perfect, but the least you can say is that public money, at least in part, goes to providing public services. Take a look at the RCD. When they ran Bukavu they invested nothing. Pensions and government salaries were not paid, only a few civil servants who occupied strategic positions received money. When you pay rebels, you are fuelling the conflict.

Beer logos at school and the police station

My next destination is Kinshasa, home to Congo's largest brewery and the single biggest local beer market. The flight from Goma takes two hours on a second-hand Airbus belonging to the recently established Congo Airways, but when I try for a ticket I am told it is already fully booked. The alternative is a much older and slower Fokker 50 operated by the Compagnie Africaine d'Aviation, the subject of rather macabre local jokes. A similar aircraft of the same company crashed near Goma airport in 2013, and most are convinced that its sister plane awaits the same fate. The only question is when. I comfort myself with the thought that this plane has been making many flights a day for years, and the chances that something will happen when I'm on it are statistically larger than in other places but still vanishingly small. Also, the weather is good on the day of the flight.

And indeed, once on board, the turbulence is not so bad, and confidence that all will be well grows with every can of tepid Angolan beer the flight attendant serves. (Beer in Africa has its benefits too, I will not deny.)

But in Kinshasa the next ordeal awaits me: the intelligence service. On previous visits, I did not have the impression that I was on their radar. But this time around and at my very first appointment, lo and behold: there they are. As I am interviewing a former Bralima director on the empty terrace of a coffee bar, a man sits himself down at the table next to ours. He glances at his phone with studied indifference (phones having taken the place of the classic newspaper with a hole in the middle) and trains his left ear on our conversation. We decide to move to another terrace a few streets away, but there is a second man there, whose behaviour is identical to the first's.

My contact is suspicious and tells me to take a new phone number and stop arranging meetings via SMS. Also, as a European, I am far too conspicuous in the middle-class neighbourhood where I booked a cheap hotel. I should also stop using shared taxis and motorbikes. My contact tells me that being a foreigner means you can be easily accused of spying; you must avoid being arrested, even if they have nothing against you. Before you know it, someone will have to come and bail you out, which in the case of a freelance journalist can take some time.

Am I a threat to state security? Have the intelligence services seen my critical article in *Le Monde* about Heineken in Congo? Are they tapping my phone? Or am I simply regarded as a potential wallet full of cash? I probably will never know, but the information I have gathered about Bralima and the Congolese authorities over the years does not put either party in a particularly favourable light.

Kinshasa's streets show what an eager multinational can get away with in an underdeveloped nation without strict regulation. Entire neighbourhoods have been painted light blue, the colour of Bralima's popular Primus brand. Not only does the company paint beer logos on shops and bars but also hair salons, a cement depot, garages, pharmacies, a school bus—even a police station does not escape unscathed. For its part, Bracongo tries to paint as many bars as possible yellow, the colour of its Skol brand, but it is no match for the Dutch.

A former Bralima director confides: 'We should be more discreet. Our logo on the wall of a police station—no, that should never have happened. The state should act, but it is too weak. Having said that, we must also take our own responsibility.'

No bribes, no business

The brains behind this campaign is Van Mameren, the man who boasted to a Dutch newspaper about running the biggest agricultural project in Congo. In Kinshasa, he was called 'the walking icon of Dutch business'.[11] He ran Bralima between 2003 and 2012 and during that time acquired two more nicknames: 'African Sun King' and 'Big Baobab'. An old hand in the tropics, Van Mameren thrives in obscure outposts, not in neatly organised Dutch villages like Zoeterwoude and Bunnik where Heineken has its factories. He has been roaming around Africa since the late 1970s and sometimes beyond the continent. Starting out in Chad, he went to Sierra Leone, Congo-Brazzaville, Rwanda, Malaysia, Bunnik (briefly), Nigeria and Rwanda again.

Few inside the company have fond memories of Van Mameren or appreciate his qualities as a manager. 'He liked the good life and strove to make his own as comfortable as possible,' is one of the milder descriptions of the man. 'He did very well for himself', his former boss in Nigeria says. 'Heineken did not fire him. They sent him to Congo instead.'

Emmanuel de Tailly, top manager at Bracongo, thinks that over the years Van Mameren lost all sense of reality. He points to his obsession with the Primus blue colour and the exclusivity principle—more than 68,000 bars were only allowed to sell Bralima products.[12] 'Their ideal is to paint the entire country blue and have total exclusivity. "This is our country"—that's what they believe. You used to have Mobutu's one-party state, now you have Bralima.' (It must be said, though, that Bracongo does not hold the moral high ground and that the parent company, Groupe Castel of France, has a track record of unethical business practices that matches Heineken's, according to many sources.)

As we saw earlier, Van Mameren does not have a high opinion of the Congolese, who, he says, have never learnt at school how to punch little holes or colour inside the lines. Congolese politicians did not impress him either. 'Thieves, all of them,' a former colleague claims he heard him say.

Van Mameren once explained to a Dutch journalist how he handled them. 'Look, here's one,' he said, taking a blue file from a pile on his desk. 'This is a minister's letter. He writes that all our contractually agreed advantages with the state have been rescinded. The request is to pay all these taxes directly to him. We had quite a few letters going back and forth but in the end the decision was reversed.'

'Letters?,' the journalist asked. 'You mean written threats? I take it you let out the odd swear word or two.'

'We appealed to good governance.'

'And when you do that, the minister will think: ah yes, of course, this is not the way we're supposed to be doing things.'

'Hm. Well, maybe we have been asking some of his colleagues about the general opinion of this man. And based on that, we may have made an effort to figure out how we could put a little pressure on him. After all, someone like that must be in very good books with the president, otherwise he wouldn't tackle us in this way.'

'So that means you're pretty powerful.'

'Oh well.'

'Well, are you?'

'Let me say that with our taxes and duties we constitute an important source of revenue for the authorities. And for the population beer is a barometer for the state of the country and the economy. If one brewery stops operating, the price of beer will go through the roof.'

'So you really are a pretty powerful man.'[13]

Van Mameren omits to mention that Heineken has other ways to increase pressure. Two former directors, Faustin and Albert, both tell me independently of each other that under his directorship Bralima did not hesitate to reward high-ranking officials, in order to be left alone or to have files processed quickly.[14] Faustin will not name names, but he says that it is particularly important to have friends at the Ministry of Economic Affairs, at customs, the revenue service and among officials at the Ministry of Finance. He knows with absolute certainty that Bralima gave someone at the Ministry of Economic Affairs 50,000 dollars in return for his cooperation. 'Van Mameren never made a secret of it,' he says. 'I was ashamed for my people. It was humiliating.'

Albert thinks Van Mameren is 'a real African'. 'When the taxman finds you have made an error, you run the risk of a tax return that's worth thirty times as much,' he explains:

> You can go and see a judge and start a very long procedure and then be restored in your rights. But you can also talk. And then maybe you'll arrive at a sum of, say, 30,000 dollars that you slip discreetly under the table. It's the kind of thing that happens at the highest level, and Van Mameren has always understood that. If you do everything in accordance with the rulebook, you will not get the same results. Sure, ethics don't allow it, but in Congo other conventions apply: no bribes, no business.

Both my sources tell me that the method is old-fashioned: a pile of banknotes; Albert says this can go up to 100,000 dollars. But there are also times when things are done more subtly. Faustin: 'I'm not saying that this happened, but you can, for instance, help someone build a house. Or send someone's child to a course in Belgium. It went against everything in our Code of Conduct, but the alternative is to wither away.'

Another source, European this time, acknowledges that this is the way things are done at Heineken in Congo. 'This is the game you play as a company. You try to move forward in the space that's available to you and ethics go out the window at times. Managers are not made to account for their ethical decisions.'

According to Albert, the most important pillar in the power structure was Augustin Katumba Mwanke, a presidential advisor whose influence was considered unsurpassed. Albert is certain that Van Mameren paid him. Castel's general manager De Tailly confirms this has happened. 'If paperwork was delayed or blocked, he was called,' says the former director. Desperation was palpable when Katumba died in a plane crash in 2012.[15] The word at Bralima was: 'We have lost our most important ally.'

Another key figure in the relationship between the company and the seat of power was Chantal Mabunda, the public relations director we met earlier when she extolled the virtues of Bralima as a development organisation. Her sister, Jeanine Mabunda, was minister for portfolios, a department that is in charge of state-owned enterprises. She was not dealing with Bralima directly in that capacity, but she was considered an influential person who could get things done. Albert and Faustin are certain that Mabunda was given her position thanks to Van Mameren, and they were unsurprised that she was asked to leave after the director's departure.

Kabila's sleepover parties

The president merits special attention, as becomes apparent in Boma in western Congo. When Joseph Kabila pays a visit to this port town, he stays in one of Bralima's villas. 'The president does not have a residence here and there is no hotel of sufficient standing,' says Jean-Pierre Pambu, the local chairman of the Parti du Peuple pour la Réconstruction et la Démocratie, Kabila's party:

> The villa's location is beautiful and calm, with a swimming pool and a large garden. It's on Bralima's premises, where he can meet politicians and high-ranking civil servants in all tranquillity. When I was there, they were organising a dinner party with some thirty guests.

Bralima's directors were present. Just before the elections in 2011 he visited again, and I suppose he stays there more often.

In other towns, Heineken also offers its accommodation to VIPs. The governor stayed in the villa in Bukavu for a couple of months, and President Kabila's wife visited on various occasions. What are the advantages of such sleepovers? Pambu says: 'They are worth their weight in gold. Whenever there are problems, they have immediate access to the right people. And there are always problems. Of course it has advantages. This is Congo!'

Heineken admits this is happening. As Africa director Pirmez confirms: 'It is an order given to us, which we obey reluctantly.'

In Congo, bribery and corruption are present at every level. In that sense, Bralima is very much 'a Congolese company', as one insider describes it. Rémy Bambaka of the local NGO Gouvernance Alerte puts it like this: 'There is a local context with managers who are from here. Bralima reflects our society. Most of those managers have been raised in an environment where you have to enrich yourself at all costs.'

There are countries where it is taboo to give crates of beer to the judiciary; Congo is not one of them. Albert explains:

> For us, it's necessary. If we have a court case and the judge rules in our favour on all points except one, then we lose and have to appeal to get the entire judicial machine working again. A complete waste of time! If you maintain your relationships correctly, the judicial institutions will do a better job of it and you can prevent the worst.

For reasons like this, Bralima plays host to a public prosecutor on its Bukavu premises. Officially, he is a civil servant, but Bralima pays him. He is the go-to person for employees who want to fight their dismissal. 'Bralima gives him a car and pays him allowances,' says Bambaka. 'But it's not at all clear what the criteria are for payment. Are these allowances not also encouragements, designed to ensure that he will always take Bralima's side? Business and justice should be strictly separate.'

As we saw in Nigeria, Bralima abides by the custom of reciprocity: suppliers grease the palms of the right people in the company and get the contracts. Albert: 'We tried to stop this practice because there is a risk that such matters become public knowledge. After all, these are usually small sums, a few hundred dollars at the most, even though for most people that's easily a few months' salary.' He pauses. 'In Congo, it's very hard to respect ethical standards.'

'Impossible?,' I ask him.

He replies, laughing:

> I said: very hard ... What's happening is this: just like any other company, we have done our research and found the politicians with whom we could be working most effectively in order to get our dossiers sorted out, without anybody else noticing. As usual, we must make some under-the-counter payments. But a few years ago they put integrity on the agenda. You're not allowed to give presents any more, and if you do their value must not be more than 150 dollars. For the authorities, that's peanuts.

He recalls a workshop about corruption. It was held in the stately Park Hotel, in Amsterdam. The main question was: how to behave in a corrupt country? 'I was sitting next to another African manager, and we were left speechless. We thought: "Really? Is that the way you think we can work? You might as well close Bralima now."' Thinking back on the event, Albert still cannot stop laughing.[16]

'Is was pure theory,' he continues:

> It had nothing to do with our world. We saw ethics as an obstacle. In Congo, if you forget something when returning your tax forms, the sanctions are colossal. Additional taxes—boom: 1 million dollars. Do you pay? No you don't, you negotiate, and you reach a settlement with a civil servant. In accounting, we have numerous euphemisms for this, like unforeseen expenses, contributions.

Bralima spokesman Sylvain Malanda says that Heineken does not really care how the money comes in, as long as it does. He told *Foreign Policy*: 'What matters to Heineken is sales targets. If you reach those, all is well. If you don't, there's a major problem.' When he spoke these words, his interviewers noticed he was making gestures that resembled beating someone with a stick.[17]

Is Head Office aware of the way Congo conducts business? Albert says he cannot be certain. 'But there are people in high places who are aware of our business ethics.'

Beer sends people to sleep

Eighty years. That's how long Heineken has survived in Congo. The Dutch brewer has found a way to operate in this lawless land that has not only been successful; it's been noticed. In a memo released by WikiLeaks, one American diplomat writes how Bralima could serve as evidence that enterprises can survive in Congo's extremely difficult business climate. Provided, the diplomat warns, that you have deep roots and heaps of experience in the country. Oh, and it may also help to sell drinks. 'Others should be wary not to take too many lessons from this particular story, as the beverage industry seems to stand nearly alone in many post-conflict African countries as a successful manufacturing sub-sector.'[18]

Fidel Bafilemba is a Goma-based researcher who keeps an eye on multinational corporations. As he puts it:

When I was born, you had several industries in this region. There was a brewery, a soap factory, a pharmaceutical laboratory, even an agronomical research centre—a national showpiece. Now I'm in my forties and the only one left standing is Bralima. Everything else has collapsed, it's only the breweries that do well.

He is not sure whether they deserve any credit for that:

Beer is politics. It's an instrument, like religion, it sends people to sleep. It's a virus. Please, do not misunderstand, I have nothing against beer. In the social sense, it can do miracles. But if there is no context, like there is in Europe, then we have a problem. You must know that here in Congo we have never been taught how to develop a critical mind. At school, you learn to obey. Nobody encourages you to think for yourself.

Bafilemba regards breweries as extensions of the system. Just like the extractive industry, it is a source of nourishment for the powers that be, sharing the same interests:

I don't think brewers ever ask themselves moral questions. What is it that Bralima has given us over the years? How many people have jobs thanks to them? One thousand, maybe two.[19] A drop in the ocean; we have well over 70 million people here. And what else? If your investments end up perpetuating a regime that is authoritarian, immoral and irresponsible, should you not reconsider your position? I have never heard anyone in the beer industry complain about where their tax money goes. They pay millions and millions, but Congolese lives don't improve as a result. Their conscience is clear; they do their business while they are lining the pockets of the predators that rule us. Such an enterprise becomes what it feeds: a predator.

'We are present in 172 countries and we are still thirsty'. Advertisement in Bujumbura, the capital of Burundi

A promotion girl in Nairobi, Kenya. 'In the dresses we have to wear, we are often seen as prostitutes'

'One history, one beer.' Primus, a Heineken brand, celebrating the 50th anniversary of independence in Burundi

Heineken coming to Mozambique, at a beach in the capital Maputo

Old advertisements for Heineken and Amstel (continued on next page)

Heineken's brewery in Freetown, Sierra Leone

'To love Primus is to love Congo'.

Advertisement on the beach in Freetown, Sierra Leone

12

CONFLICT ZONES

WAR, TYRANNY AND BUSINESS ETHICS

Speaking about predators: at the beginning of this century, the authoritarian President Zine el-Abidine Ben Ali held his country—Tunisia—in an iron grip, winning elections with scores of between 99.3 and 99.9 per cent. He had been ruling the nation since 1987 and considered Tunisia his private property. The president, his wife Leila Trabelsi and their respective family clans helped themselves to all the riches of the land, both in the public and the private sector. There was no space for opposition or any other form of criticism; torture and executions were commonplace. The West left him alone but in 2005 called for a little leniency. Ben Ali agreed, mainly because he had been promised money in return, but he continued to ban all gatherings of human rights organisations and journalists. His party still garnered 94 per cent of the vote at local elections, while hundreds of Tunisians languished in his jails for the crime of disagreeing with the government.[1]

Now that's a perfect place for a new brewery, thought Heineken's management. In a confidential investment proposal, written in

2006, Tunisia was praised as 'politically and economically stable' (see fig. 8). Hiring people was cheap, and while the beer brewer did not expect any 'progress towards real democracy', it was looking forward to excellent growth figures. Tunisia was a strictly secular country, and those who advocated a more prominent public role for Islam were ruthlessly prosecuted and jailed. 'The Heineken brand has wonderful prospects,' said the proposal.

There was a snag, though: foreign investors were obliged to cooperate with a local partner. Well, Heineken had set its sights on one. He was Saïd Boujbel, a businessman with special qualities. 'Mr Boujbel is married to the daughter of the sister-in-law of the Tunisian president, which will help to get the necessary approvals.' (In 2011, five years from the date on this proposal, Heineken claimed it had not known about his connection with the ruling clans when they established the joint venture.) The Executive Board gave its green light for the investment.[2]

A few years earlier, Heineken had entered the Egyptian market essentially by buying back their own breweries for almost 300 million dollars—these were the factories that former president Nasser had nationalised in the early 1960s. Had he been alive, the company's iconic CEO, Freddy Heineken, would have been against payment out of principle—you don't buy back what has been forcibly taken from you—but he had died in 2002.

Like Tunisia, Egypt was a stifling dictatorship under President Hosni Mubarak, who had managed to hold on to power even longer than Ben Ali and easily qualified as one of the world's worst dictators.[3] Heineken's purchase, the largest foreign investment in Egypt at the time, was part of a wave of privatisations, intended to give the government a shot in the arm. Osama Diab, a Cairo-based corruption expert explains:

> Those foreign companies basically gave the tottering regime a 'kiss of love'. It provided our leaders with a façade of transparency: 'See how many companies we attract? We are definitely doing something

Heineken
International

Authors
Peter Vogelsang
Hans Jakop Burkens

Strictly private & confidential

Investment proposal in greenfield project in

Tunisia

Dated April 12th , 2006

Description partner
Since 1992 Mr Boujbel is hotel operator, mainly selling so-called "inclusive packages"
He operates two microbreweries in Hammamet (one in one of the hotels, the other
stand-alone), which produces draught beer. The microbreweries mainly cater for
Boujbel's hotel, but sell a small part to other hotels in Hammamet. SPDB will buy one
microbrewery that operates independently to avoid a conflict of interest.

We consider Mr Boujbel a good and trustful businessman with an excellent reputation.
His knowledge about beverage and beer business is limited to the hotel sector, but

Tunisia
Middle East – North Africa / date and issue number: April 12, 2006

5 / 19

Heineken
International

understands that he can only operate industrial wise, if the business covers each
segment. He clearly understands his limitations and requests Heineken to lead his
business to success.
Mr Boujbel is married to the daughter of the sister-in-law of the Tunisian President,
which will help to get the necessary approvals.

Fig. 8: 2006 Tunisia investment proposal, relying on Boujbel's connections
to the regime

right ...' Egypt became one of the largest recipients of foreign direct investment in Africa, and it led to an economic boom. This, in its turn, legitimised the government, and enabled it to survive longer.

For Heineken, the presence of a dictatorship or the prospect of supporting a controversial regime are apparently not reason enough to reconsider its investments. We saw the company keep a succession of autocrats in power in Burundi, without any tangible benefits to the country. When he wanted to stay in one of Heineken's villas, the company gave Congolese President Joseph Kabila the red carpet treatment. We also noted Heineken's reported predisposition towards sweetening deals with high-ranking government officials in the same country. The company allowed itself to be exploited by Mobutu, and in apartheid South Africa even the Sharpeville Massacre did not sway Heineken towards disinvestment. On the contrary: the brewer rejected the idea of a massive trade embargo against the apartheid regime. In Burundi and South Africa, activists, journalists and concerned citizens wondered whether there was any justification for Heineken's presence in their countries. At the most extreme end of the spectrum is Heineken's role in the Rwandan genocide, which we will discuss in the next chapter.

Where does complicity begin? Is there a line one should not cross?

Siding with rebels: it could be a crime

Heineken is no island. When operating in Africa, multinationals are supposed to be bound by local and international legislation. They are also supposed to adhere to a number of principles and codes of conduct, including their own, the OECD Guidelines for multinational corporations, the UN Guiding Principles for Business and Human Rights and the UN Global Compact, which Heineken signed in 2006. The latter consists of ten principles that underpin corporate social responsibility.[4]

All this looks good on paper. Reality, however, is often different. Heineken has been on a very slippery slope, especially in Central Africa where we have seen the company making promises to maximise income for a rebel outfit in eastern Congo. Human rights lawyer Channa Samkalden sees a parallel with a case against Shell in Nigeria, in which she represents four Ogoni widows whose husbands were murdered by the dictatorial regime of General Sani Abacha. She commented:

> In both cases, we are dealing with companies that work towards maximising their profits in highly unstable countries where authorities were known to be involved in large-scale human rights violations. If a company is facilitating those violations or encouraging the authorities to continue, then you can legally argue it is co-responsible. Not only is this reprehensible, it may even be punishable by law. Siding with rebels in Congo—that could be a court case.

Peer Schouten, a researcher at the Danish Institute for International Studies, also concluded that Heineken had been complicit in human rights violations as defined in the UN Global Compact principles. The United Nations works with three levels of complicity. A company is:

1. Directly complicit when it provides goods or services that it knows will be used to carry out abuses;
2. Beneficially complicit when it benefits from human rights abuses even though it did not positively assist or cause them; and
3. Silently complicit when it is aware but silent or inactive in the face of systematic or continuous human rights abuse.[5]

According to Schouten, Heineken would have been silently complicit if the Bralima management was aware the company was financing the rebel group. The financing part of this allegation was certainly true.

As noted earlier, Heineken had only signed up to the Global Compact principles in 2006 and was, at the time of events, not yet committed to complying with them. But the company responded as if it had been stung by an adder and threatened legal action:

> We utterly reject the accusation that we are a silent accomplice to the human rights abuses carried out by RCD-Goma troops or were in any way an active 'accomplice' with the rebels. As we emphasized during our conversation, the use of these words may have legal consequences. We request that you not use them.[6]

Schouten was not to be intimidated. He published his findings; there were no legal consequences. Heineken was not naïve enough to make a solidly researched piece of analysis into a potentially damaging court case.

Besides, Schouten's approach was understated. One could argue that Heineken's complicity was more than 'silent' and that the company benefited from the abuses. After all, the RCD allowed mass redundancies at Heineken, and a lucrative deal for Bralima was secured that outlasted the rebels' presence in Bukavu and Kisangani. As a result, Heineken derived long-term benefits from the collaboration. Their presence and tax payments gave the rebel movement legitimacy and helped maintain instability and conflict, in much the same way as the more recent case of the M23 rebels who derived their income from 'taxing' beer transports. As David Van Reybrouck wrote in his book on Congo: 'The war was not started for reasons of profit but now that everybody was making money out of it, the war continued.'[7]

The situation in eastern Congo is not an isolated case. In Burundi, the authoritarian regime of Pierre Nkurunziza is a deadly menace for members of the opposition and critical journalists; it also relies to a high degree on Heineken, which is the single largest taxpayer and a business partner of the government at Brarudi. This looks like silent complicity in human rights abuses, which is how the United Nations qualified the actions of the regime in Burundi in September 2017, after a long inquiry.

Sylvère Nimpagaritse, the Burundian judge living in exile, is adamant: 'Heineken is an accomplice to the regime's atrocities. It played an important role in securing President Nkurunziza's third term, which has brought the country to the brink of civil war. Money is the only thing that matters at Heineken. The fate of the people leaves them cold.'

We saw the dissident Léonidas Hatungimana draw a similar conclusion. Criminal lawyer Michiel Pestman goes even further and asserts that Heineken is playing with fire in Burundi:

> The world is changing, also in the legal sense. These days, companies are expected to make sure that their money is not used to enable corruption or serious human rights abuses, even when this would not be their direct objective. The time when you could say you did not know what was going on in a faraway land is definitely behind us. Current trends indicate that companies are increasingly being held accountable for the consequences of their activities.

And what about the situation in Burundi in the 1990s? The belligerent regime of the putschist Pierre Buyoya largely relied on Heineken for its finances and its war effort. The soldiers doing the killing enjoyed a few bottles of Primus in the morning. As was noted above, 'without beer, this Burundi war would have ended ages ago'.

In the next chapter, we will see that by today's criteria the company may even have been directly complicit in crimes against humanity during the Rwandan genocide.[8]

Guard against getting involved

Heineken could argue in its defence that corporate social responsibility was less of an issue back in those days, and the wars and massacres in central Africa were almost unprecedented. But you could be forgiven for wondering how a company that claims to be ethical could be so callous and amoral in its decision-making.

Today, there are people working for the Dutch brewer who present themselves as true activists for a better world. Zita Schellekens is one of them. She works for Heineken because she wants to 'make a difference'. She says: 'International solidarity sounds rather vague but to me it is still very relevant, like working towards an equitable world where everyone gets a fair chance. There is too much inequality in the world and there is very little social, economic and democratic development in too many countries.'[9]

Most Heineken managers are, in all probability, decent, well-meaning people.[10] I have spoken with dozens of Heineken workers, both in Europe and Africa. Almost all of them were likeable in their own way. They often really think that their work for the company helps to reduce poverty, and they do not appear driven by financial gain above all else.

Still, none of this guarantees good corporate governance. After all, a company is not just the sum of its workers; it has interests that create their own dynamic, or indeed—as some would argue—a corporate identity.[11] When on the company payroll, managers are told that they should be guided by professional objectives, not personal convictions.

'Don't get involved,' is Homé's advice about doing business in Africa. 'Stay professional; don't let your own moral judgement prevail. In business you should act according to what fits with the long-term objectives of the company. It's a prerequisite that you look for profit.'[12]

Such convictions—profits first, moral judgements later (if at all)—push salesmen to cross boundaries. In Congo, we saw how managers were rallying the troops with war talk. The message is not 'try to sell as much beer as you can but stick to the rules', it is 'we are at war, the enemy must be defeated no matter what and if that happens you will get paid extra'. It is easy to imagine what this can lead to.

Another contributing—and unhelpful—factor consists of the unrealistic targets that managers are sometimes saddled with. Dennis Heijn experienced this when he led Heineken in Italy:

> In 2002, we had the best summer in two centuries. You don't need to be a commercial genius to sell a few beers. Let's say you sell 100 units and the next year you sell eighty. What you do is check whether there have been any pointless expenses, and if not you'll compliment everyone on a job well done and tell them to carry on. But no, we're part of a huge listed company where growth is paramount. So we had to grow again: they wanted 10 per cent for the following year.[13]

The end result was a persistently depressed workplace and the impression that unnecessary cuts were being made to reach the targets. Heijn concludes that this relentless drive towards growth and more growth is unnatural, even risky. It can lead managers to take immoral decisions that they may not support personally but can be justified professionally.

The importance of bonuses for senior management became apparent in 2013, when after a disappointing year the company decided to reduce the targets. Otherwise, the 750 top staff worldwide would have missed their bonuses. Earlier in this book, we met Paul Stanger, the local sourcing director, a dedicated worker I thought. But his primary concern turned out to be his bonus and not the farmers or communities he claimed to help. 'We fear that managers will otherwise have no incentive to reach their financial targets or simply move to another company,' explains Maarten Das, a member of the Supervisory Board.

Many shareholders begged to differ. 'Shocking,' was the verdict of Faryda Lindeman of the MN pension fund. She felt the idea that managers could only be motivated by bonuses was sending 'the wrong message'. André Jorna of the Dutch Investors Association agrees:

> It is inappropriate to change incentives if you miss targets. It's like the owner of [the football club] Ajax telling the players and staff: listen, you will not be champions this year, as was the plan, but if you don't get relegated, we'll give you the same money we promised anyway ...[14]

What matters is the protestor in San Diego

Is there a line in the sand for Heineken? When circumstances in a country have changed so much that you can no longer operate there in an ethically responsible way, do you then leave? The beer behemoth has never done this and, as we've seen, has often cited concerns about its staff's welfare as its main reason for staying. On top of that, the company thinks that by staying it can help secure peace and stability, as former manager Katinka van Cranenburgh and academic François Lenfant have written in an article.[15]

Heineken claims this argument has received support from many sustainability experts. The departure of multinationals would be bad for employment, they argue. It would diminish prosperity and cause suffering among ordinary people. Boycotts and sanctions rarely have the desired effect and serve primarily to soothe the conscience of those that call for them. It sends the message that at least they did not stand idly by.[16] A business ethics specialist writes: 'No dictatorship can withstand prosperity in the long run. Dictators thrive amidst poverty, not wealth.'[17] The business world stresses the long-term character of investments, stretching into scores of years, while governments come and go. 'A company is not like a lamp you can turn off today and on again tomorrow,' writes Morris Tabaksblat, former chairman of the Board of Directors at Unilever.[18]

And besides, runs the argument, what is the alternative? If Heineken gets out, demand for beer will not dry up. A local company or an Asian investor is likely to fill the vacuum, and it remains to be seen whether they will be more concerned with business ethics or human rights.

However, the reverse of each of these points can be argued with equal force. In corrupt states like Tunisia and Egypt, a tiny elite close to the dictator has profited from the stability and increased prosperity that foreign investors brought in. As bank accounts in tax havens swelled, the people remained poor. And even when conditions improve for the population at large, this can serve to legitimise authoritarian regimes, as has happened in East Asia.

Boycotts can work. Sanctions against the apartheid regime in South Africa contributed to its demise. Elsewhere, Heineken and other multinationals have the power to break authoritarian regimes that commit atrocities against their own people, making improvements possible—at the very least. The conclusion reached by the authors of a book on this issue (*When Good Companies Do Bad Things*) is even-handed: 'Though it is hard to find proof that sanctions work to bring about desired reforms, it is equally hard to prove that foreign investment help move such reforms forward.'[19]

After all, what have been the benefits of Heineken's unwavering presence for long-suffering countries like Burundi, Congo and Sierra Leone? They are among the poorest countries on earth, they lack stability and Heineken has not acted as a great catalyst for other foreign investments. The American diplomat in Kinshasa probably had it right when he said that the success of the beverage industry in unstable African countries is a story that cannot be easily replicated.

And yet, the company does not regard being present as its sacred duty. We have already seen that Chad and Angola did not yield enough in profits back in 2004. In South Africa, the company was close to giving in to anti-apartheid activists. In 1996, Heineken withdrew from Myanmar after it had come under fire for its collaboration with the junta, one of the most brutal dictatorships on the planet at the time, a regime that committed murder, torture and forced labour on an enormous scale and used child soldiers. Opposition leader Aung San Suu Kyi had won an election at the beginning of the decade, but the regime ignored the result and put her under house arrest. She called on foreign businesses to delay their investments in order to help her protest, but Heineken remained impervious to her demands. It only changed its opinion once other companies had started to withdraw, including its direct competitor Carlsberg. CEO Karel Vuursteen declared at the time: 'The opinions regarding this market have changed to such an extent that there may be negative effects on the Heineken brand and the reputation of our enterprise.'[20] In other words, the company made no secret of the fact that this was not a moral decision but a business one, a risk-management issue. Damage to reputation could surpass the value of lost investments.

A dictator can commit crimes, aided and abetted by Heineken's tax contributions, and all is well. Alarm bells will go off in Amsterdam as soon as there is any kind of revolt in the West. Homé comments: 'Working in developing countries implies not merely taking financial risks; in fact, the biggest risk is reputational. How can we operate in Congo and not damage our good name in the United States? Our problem is not the African government—it is the protestor in San Diego.'[21]

No 'evil empire'

In the Corporate Human Rights Benchmark 2017 (a joint initiative by investors and civil society organisations to measure corporate human rights performance), the first of its kind, Heineken was awarded just thirty-two points out of a possible 100. The reporters say that in virtually every area connected with human rights, Heineken's performance leaves much to be desired. Its corporate culture and management systems pay scant regard to protecting human rights and do nothing to sanction abuses of them. The company was awarded points for its 'reaction to serious allegations of human rights abuses', which, according to the report, had not happened. However, there were indeed allegations, as we shall see, and should this have been taken into account, Heineken's position in the index could have been even worse.[22]

A conversation at Head Office about the worrying situation as regards human rights is a fairly peculiar experience, as Egbert Wesselink, of the peace organisation PAX, can confirm. 'I must say that I was taken aback. They really have a long way to go. It's like Shell twenty years ago. They have not thought about the essence of human rights and only react when there are problems.'

I am discussing the same matter with Rutger Goethart, in charge of international labour relations at Heineken, and one of his former colleagues who was intimately involved with human rights issues and does not want to be named. He says that my critical approach has affected him personally, and he is disappointed that I have not fully understood corporate ethics. For instance, am I not aware of the fact that the OECD Guidelines for multinationals do not apply to multinationals? They exist only for the benefit of governments, who can transform these guidelines into laws.

But why, I ask him, does Heineken then highlight the fact that it respects the guidelines?

'Heineken does no such thing.'

This is all a bit too much for his colleague Goethart. 'We do have a statement saying that we support the guidelines. We are attempting to make policies that match them.'

Both men employ cliché-ridden woolly discourse. They recognise that Heineken makes mistakes, but they assure me that the company is 'part of the solution', not part of the problem. Making and implementing a human rights policy is not a matter of 'flicking a switch', no: it is 'a journey'. Moreover: 'You cannot solve everything. Where do you begin, where should your focus be?'

Not with the promotion girls, that much is certain. In collaboration with Shift, a specialist consulting agency, Heineken has formulated a number of specific policies relating to human rights—but the promotion girls were not included.[23] Child labour is an area of concern, but Goethart cannot give any details about the size of the problem and how it is being addressed.

Can Goethart and his colleague cite an example of a successful intervention based on the human rights policy? Indeed they can.

'There was a complaint in a North African country concerning a manager who used social media to ridicule Islam and Muslims,' says the former colleague. 'So we took him out of Africa. We did not fire him, because he is basically a good manager and everyone deserves a second chance. We have given him a new job in Europe—but rest assured that this will affect his career prospects.'

The managers emphasise more than once that I should not doubt their good intentions. Fine, one tends to think, but what use is that to the victims of human rights abuses in Burundi and Congo? And what would the thousands of Africans laid off because of austerity measures think about this racist manager getting a second chance?

Goethart continues: 'Over a ten-year period I have not seen this company commit an act of conscious human rights abuse or attempt to hide something.'

But a close insider says that some cases have most definitely been covered up. When Heineken receives information about possible complicity in human rights abuses, it is required to report and investigate them, even if the informants are third parties. This, I have been reliably informed, has not happened on two occasions: the road blocks in eastern Congo discussed in the previous chapter and a Congolese manager who was ordered to negotiate with RCD rebels in a war situation. An insider says: 'Both Van Boxmeer and Siep Hiemstra [the Africa director at the time] know about these two complaints but investigations were not allowed.' Heineken denies that this was the case.

I ask Goethart and his colleague about the east Congo road blocks.

'I was not involved,' says Goethart. 'I know the case was looked into at the time.'

Me: 'Has anything tangible come out of this?'

Goethart: 'The Code of Conduct is constantly being amended, and our communication about this issue circulates throughout the organisation.'

'Which parts in particular have been amended?'

Goethart: 'Well, these kinds of incidents make us more aware of the necessity to have clear norms and communicate about them.'

'But as far as you know this case has not led to tangible changes or new policies?'

Goethart: 'I would have to double check that.'

His former colleague: 'I cannot for the life of me imagine that nothing has been done with it.'

'But you were responsible for that, were you not?'

'No.'

'Then who was?'

'No idea. It could have been someone who works on taxes in Africa. I don't know.'

'It's an accusation of indirect involvement with human rights abuses. That was your remit, was it not?'

'Well, I don't know that. Were these human rights abuses?'

'We are talking about a violent rebel movement that had Heineken as a significant source of income. *Foreign Policy* mentions 1 million euros.' His reaction:

> You know what I find so beautiful about this? When Trump goes to Saudi Arabia for a multi-billion dollar arms deal nobody bats an eyelid, and these kinds of things ... I can assure you that these things are studied with a very critical eye. Of course! What do you think? This is not some kind of an 'evil empire' that wants to brew beer no matter what the cost.

Later, Heineken explains in writing that the complaint did lead to an investigation and subsequent action and that Siderius was the person ultimately responsible for the matter. However, the company will not release the report containing the conclusions. It does send me a picture that shows Siderius in the company of a group of Congolese. The picture was supposedly taken during a training session, specially designed, Heineken claims, to put an end to these practices.[24]

How much extra beer do I sell with this?

For Goethart and his former colleague, the very existence of a policy and a whistle-blowing process proves that Heineken is serious about human-rights issues. Not every multinational has such policies, they stress. However, this does not mean that the company follows its own rules. Worse, four years after writing it, the company has yet to fully implement its own human rights policy. Or, as Goethart puts it: 'In order to further embed the policy we need more awareness internally, local analysis and an adequate planning of action.'

But these are the words of someone close to the fire:

> Just imagine. It takes years before a policy is approved and then you think: fine—let's get to work with it. But when they then do some

local research and find out what is going on, it turns out that there are things they'd rather not know about. At Head Office, they're afraid of problems without solutions. So they decide to sort out complaints at the local level and keep Head Office out of the loop. Don't ask, don't tell.

Van Cranenburgh, who was closely involved in devising and implementing the policy, says: 'The decision to handle human rights-related issues locally was defended by the argument that people there would know more about the local context.' Today, Heineken says that it weighs whether or not a complaint should be processed locally or centrally on a case-by-case basis. It guarantees that every complaint generated through the whistle-blowing process is being checked at Head Office. Apparently, this guarantee does not apply to other complaints.

Other corporations have shown more diligence. 'Look at Nestlé,' says Van Cranenburgh. 'They became a model of good behaviour after discovering that one of their suppliers in Thailand was using forced labour. They commissioned the inquiry, made the results public and implemented measures. Even campaign groups praised their work.'[25]

At Heineken, these things take a lot of time. An insider comments: "It's always the same message: we're working on it. There are intentions, discussions, working groups, items on the agenda but never concrete action. The more we play for time, the better.'

Former HR manager Hans Wesseling had ample experience with this. In the late 1990s, he wrote a series of statements on almost every sensitive subject you can think of: bribery, child labour, conflicts of interest, union rights, environmental protection, gifts, human rights, discrimination, health and safety, doing business in politically sensitive areas and sexual intimidation. Everything mentioned in the 2012 human rights policy (and more) was already written into these papers, and the wording differs hardly at all from the final version of the policy. Those 1999 texts were discussed at all levels, all the way to the Executive Board, but were then put on a shelf to gather dust.

Wesseling:

> At the time, there certainly were staff who saw the value of it, like Jean Louis Homé. But in the end someone would always ask me: all well and good, but how much extra beer do I sell with this? For someone like Van Boxmeer, these ethical questions were of no importance whatsoever. With him and his money man Hooft Graafland at the helm the whole dynamic changed and there was a shift from 'how' to 'how much'. Just as we were busy entrenching ethics in the entire Heineken corporate structure they came along and we all went back to 'we're only in it for the money'.[26]

Human rights at Heineken? The company still has a long road ahead of it.[27]

13

RWANDA

BREWING BEER FOR MASS KILLERS

It was 4 September 1993. For thirteen years, Max Boreel had been general manager of Bralirwa, Heineken's subsidiary in Rwanda. Now the Dutch expat was about to give his farewell speech.

The small central African nation was on tenterhooks. Since the Rwandan Patriotic Front (RPF) had launched its invasion from Ugandan territory in early 1990, the country had been in the throes of civil war. The demographic balance was similar to that of neighbouring Burundi, with a Hutu majority and a Tutsi minority. The rebels, mostly Tutsi, and the Hutu-dominated government had signed a peace treaty in August 1993, but the extremist radio station Radio Télévision Libre des Milles Collines (RTLM) kept broadcasting messages of hate about the Tutsis who had to be exterminated 'like cockroaches'.

In business terms, Boreel had much to celebrate. These were the golden days for Heineken. An in-house magazine had this headline at the end of 1991: 'Bralirwa Is Moving Like an Express Train'.[1] People drank as if their lives depended on it and did not put aside a single franc for later. The army was a major consumer: the soldiers were given a daily ration of beer to keep morale from sagging. A former manager recalls: 'The [soldiers] drank more than they ate. When I left in 2000, their levels of consumption were still below what they drank during the war.'

As is the case in Burundi today, Heineken held a monopoly and maintained close ties with the government, which was joint shareholder and a partner on the Board of Directors. It was also highly dependent on Heineken for its tax revenue. According to insiders, the company did not pay all the taxes it was supposed to pay, but the authorities looked the other way. As long as Bralirwa scrupulously maintained the maximum quota of ten per cent Tutsis among its workers, things were fine. 'But if you exceed the limit, the government would act,' says a former human resources manager.

Before a multi-party system was introduced in 1991, the brewery was home to a special propaganda cell of the governing party, just like every other enterprise. Said the same source: 'Every week we sang the praises of the Leader and danced for the party, on company time. Three or four employees organised all that, expenses paid by Bralirwa.' The 'Leader' was Juvénal Habyarimana, who had ruled the country single-handedly since 1973.

A dangerous virus

Boreel started his farewell speech. His voice was trembling. He was going to miss the scenery. The factory was in the most pictur-esque of settings: on one side, the receding shoreline of a Lake Kivu bay, on the other, a hillside with small mud houses and banana plants. In the distance loomed Mount Nyiragongo, a men-acing presence, 3,475 metres feet high. The active volcano was known for its regular and devastating eruptions.

Boreel was proud that under his stewardship Bralirwa had become larger, richer and more mature. But he was also deeply worried. 'I am talking about a new phenomenon that is increasingly rearing its head in Rwanda: regionalism, to give it a name. A ridiculous phenomenon because Rwanda does not have linguistic or cultural differences, like Belgium. Tiny Rwanda, where everyone speaks the same language, cannot afford this luxury.'

The audience pricked up its ears. They knew what he meant with 'regionalism'. It was not just a geographic delineation; it was also ethnic. 'It is ridiculous when people are being chased away because they are seen as foreigners, or spies,' Boreel continued. 'Make sure that this company does not get caught in this manipulative game! As the most important company in Rwanda, Bralirwa has the right to employ the best people, wherever it wants. Be careful, a very dangerous virus has contaminated your society!'[2]

In a country where silence is considered golden, Boreel's outburst made a deep impression. 'Dear friends,' he concluded. 'You may think: "What business is it of this *muzungu* [white man]?" But I consider you all my friends, and among friends you should be able to tell each other the truth.'[3]

It is highly likely that Boreel knew the virus was also active within Bralirwa, but one insider says that until he made his emotional address the matter had never come to the fore. 'Expats pretended as if the ethnic issue did not exist. They made an effort to regard Bralirwa purely as an economic concern: we're here to brew beer and that's it.'

After Boreel's speech, the mood at the brewery darkened. A high-level source remembers: 'Hutus and Tutsis became ever more hostile towards one another. They were listening to RTLM or an extremist Tutsi radio station and spirits were getting more and more inflamed.' Within the company, the hard-line Hutu Power party was active, the Coalition pour la Défense de la République et de la Démocratie. Several sources say that there were lists circulating with names and addresses of Tutsi employees.

HEINEKEN IN AFRICA

On 20 March 1994, Heineken CEO Karel Vuursteen was visiting Africa for the first time. He stopped at Gisenyi, where the National Ballet of Rwanda gave a memorable performance, on the shores of Lake Kivu. Homé, who accompanied Vuursteen on this trip, recalls 'a magical evening'.[4] Seventeen days later and at the same place, the first corpses were seen floating in the lake.

Genocide at the brewery

The genocide in Rwanda has been called the most efficient act of mass murder since the dropping of atomic bombs on Hiroshima and Nagasaki.[5] It began on 6 April 1994. Shortly before it was set to land at Kigali airport in the Rwandan capital, a plane was shot down. On board were the presidents of Rwanda and Burundi; they and all other passengers died instantly. It is still unclear who shot the plane down. Heineken was directly involved, because Juvénal Renzaho had also been on the doomed aircraft. He was not only a presidential advisor, but also the chairman of Bralirwa's Board of Directors.

President Habyarimana's death triggered slaughter on an unprecedented scale. The army, police and Interahamwe militias close to the regime had prepared the killings, which were mostly committed by ordinary civilians. They went after Tutsis and Hutus who were considered 'traitors', using machetes and other weapons. The death toll is estimated at 800,000, 90 per cent of whom were Tutsi. The number of perpetrators may have been as high as 200,000.[6] They killed their own colleagues, neighbours and sometimes friends and family.

Heineken was in the thick of it all. 'I was one of the first who had to die,' says a former manager:

Colleagues came for me at the hotel in Gisenyi were I was temporarily lodged. Fortunately, I happened to be in Kigali. I am a Hutu from the south of the country, and I was not a party member. In short, I was an enemy. And what's more, I had a job that lots of people wanted. Motives during the genocide were ethnic, regional but definitely also economic.

Heineken is present in Rwanda at two locations. The brewery is in Gisenyi, the main office is in Kigali, which is also home to the factory where Heineken produces soft drinks under licence from Coca-Cola, as in Burundi and Congo. Hutus murdered their Tutsi colleagues at both locations. Heineken has never revealed how many victims there were, but they number in the dozens.[7] As was the case in Burundi, the mortal remains of the slain president, Habyarimana, were held in the brewery's cold room.

The first concern at Amsterdam Head Office was the safety of the expats. Boreel's successor Edwin Botterman happened to be out of the country on holiday, and the other Dutch and Belgian citizens were evacuated from Rwanda in a matter of days. Among them was Kees Klute of the technical division, who had tried to hide two neighbourhood children from the killers in his expat villa. In vain; they were found. At Heineken, they were not amused. 'It was clumsy, it breached neutrality,' says an internal source.

Luc Jolie, the director of the Gisenyi brewery, moved temporarily to Goma, just across the border. Botterman joined him later, and Henk Bont, head of security for Heineken, was also present. In his book, Homé calls it Bralirwa's temporary headquarters. 'Every day, technical managers crossed the border.'[8]

Thus Heineken continued to brew the local Primus brand while corpses were piling up across Rwanda. *Bier soll sein*, also during this genocide. Production was lower than usual, since many workers had been killed or fled, but still Heineken succeeded in providing large parts of the country with freshly brewed beer. Anti-aircraft guns appeared on top of the brewery, and some thirty soldiers protected the facility while Tutsi drivers were replaced with Hutus.[9]

Every day is party time with Primus

That was good news for the mass killers, for whom beer was the tipple of choice. Numerous eyewitnesses have stated that they committed their atrocities when under the influence of alcohol and drugs. Large bottles of Primus beer and banana beer: these were the principal culpable stimulants. There are accounts of 'tropical SS officers, drunk on alcohol and a purifying rage' and of mass killers who downed another Primus 'in between killing sprees', which spurred them on.[10]

'The killers killed all day in Nyarubuye,' writes Philip Gourevitch in his seminal work on the genocide, *We Wish to Inform You That Tomorrow We Will Be Killed with Our Families*:

> At night they cut the Achilles tendons of survivors and went off to feast behind the church, roasting cattle looted from their victims in big fires, and drinking beer. (Bottled beer, banana beer—Rwandans may not drink more beer than other Africans, but they drink prodigious quantities of it around the clock.) And, in the morning, still drunk after whatever sleep they could find beneath the cries of their prey, the killers at Nyarubuye went back and killed again.[11]

Wholesalers and other influential individuals who supported the Hutu cause used beer to encourage inexperienced killers. Etienne Nzabonimana was a distributor and according to one of his former employees a lynchpin of the beer trade during the genocide. After they had been killing people during the day, militia members would drink his beer to quench their thirst.[12] Later, a Belgian judge was to sentence Nzabonimana to twelve years in prison for his part in the genocide. A parliamentarian, Bernadette Mukarurangwa, also incited citizens to participate in the killings. She rewarded them with beer, stolen goods and the opportunity to sexually abuse Tutsi girls.[13]

In his critically acclaimed book, *Machete Season*, a portrait of one group of Hutu friends who turn into genocide participants,

author Jean Hatzfeld shows the various functions that beer per-
formed at the time. With every page you read, it becomes clearer
how important Primus and banana beer were for the killers.
Before the genocide, the friends used to get together in a small
neighbourhood bar at the end of the afternoon; most of them
worked on the land. They would enjoy their Primus and beef
skewers but only on special days. To them, those three months
from April to July 1994 were an escape from their day-to-day
tedium. 'Our lives improved enormously because we had everything we could normally only dream about. A Primus every day,
beef on a skewer ... everything. It was a happy season,' says
Alphonse. 'While the massacres were going on, there were no
marriages, baptisms, no football matches ... those Sunday futili-
ties no longer were of any interest to us. We were exhausted from
our work, we were greedy, we partied hard and we drank as much
as we could.' Every day was party day.

For some, killing was not at all easy at first, and beer helped
to deal with the gruesomeness. Jean-Baptiste, for example, was
married to a Tutsi, but the Interahamwe forced him to kill a
supposed enemy collaborator, a Hutu who had been accused of
helping Tutsis escape. If he refused, they would kill him instead.
A crowd gathered around while he took a machete and hacked
down time and time again on the victim below him. At one
point, Jean-Baptiste wanted to turn away, but the crowd pushed
him back and he hit the man again, with his eyes closed. He
then collapsed on a bench at a nearby bar, ordered a drink and
tried not to look at the victim. He was told later that the man
had convulsions for another two hours before he died.

Beer was also the go-to tranquiliser to prepare for another day's
work. 'We met at night in the bar,' Jean-Baptiste recalls. 'We
ordered boxes full of Primus, we drank and we joked to regain our
composure. Some would stay up all night, drinking one bottle
after the next without sleeping. They would be even wilder.'

Exterminating Tutsis became so banal to some that they thought of new games to keep it fresh and exciting. They organised a contest: Who could kill the most in a single day, or who would be able to predict how many would be killed tomorrow? The prize was an extra Primus. 'Even when you lost you'd be happy.'

As the genocide was ending, the fun was taken out of it. The thrill of the chase was diminishing since the only Tutsis left were the bravest and smartest. 'Some of our comrades just wanted to open another bottle of Primus,' Pancrace, another of the group, recalls.

Even from jail, one of the killers says he has put his hopes on beer to help him in the reconciliation with the relatives of his victims. 'I have confessed and admitted my mistakes to the relatives of the people I have killed. When I am free, I will come with presents and food and drinks. I will make sure that during the reconciliation meeting there will be enough Primus and brochettes.' Could that be enough? Surely not. 'If a man has had one Primus too many and he hits his wife you can forgive him,' is the verdict of Francine, a farmer. 'But if you kill throughout the month, and even on a Sunday, what's there to forgive?'[14]

'Not the Red Cross'

It took some time for the world to realise what was happening in Rwanda. Many Africa correspondents were in South Africa in April 1994 to cover the first free elections in the country's history. But at Heineken they immediately realised the gravity of the situation. A few days after the president's death, Homé understood that 'the worst' was about to become reality.[15] And yet Heineken never contemplated turning off the beer tap. 'Why? As long as there is demand and we can produce, then I think there's no need for it,' was the comment of a spokeswoman at the time.[16]

Former staff and workers confirm that the role beer played in the slaughter was never considered reason enough to halt production: 'Business is business. For us, volume was paramount,' says one. Another adds:

> Bralirwa is not the Red Cross. If you have the raw materials, the empty bottles, the machines and sufficient staff and there is demand—then you must make beer. You can even try to increase production, in order to satisfy all demand. If you fail to do that you run the risk of being seen as a saboteur. And that would have been really bad.

In a whisper, he adds:

> If Bralirwa had stopped brewing, it would have meant—according to the army—that we were supporting the Tutsis, that we were abetting the RPF. Do you understand? They would say: 'There is a beer shortage because Bralirwa is supporting the Tutsis.' We don't sabotage, we prefer to increase production. That's logic. Demand is there—you satisfy demand.

Bralirwa remained loyal to the authorities until the very end, confirms yet another inside source:

> We called Bralirwa the government's big brother at the time. During the genocide, they continued paying taxes. Had Heineken decided to close the brewery, it would have been a setback for the killers. It would not have stopped the killing but the company could have influenced matters.

In a 2010 interview, Van Mameren admitted implicitly that Heineken played an important role in the genocide. Between 1998 and 2001, he led Heineken in Rwanda. When a journalist suggested that machete-wielding Hutu militiamen were often drunk on Primus, he said:

> The Rwandan president once told me: you supported the rebels. [Van Mameren is probably referring to the militias.] Well—that's difficult. I don't think you have a lot of choice when there's a gun pointing at you. And quite apart from the beer, there was of course an intense hatred.[17]

No choice? Nonsense, says a former expat who lived in Rwanda for many years prior to the genocide:

> Of course Heineken could have said: OK people, we're pulling out until things get back to normal. It is deeply unpleasant to see Bralirwa doing better than ever in a time of war. It really beggars belief: the entire country is in ruins and those fancy Primus trucks just keep on rolling.

But in marked contrast to Burundi, criticism of Heineken in Rwanda was distinctly muted. A provincial newspaper in the Netherlands published a negative article, entitled 'Rwanda, Beer and Death':

> In this mess, one thing remains standing: Heineken's brewery ... The local population in Rwanda and neighbouring regions will no longer touch any fish from the Kagera River because of all the corpses that have been dumped there but Dutch salesmanship is not affected by such superstition. When a war gets more twisted, drinking starts making more and more sense. If you stay sober you'll tire of this madness soon enough.[18]

The Dutch daily *Trouw* also featured a critical story. Headed 'In Blood-Stained Rwanda, Heineken Merrily Keeps on Brewing', the article says: 'There are reports claiming that the killing sprees of the past weeks were always preceded by binge-drinking.'[19] And five years after the events, another Dutch newspaper wrote that Heineken's image is far from spotless in Rwanda: 'During the genocide, between April and July 1994, the company kept operating and if the Tutsi intervention had not happened it seems the company would simply never have stopped.'[20] A Dutch entrepreneur in Kigali comments: 'There's hardly any other way to describe this attitude: it was collaboration.'

It was a surprising turn of events, maybe even a blessing in disguise for Heineken, that in April 1994, the same month the genocide erupted, the Dutch branch of the multinational was hit by a strike. That lasted just over a week and followed failed negotiations for a new collective labour agreement. It was all over the newspapers. 'Heineken's Stock Running Dry' was the slightly worrying headline one Dutch daily decided to run on its front page. The nation was a few days away from Queen's Day, the biggest national party on the calendar, and there was the distressing prospect that there would be no Heineken or Amstel to drink.[21] A Dutch commentator took a different angle: 'Isn't it fascinating that a strike at a brewery is a bigger talking point than the wars in Bosnia and Rwanda put together.'[22] Heineken was doubtless happy to see extensive coverage of the strike in the press and on TV, rather than an in-depth investigation of the company's role in the genocide. The strike ended just in time and on Queen's Day there was more than enough fresh beer to slake the joyous nation's thirst.

'Heineken had lost control'

Eugène Ubalijoro is waiting for me. He is seated in a comfortable lounge chair in the lobby of the sumptuous De l'Europe hotel in the heart of Amsterdam. The meeting place with the Heineken expat is no coincidence: the company owns this hotel, and for a drink you go to Freddy's Bar—how appropriate. A spacious meeting room has been put at our disposal.

Ubalijoro, formerly based in Miami and now general manager for Ethiopia, was marketing director in Kigali between 1992 and 1995. He has been flown into Amsterdam by his company to give an account of what Heineken claims to be the true story of what it did during the genocide. CEO Van Boxmeer and Africa director Pirmez had come up with a new version of the facts in conversations at Head Office. And Ubalijoro was the man who could tell me everything.

In his version, the brewery at Gisenyi fell into the hands of extremists almost immediately after the genocide had started. Admittedly, these were Bralima's own staff, but they were now operating independently. 'Heineken had lost control. The brewery was still producing and delivering beer for the soldiers to ensure that they kept on fighting, but this was out of Heineken's hands,' Ubalijoro says.

So after the earlier implicit confession by Van Mameren, Heineken now admits wholeheartedly that beer from its own fermentation tanks had been of major importance during the genocide. It's just that the company itself no longer had anything to do with it, even though it was its own staff that remained involved in the operation.

I ask Ubalijoro why the Heineken spokeswoman at the time talked about supply and demand when asked why the company continued production. He replies: 'That's the first time I am hearing this.'

I read him the passage from Homé's book that describes how company employees crossed the border every day in order to maintain contact between the directors in Goma and the brewery at Gisenyi. Every day. Ubalijoro replies: 'Heineken was present, but it is naïve to think that in Goma they were aware of what was going on in Gisenyi.'

The value of Ubalijoro's testimony is questionable. He was in Kigali when the genocide began. Despite being a Hutu, the killers pursued him because his father was a member of the opposition. He never came anywhere near the brewery before he escaped Rwanda on 8 May.

Nevertheless, Van Boxmeer and Pirmez are in full support of Ubalijoro's story. Heineken puts all the blame squarely on local staff, led by Emmanuel Sinayobye. According to the company, he is the mastermind behind the mass murders at Bralirwa, and it was thanks to him that the brewery continued to produce fresh beer for mass killers.

But the exact role Sinayobye played remains unclear. There are expats who swear that he is innocent and have supported him after the genocide, when he was accused of being complicit. He has never been convicted, and at the beginning of the genocide, he was not even in Rwanda, but in Kenya. According to Heineken, he then quickly returned to the brewery, but other sources refute this. Sinayobye, like the other key figures Jolie and Botterman, no longer wants to discuss the matter.

Homé, the Africa director at that time, does agree to talk about Heineken's role in the genocide. When asked if the brewery had become fully autonomous, he makes a dismissive gesture. 'Is that what they say at Heineken? No, that's really exaggerated. There was daily contact between our people in Goma and the staff at Gisenyi brewery.'

A former expat knows that the production could only continue if there was a fresh supply of yeast. 'That was needed every month. No yeast—no beer. So if production did not stop, it simply means that Heineken continued with its supplies.'

The subject gives the brewer cause for worry. According to the criteria of the UN Global Compact mentioned earlier, this may have been a case of 'direct complicity' in war crimes, and the fact remains that Heineken continued to produce beer, knowing that its product played a role in the mass killings—and Tutsi drivers were replaced with Hutus to facilitate smooth distribution.

Shortly before the Dutch-language version of this book went to press, Heineken sent me a new statement. Head Office now recognises that two of its Bralirwa directors had relocated just across the border in Goma during the genocide and that there had indeed been contacts with the brewery. But: 'We maintain that at the time of the genocide and due to the enormous panic and chaos in the country and the region the brewery at Gisenyi was outside Heineken's control.'[23]

'Support for a genocidal system cannot remain unpunished'

In early July 1994, it was obvious that the Tutsi-led RPF was going to be victorious, and production was finally halted on

10 July. 'One week later, the RPF arrived in Gisenyi,' a witness remembers. 'When we started brewing beer again, the boilers were full but they had not yet cooled down. In fact, we should have thrown away that beer, but the director at the time refused. He said: "At this point in time people will drink anything."'

Bralirwa workers who had fled were encouraged to report to the brewery or a central depot in their own region so they could claim 'a small sum of money, just enough to survive,' in the words of a former employee. The brewery re-started in October, partly with the help of new foreign recruits and partly using existing staff, including killers. A former manager relates:

> Dozens of Bralirwa workers were active participants in the genocide. Some are still in jail today, but others were never prosecuted and are now back at work. It has been painful. A lot of people suffered from depression, wanted to kill themselves. You have seen friends, acquaintances, children die before your eyes. How should you deal with that?

The change of power meant that Heineken had a new partner within Bralirwa. The first encounter was understandably far from cordial. Of course, the RPF resented the fact that the beer brewer had been siding with the murderous regime to the bitter end. 'Support for a genocidal system cannot remain unpunished,' was the RPF's opinion. Homé responded that his company paid taxes regardless of how the money was spent. Which is what Heineken fully intended to continue doing, in the Netherlands, Rwanda or wherever. 'The atmosphere changed during our talk. We weren't exactly best friends at the end of the meeting but there was a firm handshake,' he writes.[24] A pretty optimistic presentation of the state of affairs, as would become apparent.

Heineken went looking for a new top manager, and Ubalijoro advised them strongly against appointing a Frenchman.[25] The new government was absolutely livid about how the French had armed the soldiers and the militias of the fallen regime.

Moreover, thanks to a French mission operating under the auspices of the United Nations, Opération Turquoise, many perpetrators had been able to escape across the border. So, better not appoint a Frenchman.

In the spring of 1995, Heineken appointed Yves Lafage, indisputably a Frenchman.[26] While he was in charge, Bralirwa was in constant conflict with the government. There are two versions of this episode. Former employees say that the new government was insatiable in demanding more and more tax revenue. Others, including the current minister for trade, François Kanimba, say that the company thought that it was going to be business as usual, whereas the new government demanded more transparency and rigorously enforced tax payment. 'This led to tensions because the government was under the impression that Bralirwa was still dodging taxes, as it did before the genocide,' he says.

Rwandan sources quoted in the Dutch daily *NRC* claim that Heineken was 'arrogant' in saying that its investments already constituted a significant contribution to state income, so why should the company therefore also pay taxes?[27] Questions about Heineken's behaviour were asked in the Dutch parliament, but the foreign minister did not acknowledge there was a problem. As far as he knew, Heineken was meeting all its fiscal obligations.[28] The tax dispute was still rumbling on when, in early 1998, Bralirwa was confronted with a fresh tragedy.

The ambush

Every morning, the company staff bus would leave a little before 7 a.m. and take the winding road from the centre of Gisenyi to the brewery a little farther to the south.[29] The morning of 19 January 1998 was no different. The bus took the lakeside road, across the hilly landscape, past plantations and through tiny villages. About halfway was a steep ascent, where the bus with just over sixty people on board would slow to a crawl.

An ambush.

Armed men in uniform ordered the bus to a halt. The passengers imagined them to be soldiers, until shots started ringing out. These were no soldiers, it was a Hutu militia, 'the same people who had been involved in the genocide four years earlier,' a witness recalls. There were more fighters hiding among the banana trees, dozens of them.

The driver was killed instantly. The militia then ordered the workers to form two groups, Hutus on one side, Tutsis on the other. 'We're all Rwandans,' one of the workers said courageously. Nobody obeyed the order. 'Then all of you will die,' came the irate response. This was no idle threat: the assailants threw a grenade into the bus and started shooting straight at the passengers. They then doused the bus in petrol and set it alight.

'When they opened fire, I hid under a chair, but I was hit in my left leg,' says Alphonse Bahati, who was a cook at Heineken. He managed to jump through the window and run away despite his injuries. 'One of the attackers overtook me. He said they would forgive me, being a Hutu. Some had worked at Bralirwa and knew who was Hutu and who was Tutsi. I had just started so they did not know what I was. I'm Tutsi.'

Jean-Bosco Karoretwa, who worked in the bottling plant, also managed to get away:

> They shot at me. There was a bullet that went through my neck. I was covered in blood, and when I fell down they thought that it would soon be over. I staggered on for another kilometre or so and then a villager offered me help. He took me to a hospital in Gisenyi in a wheelbarrow.

There were thirty-six dead and twenty-seven injured. Homé was devastated. 'What happened in Gisenyi happened to us all,' he writes. In a closed room, he and his deputy fell into each other's arms and wept. Production was temporarily reduced and limited to the day shift only. There was army protection. Heineken says its attitude towards the absentees was flexible. Pay continued for everyone.[30]

However, there were limits to the multinational's understanding and amenability, as became apparent in an interview with Karel Vuursteen four years after the events.

> You really can't do a bloody thing. All you can do is be sympathetic. You're sitting there on a crate with a hand-rolled cigarette, and you're surrounded by people who say: 'You were here two years ago when I had a family with three children that I had to take care of. I still have the same job at the brewery except that now I'm also taking care of my brother's five children, my mother-in-law, or my sister and her two kids and I'm still making the same money ... that's just unfair, is it not?' Well, there's very little you can do about that.

'Give them a raise?' the journalist suggested.

'No, we can't, we're a commercial organisation, we really are very concerned about people but we cannot for that reason structurally increase salaries.'[31]

The surviving passengers were similarly acquainted with the limitations of a commercial organisation. Just under two years after the attack, Bahati's contract was not renewed, and he was made to pay for his own medicines:

> Of course I was incensed but what can you do? There are people working for them who have been studying for many years. You can take them to court but you will not win. And I wasn't the only survivor they sent away so soon. Fortunately I have no trauma, no nightmares. But I do feel physical pain.

Karoretwa is extremely lucky to be alive. He tells his story:

> In the hospital, the doctor made a hole in my throat that enabled me to breathe again. But talking was impossible. My situation did not improve, and I was taken to Kigali, where a Dutch doctor said it would be wise to send me to a university clinic in Belgium. But the

directors considered that too expensive. Four months later, I was allowed to go to Nairobi, where an Indian doctor treated me. Four times I was operated on, and I was unable to speak for a year. I communicated using a notepad.

Karoretwa, who still speaks with difficulty, was able to return to work in the end and his pay had continued throughout his time off duty. He did well and was promoted to team leader:

What did hurt was that I only received a part of the insurance money. The insurance company tried to downplay the consequences of the accident, which was painful. Neither Heineken nor Bralirwa paid any damages, even though it was an occupational accident. As soon as you take your seat in the company bus it's the employer who is responsible. But we were always told: the brewery cannot pay all survivors. Even the expenses of the annual commemoration are not covered by management. They take care of transport and drinks, but we must always provide our own food.

Brought to you by Heineken

Now that the machetes serve once again as kitchen utensils and Kalashnikovs have fallen silent, Rwandans can turn their full attention to the local beer war. This one started in 2010 and pits Heineken against its challenger, Skol Brewery, owned by the Belgian Unibra company. So it's the Netherlands versus Belgium, slightly south of the equator.[32]

During one of my visits to Rwanda, the country is preparing for the twentieth annual commemoration of the genocide. Kigali is booming and will play host to high-level guests from all over the world. Since the genocide, the city has been transformed, and Rwanda is in many ways an economic miracle on African soil. The flipside of this equation is the fact that the former commander-in-chief of the RPF and country's president since 2000, Paul Kagame, tolerates no disagreement. He has engineered a change in the Constitution that will allow him to continue running the country until at least 2034.

During the commemoration, the president addresses a 30,000-strong crowd in the national stadium, which in 1994 was a refugee camp. There are billboards all over town on which companies, Bralirwa included, declare solidarity with the government and its slogan: 'Remember, unite, renew.'

I visit the impressive Kigali Genocide Memorial on a hill where a mass grave was found after the genocide. Photographs and captions tell me about the slaughter of Tutsis. In this highly religious country, they were even pursued into the churches in which they had taken refuge. Men who were known to be HIV-positive raped women and then often 'spared' them immediate death, exposing them to long-term suffering instead. There are fragments of radio broadcasts, exhorting the Hutus to exterminate the 'cockroaches'.

Numb from the thousands of skulls exhibited, the photographs and all the names of the victims, I walk into the peaceful garden, full of flowers. It overlooks the city. My eye is drawn to a small sign that bears the logo of the local Heineken subsidiary. Yes, that is what it says: the memorial gardens are supported by Bralirwa.

Did the directors consider making this modest donation anonymously? Or at least have a sense of dignity and leave out the name and the company logo? I suddenly remember the words of a former manager: as a company, we don't do charity for free. 'There must be a clear signature,' he said. And after all, Heineken is not the Red Cross.

14

WHAT ABOUT HEINEKEN?

RESPONSES AND STRATEGY

Travelling through Heineken's Africa, one thing becomes clear: business is booming. True, profits may fluctuate from time to time, but African markets are, generally speaking, among the most lucrative in the world, and the expectations are that this will continue. Unsurprisingly, Heineken has not been universally happy with my critical research. There is incomprehension among company staff who are working on the continent or managing business there from Head Office.

One would expect a manager who is involved with corporate social responsibility to be highly curious about the contents of my book and use its findings to get his superiors more involved with his work. But instead, he stopped reading after a few pages and disregarded it because what he read did not reflect his own experience. This could simply not be true.

A former expat wrote this to me: 'Why are you so negative about the huge efforts we have made to provide Africans with the pleasure of a beer while working in places where we are confronted with war, ethnic discrimination, Aids, malaria, corruption and dictatorship? Is pleasure only reserved for rich, white Westerners?'

Many employees who busy themselves with Africa are convinced that they do not just have well-paid and adventurous jobs. They think that with Heineken they also contribute to a better world. The job adds meaning to their lives, and this comes as no surprise. There is praise for Heineken all the way to the United Nations General Assembly and the US Congress, and the beer brewer often wins sustainability prizes. Managers are invited to congresses and debates where they regale participants with pleasant stories no one will verify.

And then some 'individual with an opinion' shows up (that's how Heineken describes me) and tells the world that the success stories are, in the main, mirages.[1] What action do you take?

Heineken's defence

After the first edition of the book was published in the Netherlands, Heineken advanced five arguments to challenge my findings. I was accused of using subjective sources, making mistakes and turning sweeping statements about incidents into generalities; I judged yesterday's events with today's values, and my work was supposedly motivated by an agenda that was against multinationals working in developing countries.

Heineken does not specify what it means by 'subjective sources', but I assume these to be former employees who did not leave the company on good terms. And indeed, this has been the case for a few of my interviewees, but their statements have always been cross-checked with other sources or confirmed with supporting documents.

About the 'mistakes' Heineken mentions, it was Van Boxmeer who stated in a public debate that 'many facts are absolutely correct but others absolutely not'.[2] In conversations with interested parties, the company stresses that not everything is correct and that there are some issues I simply fail to understand. What Heineken omits to say is that it was given the opportunity to correct the manuscript prior to publication but chose not to.

When talking with Van Boxmeer at Head Office, I ask him about the perceived errors. He replies: 'I'm not going to go into that, page by page.'

Now it's my turn to protest: as I am being publicly accused of telling absolute inaccuracies, at the very least I have a right to know what these are.

'But you're not going to re-write the book.'

'That's exactly what I'm doing.'

'This story will never end.'

By contrast, I found former Africa director Tom de Man perfectly willing to go through the inaccuracies he had found, in a session that took a full five hours. The conclusion is that I have indeed made mistakes. For one, sugar is not added to beer to render the taste less bitter, as I had presumed. There is only one thing that determines a beer's bitterness and that is the quantity of hop used. And I was also unaware that the land on which a new brewery was built in Nigeria in 2002 had already been acquired, in 1984. Proof enough, according to De Man, that Festus Odimegwu, who comes from the same region where the brewery was built, had no influence on the choice of location and did not enrich himself in the process, as one high-level source had told me.[3]

The remaining inaccuracies, says De Man, concern suggestive remarks and differences of interpretation. Heineken, for instance, does not agree with my qualification of Jean-Pierre Bemba as a business partner. The company also resolutely maintains that during the genocide in Rwanda it had lost all control of its local brewery and can as a consequence not be held responsible for all that fresh beer that kept flowing from the facility.

Heineken's third argument is that I seem to focus on incidental mistakes. Willem de Jonge, director for sustainable development, puts it like this: 'When you are at work you do ninety-eight things right and two things wrong. What you do is constantly write about those two.' Well, how susceptible would a judge be to a plea that says the suspect may be doing things that are very bad but only 2 per cent of the time, while during the other 98 per cent his behaviour is impeccable ...

I must confess that I was grappling with these issues early on. Was I writing about a series of isolated incidents and in doing so obscuring the fact that Heineken is reasonably well behaved given the African context? The answer is that I am convinced, given the scope of my research, the time it took and the areas I covered, that my findings accurately represent the way Heineken does business on the continent. In many countries, I found the same type of behaviour, from having ties with authoritarian regimes to violating advertising codes, from engineering mass redundancies to pressuring authorities to reduce taxation.

Moreover, as I got to know the company better and gained access to more and different sources, I gathered information that shed light on structural bad practices: there were quite a few things rotten in the state of Heineken. Basic assumptions, that Heineken has supposedly created thousands of jobs throughout the continent and that it benefits the local economy, for instance, proved to be illusory. One almost starts wondering what else the company might be hiding. Has this research merely revealed the tip of the proverbial iceberg?

Heineken is stung by the idea that events from twenty to thirty years ago are presented as if they are happening now. 'Make no mistake,' Van Boxmeer repeatedly said, 'Thirty years ago the payment of bribes was tax-deductible in the Netherlands.' (He claims to have never used that facility.)

That may be true, but the 1990s were not exactly pre-Enlightenment times as far as corporate ethics were concerned. Back then, delivering beer to mass killers participating in a genocide, cooperating with pillaging rebels and hiring women in exchange for sex were generally not considered to be normal business practices.

Heineken was a relative latecomer in devising a global business code (in 2005). But even in that 'era of ignorance' a lot of thought was going into acceptable corporate behaviour, even though no tangible action was forthcoming. Indeed, in those very same 1990s a series of statements were committed to paper about every potentially controversial issue Heineken is grappling with today, as former HR manager Hans Wesseling can testify: he wrote them before they were left to gather dust on a shelf.

Finally, I was said to be opposed to the work of multinationals in developing countries. In a statement, Heineken writes:

> In essence, the book reflects Olivier van Beemen's opinion that companies should not be working in developing countries and countries with a challenging political climate. With all due respect to Olivier van Beemen, we see things differently. And this vision is shared by organisations such as the United Nations, World Bank and OECD. They believe very strongly that the presence in developing countries of large companies like Heineken promotes economic growth and as a result more development.

The company refers to general statements written by each of these different bodies, none of which have anything in particular to say about Heineken.[4]

Heineken ascribes to me an ideological conviction. It implies that in my eyes, the company can never do any good in Africa, simply because I am against the presence of multinational corporations in poor and unstable countries. In reality, I think business can indeed play a positive role, but this should not be an automatic assumption. Companies should be subjected to a critical assessment: what does a particular enterprise bring to the host country and what are its business practices? In the earlier Dutch edition of this book, I wrote: 'Business-powered economic development, like mobile phone companies, appears to be more effective than aid but it is highly contentious whether this is also true of brewers that are fighting aggressive beer wars in countries where the authorities are too weak to protect the population.'[5]

Heineken gets away with it

As Katinka van Cranenburgh is reading my book shortly after its first publication in the Netherlands in 2015, she holds her breath. She has just left the company and still feels a bond with her former employer. 'This is trouble,' she fears.

While the book was being written and researched, Heineken refused all cooperation: no interviews, no reaction to the contents of the manuscript I had sent to the press office. Should the company wish to remove possible mistakes, that would be admitting, implicitly, that the rest of the story was correct, which would contribute to the credibility of the book. Heineken wanted to avoid this, admits an internal source.

After publication, the company continued with the same tactic, eschewing all discussion—at least in public. But Heineken did table a new publicity campaign—not advertising a new product, mind you. This one was designed to create good feelings: Heineken stands for 'pure', 'refreshing', 'reliable', 'clear' and 'magical'.[6]

It is only when Labour Party and Socialist Party members of the Dutch Second Chamber and the European Parliament begin to ask questions about Ibecor's controversial business practices that the beer brewer finally decides to respond in public. A new section is added to the corporate website, called 'Growing Together in Africa'. It features short films about happy Africans who enjoy better lives thanks to the company, and short texts about its agricultural projects, Aids policy and the Heineken Africa Foundation. And then it adds the company statement about my supposed aversion to business in developing countries.

WHAT ABOUT HEINEKEN?

But that is pretty much where all the commotion ends. Newspapers and magazines publish a steady stream of articles, and I am invited to several radio programmes, but the far more widely-watched TV talk shows ignore my research. One current affairs programme has taken a serious interest in filming a report in the field but tells me that when it comes to reporting on Africa, it prefers to cover hunger and other catastrophes. The editor also considered it problematic that my sources—including those working for the local Heineken subsidiaries—are all black. He thinks Dutch viewers will find it difficult to identify with my interlocutors.

For a week and a half, *Het Financieele Dagblad*, the newspaper I served for four years as a correspondent in France, does nothing with the freshly published revelations. When I ask them why, they reply that no one has properly read the proof and it is now too late anyway. However, the paper thinks that a background article about corporate social responsibility is an option but will only publish if Heineken can be bothered to cooperate.

The company may be quiet in public, but behind the scenes it is busier than ever. When fresh questions are launched in the Dutch parliament, the two political parties involved (the Socialists again and a small Christian party) are the immediate targets of a visit by a company delegation. Interested journalists, academics and NGO workers all receive invitations to come and talk with Heineken.

I am quietly astounded at how easily Heineken gets away with it. Take the ASN Bank, a self-declared idealistic financial institution that claims to be guided by the principles of sustainability. During its annual shareholder meeting in 2016, the bank is asked whether investing in Heineken is still compatible with its strict corporate social responsibility rules. The bank therefore announces an in-depth inquiry. So what happens? 'We had a frank conversation with Heineken,' says Mariëtta Smid, ASN's sustainability manager. The brewer pledges that it has put its house in order and that further improvements will be made. And that is pretty much the end of the story, even though ASN states it will keep an eye on the matter.

Van Cranenburgh comments:

> I was genuinely surprised. If someone wrote similar things in a book about Shell, there would be hell to pay. But somehow Heineken brings about feelings of pride and pleasure among the Dutch. The brand has an excellent reputation, which is probably why they can brush aside these allegations.

Early 2016, Heineken will have breathed a sigh of relief, and frankly, after three years of research, I also think it is time to move on.

Leiden University's helping hand

But then I am given new leads about fresh issues, like the judge as a paid-up member of the Board of Heineken's Burundi subsidiary and the big fraud case with the Verveldes in Nigeria. Foreign publishers have started to express an interest and university professors encourage me to use my research for a thesis.[7] I cannot escape Heineken in Africa.

Early 2017, the University of Amsterdam organises a debate with Van Boxmeer about my book. At the request of Heineken, journalists are not allowed and I'm not informed about the debate either, but a contact at the university tips me off. After the debate, I finally get to speak to Van Boxmeer and at this moment he tells me not to go on a crusade against his company, as mentioned in the foreword. 'You're too young for that,' he adds. Is he threatening me? The corporate affairs director for the company, Blanca Juti, takes another approach: she invites me straight away for dinner. I reply that a coffee at Head Office would be great.

So this is Heineken's new tack. The castle doors open, and most of my requests for interviews are being honoured, including the one with Van Boxmeer himself. Their corporate time is at my disposal. The managers show me the company's human face: we make the occasional joke and talk about holidays and children. The charm offensive has begun.

My first talk at Head Office is marked by both Juti and spokesperson Schuirink saying repeatedly that this rapprochement is not a PR stunt. 'Transparency is in our DNA; it is strange that things have gone this way.'

Shortly after Donald Trump is elected as president of the United States, Juti tells me that I am looking at Heineken in Africa from a particular perspective and that there are 'alternative perspectives' that can be equally valid. I cannot help myself and ask if she also has 'alternative facts' for me, like the White House.

In short, the doors are open, but Heineken continues to regard my findings as 'an opinion', which can be countered with another opinion. The saying 'Let's agree to disagree' pops up frequently in our conversations.

Heineken feels that action of some sort is now required. This has become all the more urgent because of the prospect of the book being published outside the Netherlands, where pride, goodwill and reputation are unlikely to play similarly decisive roles in the assessment of the company. At the end of 2016, Heineken calls on the African Studies Centre (ASC) at Leiden University. Ton Dietz, about to end his tenure as director of the ASC, is an advocate of close cooperation between the university and the business world and has never made a secret of his fondness for the brewer. He is reportedly very proud that the ASC gets a mention in Heineken's annual report.[8]

Dietz organises a meeting behind closed doors with so-called stakeholders: representatives from government, business and civil society. The brief for the meeting says that Heineken wants to listen to these stakeholders' experiences under difficult circumstances and wants to pick up suggestions for improvement. But those present see a series of presentations ostensibly intended to demonstrate that Heineken is not performing so badly after all. The company sends a ten-strong delegation, three of whom are flown in from Congo, Burundi and the United States. After the event, Heineken re-christens the meeting an NGO Summit and for months afterwards uses this 'summit' as an argument to demonstrate that they really are open to outside criticism. This is part of the 'soul-searching' Van Boxmeer was talking about in response to the publication of the book.

There is more to come. In April 2017, Dietz is working on a series of research proposals for Heineken, on behalf of the ASC. He offers to develop a code of conduct for conflict zones, in a consultancy-like capacity. The expectation is that such a policy can be devised fairly quickly, giving the company tangible proof of progress on the issue. We saw earlier that Heineken had already developed guidelines for similar circumstances, which were left to gather dust on a dark shelf somewhere. In the end, this job falls to Shift, the American consultancy agency that was also hired to sort out the company's human rights policy.

The ASC has also proposed a wide-ranging review of the influence Heineken may have on the United Nations' Sustainable Development Goals (SDGs), with company staff working alongside academics to help improve its performance as regards the SDGs. The ASC hopes to obtain research funding from Heineken of around 2.5 million dollars for this study, an absolute fortune in the social sciences.[9]

Is it the role of a university to hold out a helping hand to a company in trouble? The question is justified. After all, the conditions the ASC poses for its research project are rather convenient for the company: Dietz wants to install a supervisory committee, entirely composed of former Heineken employees and no academic staff. He also gives the company the right to reject researchers for whatever reason. When asked for clarification, he writes that when it comes to selecting researchers, the ASC will have the final word after all.

As of early 2018, the project has not yet got off the ground, and nothing can be said publicly about the conditions. This doesn't stop Heineken from already talking about it as proof of its serious efforts to learn more about the consequences of its own actions.

15

MOZAMBIQUE

TAX BREAKS FOR PROPAGANDA

In December 2017, John-Paul Schuirink, the company spokes-man and my immediate contact inside the multinational, sent me an email:

As you will have seen, we announced our investment in Mozambique earlier this week: one hundred million dollars for a new brewery. This investment will create some 200 new jobs immediately and several times that number of potential indirect employment in the foreseeable future. Think suppliers, distributors, retail et cetera. We will also start with local sourcing projects in Mozambique.

A bit further down, I read:

Every year, Heineken invests some 300 to 400 million euros [around 340 to 450 million dollars] in Africa. We can do this because we are a profitable company and believe in the continent. In the countries concerned these investments represent an inflow of foreign exchange. This is how we strengthen local economies with additional govern-ment revenue, jobs and local sourcing.

One month later, I was on my way to Mozambique to see this freshly brewed miracle for myself.

The Dutch get in early

Mozambique, a former Portuguese colony on Africa's east coast, is among the six poorest nations on earth. Since the turn of the century, though, it has earned another nickname: an African lion, a rising economy with enormous potential.[1] Economic growth averages 7 per cent, and the nation is frequently presented in surveys as a highly promising business destination.[2] In 2010, one of the world's largest gas reserves was discovered, earning it yet another nickname: Africa's Qatar. Investors quickly queued up to get in, and the normally fairly cautious IMF predicted annual growth figures of up to 24 per cent for the next ten years.[3]

Mozambique was booming. But then 2015 arrived and with it the first outlines of a colossal scandal surrounding the acquisition of a fleet of fishing ships. They were paid for with money the government had borrowed, but somewhere in the process half a billion dollars had disappeared without a trace. Diplomats spoke of 'one of the biggest fraud cases in Africa's history'.[4]

Foreign donors including the IMF, the EU and the African Development Bank decided to suspend financial support, which brought the Mozambican state to the brink of bankruptcy. In another setback, commodity prices had started to slump, which meant that gas exploration would prove to be far less lucrative than predicted. Several energy projects were therefore postponed.

The currency, the metical, started losing value fast, and retail prices went up. To make matters worse, the conflict between the governing Frelimo, in power since independence in 1975, and the opposition movement Renamo re-emerged. After decolonisation, the two had been fighting each other for more than fifteen years in what became one of the deadliest wars on the continent, leaving an estimated 1 million people dead. Today, still, Mozambique is the only country in the world to feature a Kalashnikov in its national flag.

Given this context, the Dutch rapprochement with the Mozambican government raised more than a few eyebrows. President Nyusi was invited for a three-day state visit in May 2017. He went to The Hague and Amsterdam and was received with full honours by the king, the prime minister and the chairs of the First and Second Chamber of parliament. Indra Römgens of SOMO, a Dutch investigative bureau that looks at multinational businesses, called it 'a scandal that a Mozambican president gets received in the Netherlands with so much fanfare' and pointed at the controversial role of the Mozambican government in the fraud case. Investigative journalist Erik Charas of the Mozambican newspaper *Verdade* (Truth) asked himself: Why now?[5]

There was a quick answer to that question: the Dutch business spirit had overcome worries related to thorny ethical issues. Heineken and Shell could not wait to start investing in Mozambique, and President Nyusi was desperate for some positive news.

What exactly happened during that official visit? It is certain that the president and Heineken representatives held extensive talks. The Dutch brewer had been exploring the options for a new brewery project for some time, looking into water provision, among other things. In 2016, Heineken established a Mozambican sales and distribution company. According to various sources, the Dutch embassy lobbied hard for the necessary licences to brew beer locally, and diplomats were quick to point to the extensive Dutch aid effort in the country, as if to say: if you like our assistance, you must open the door for our companies. Eduardo Sengo of the Mozambican business association CTA recalls: 'These two were very emphatically tied to one another.'[6]

Internal documents and emails which were requested under the Dutch Freedom of Information Act, reveal that the Dutch ambassador, Pascalle Grotenhuis, has even tried to push for new legislation in Mozambique. Heineken should be allowed to deduct its investment costs for ten years instead of five. And the multinational, which has an annual revenue that's almost double Mozambique's GDP, has pleaded for a special excise duty status for 'small breweries', for which it would itself qualify.[7]

However, a few more hurdles had to be overcome before a final decision was made.

A multinational subsidised by Mozambican taxpayers

In the capital Maputo, I can see that people are already welcoming the imported green Heineken bottles with open arms, especially in the upmarket bars and restaurants along the Indian Ocean beaches. But the owners of the small drinking stalls called *baracas* also tell me they are happy with Heineken. Most of the drinkers order local beer because it is cheaper and comes in larger bottles, but they heartily approve of the fact that this global brand can be bought everywhere. Heineken's marketing machine is already in full swing. On digital billboards and the city's skyscrapers, the beer brewer has started spreading the message: *Abre o mundo*, the local variation on the global theme 'Open your world'.

Talks with insiders reveal that Heineken's arrival was delayed mostly because of ferocious resistance from the local beer brewer CDM, Cervejas de Moçambique, part of global market leader AB InBev. The company has a near-monopoly on the national beer market and has made major investments to boost capacity. CDM is a powerful player in Mozambique. It is one of the biggest taxpayers in the country, and the president of its Board of Directors, Tomaz Salomão, is a member of Frelimo's influential political commission. Both the Mozambican state and the ruling party's investment company are shareholders in CDM and therefore set great store by good results.

Sengo says that CDM 'did everything to keep its rival out, but Heineken has obviously managed to overcome any obstacle. I still don't understand how they got their licence.' My contacts tell me that this is possible only when you have the support of an influential local contact with good political connections, but Heineken claims they achieved all this on their own.

But there is more. Heineken not only got the papers it needed; it also managed to negotiate a substantial cut in its obligatory levy payments, as the newspaper *Verdade* discovered.[8] During the first year, the Dutch only pay half of what they owe the state, the next year they pay 62.5 per cent and in the third year they still pay only three-quarters. This is a new law and applies only to newcomers, which is the reason why CDM missed out, despite its many connections. In order to placate Heineken's rival, the government declared a tax holiday for beers with a high percentage of local ingredients. However, that rule applies to all brewers so Heineken benefits again.[9]

In short, the arrival of the Dutch means that this dirt-poor nation with a near-bankrupt state is likely to receive less revenue from beer levies than before. The local taxpayer is therefore subsidising a beer brewer's investment plans. Public finances will only improve when Mozambicans start drinking substantially higher quantities of beer and in so doing ensure that the taxes from their extra consumption outstrip the lost revenues from the government's generous tax breaks. The implication is that people would have to spend a much larger part of their income on alcohol with likely negative effects on economic development and healthcare. 'This economy needs foreign investments and new jobs, urgently,' says the Dutch development economist Jorrit Oppewal, who lives in Maputo. 'But bringing down levies in order to entice Heineken to come to your country—I find it scandalous.'

Several sources in Maputo assure me that the sweetener was not even necessary. They are convinced that Heineken, having prepared the move in the preceding years, was going to arrive on the scene anyway. Even without such fiscal largesse, there are lucrative deals to be done in a country where workers are cheap and the potential is enormous. In their view, the multinational has capital-ised on the government's desperation: the negotiating position of the state was weak, and Heineken made the most of it.

That is not how the company sees it. 'The temporal lowering of levies has most definitely had a bearing on our decision when to invest in Mozambique,' it reacts. 'Heineken has several options to invest in (new) African markets and will always compare the attractiveness and the expected return of one investment against another.'

What the company suggests here is that it can play countries off against each other in order to obtain the most favourable conditions possible, a phenomenon that is known as 'the race to the bottom'.[10]

The investment is of great importance to President Nyusi because it enables him to demonstrate to his people that Mozambique remains an attractive destination for investors. Borges Nhamire, an investigator for the Centre for Public Integrity (CIP), shows me the front page of a newspaper with a picture of a proud minister and the headline: 'We Attract Multinationals'. Nhamire: 'More than anything, it serves as a tool for internal propaganda. The rank-and-file must get the impression that the country is well administered and Heineken's arrival is proof of that. But your average Mozambican has no idea of the conditions under which such a company comes in.'

There is growing doubt whether investments like Heineken's are of any benefit to the country or actually cost money. ActionAid, an international NGO that focuses on tax evasion, has calculated that these tax holidays cost Mozambique half a billion dollars in lost income. It adds that less than a quarter of that amount would be enough to offer education to all Mozambican children who cannot currently attend to school.[11]

Critics say that the government has been using the same argu-ment in favour of fiscal sweeteners for well over twenty years: we must attract companies by offering good conditions. If one comes, more will follow, and that is good for the entire economy. 'But that's not how these things work,' says the CIP's Fátima Mimbire:

> What we see is that millions of dollars of international investments do not result in any extra orders for local businesses and that the number of new jobs created is extremely limited. Local companies do not have the requisite know-how, which means that investors continue to rely on foreign companies for almost every contract.

Although Heineken's decision to earmark 100 million dollars for investment in Mozambique sounds impressive, the bulk of this outlay goes into paying for the importation of machinery and building materials. Bottles, lorries and transport will also be sourced from outside the country. A former employee who was involved in the construction of various breweries across Africa estimates that of all money invested '10 percent at the most' benefits the local economy. 'It depends whether they work with local subcontractors. If not, it's even less.'

It is my last evening in Maputo, and I am having a plate of grilled *camarões* (large tropical shrimps, a local specialty) and a cold glass of 2M, a popular local lager. Looking at the gentle waves of the ocean, I am trying to imagine the negotiations between Heineken and the government. The beer brewer announces that it will devise a programme for local farmers and it shows the government its famous impact studies from other countries and their inflated employment figures. 'Look at all those thousands and thousands of jobs we will bring you.'

A company will of course want to invest under the most favourable conditions possible. As Van Boxmeer told me: we never refuse a subsidy. But can you really talk about corporate social responsibility when you are squeezing everything you can out of a country where the state is virtually bankrupt and the government on the ropes? Is it fair to get Mozambican taxpayers to contribute towards an investment in a brewery? And are these the lessons Heineken has learnt from the many years of 'soul-searching' it says it has been engaged in?

POSTSCRIPT

AN ISLAND OF PERFECTION IN A SEA OF MISERY

Since 2012, the Palais des Nations on the Avenue de la Paix in Geneva has been hosting the annual United Nations Forum on Business and Human Rights.[1] The neo-classical palace was originally built for the League of Nations, the precursor to the UN. Its luxurious meeting rooms are the backdrop for three days of discussions and exchanges among experts from the business world, governments and human rights organisations. The Swiss surroundings are peaceful. If you look out from the palace's impeccable central hall, you will see spotless Lake Geneva and the snow-covered Alpine peaks in the distance.

But inside those meeting rooms, robust language reverberates. 'The rebels chopped off heads, they buried people alive and did other things that are too gruesome to describe here. We were shocked that Heineken could do business with such a group.' The speaker is John Namegabe, spokesman for the group of 168 Congolese workers who are finally being compensated, after a struggle that took years. I went to see him in Bukavu, but now he is here, as an invited guest to the session entitled 'Remediation through the OECD National Contact Points: The Case of Former Employees of Bralima'.

Next to him sits Rutger Goethart, Heineken's HR manager whom I interviewed about human rights. He is being asked why Heineken had accepted mediation:

> Let me first say that I am very proud to be sitting here, next to John, because his story is truly extraordinary. When we received his complaint at the end of 2015, our initial approach was legalistic and we were defensive. This changed in the course of the process. Internally, we said: let's embrace this. Out of honesty. We are working with a new generation of colleagues who see things differently. This company has changed over the past fifteen years. We were a mostly locally operating enterprise; now we are a multinational with processes that are coordinated and controlled centrally, and these include the code of conduct and risk management.

He shows a picture of a group of Congolese complainants and the Heineken delegation, taken just after the size of the compensation had been assessed for everyone individually. 'Pictures speak louder than words,' says Goethart. Does he have some advice for other companies that are confronted with similar situations? 'Absolutely. Engage.'

'Thank you for those amazing pictures,' is the moderator's comment, who also mentions that Goethart is living up to the dignity of his family name (Goethart is an old Dutch way of writing 'good heart').

Maartje van Putten of the OECD Guidelines National Contact Point, the mediator in this case, is full of praise for Heineken. She repeats a few times that she looks back on the negotiations in Uganda and France as if they were a film:

> If you find the right person in a company, someone who is open and enjoys support at the highest level, you can resolve issues. That was Heineken's message. We knew they wanted to find a solution. They admitted that mistakes had been made seventeen years ago and said: we must bring the matter to a correct close. Which they did, with great wisdom and joy. It was great. I don't have any Heineken

shares—I don't even drink beer—but I have never seen a company
so willing to bring closure and doing this in such a fantastic way.

How had the NCP persuaded the company to become part of
the process? Van Putten explains: 'You have to show them that it
is in their interest—there's something in it for you. And I cannot
remember whether I used that word at the time but it can also
be fun. Take it like a challenge.' This she says minutes after
Namegabe talked about severed heads and people who were buried alive.

Van Putten underlines the beer brewer's generosity. 'Payments
are based on the 2017 salary structure, which was not necessary.
And those who were forty-five years and older received a little
more because it was difficult for them to find a job. The highest
sum was 45,000 dollars for a widow who never expected to get
anything.' In fact, the payments were between 500 and 36,500
dollars, and averaged 8,000 dollars.

The audience is lapping it up. A development worker says:
'How fantastic that you are sitting here, next to each other.' An
academic adds: 'You have all shown a great deal of courage.' And
a lawyer asks: 'Isn't it difficult to be so transparent?'

The hard questions, about collaborating with rebels or a company ignoring its former employees for so long, remain unasked.
This is a success story and there are only winners. A human rights
expert at the Council of Europe whom I call one week after the
event tells me: 'It was such a feel-good moment. When I was at
the airport going home I promptly bought a bottle of Heineken.'

So that's how this works. During a civil war, Heineken uses its
collaboration with a group of criminal rebels to get rid of a large
number of its workers and avoid paying the correct severance
packages. The beer brewer then proceeds to ignore their complaints for more than fifteen years but continues to highlight in
public that it has no greater asset than its personnel. Only when
damage to its reputation becomes a real possibility because the

matter comes to the attention of the Dutch authorities and I am writing about the affair does Heineken begin to take the complainants seriously. However, external pressure has never been a factor, no: we should see this as a case of 'evolving comprehension' or 'changes in corporate culture'.

After all those years, the result is a modest payment for former workers, many of whom are already dead. The company insists that this should not be called compensation and that it be kept secret. Yet Heineken gets praise for its transparency. The settlement means there will be no further proceedings by or on behalf of this group of ex-workers relating to alleged complicity with war crimes. Quite the reverse: the company gets recognition as a wise, honest and generous actor, a corporate example even, a place where you go if you need advice on 'best practices', to use the insider jargon. Two years after Prime Minister Rutte's speech at the UN General Assembly in New York, the company is again praised at the UN, this time in Geneva. Yes, Heineken never ceases to amaze.

The first time Heineken amazed me was in Tunisia, early 2011, when I discovered that the company maintained close ties with the kleptocratic family clan that had been in power for almost 25 years. It was not just the relationship itself that had me stunned—it was the fact that Heineken was brewing beer there at all. I knew that Heineken was doing business all over the world and had some vague notion that it should have breweries outside the Netherlands, but I had never realised the scale: 165 breweries in over seventy countries, including this North African autocracy.

When I told people close to me that I was planning a book on Heineken in Africa, I was mostly regaled with positive stories. A former intern told me she had deliberately chosen Heineken because of its corporate social responsibility, and she waxed lyrical about 'the combination of idealism and no-nonsense business'. She had been involved in the implementation of the company's free antiretrovirals programme and found this to be 'an honest story'. A colleague with whom I discussed the project at an early stage told me about the Heineken Africa Foundation, the charity.

I went through news archives and found enthusiastic stories with appealing headlines like 'Heineken Is Helping', 'Message to Those Who Drink Opaque Hooch: Clear Beer Is Coming' and of course 'We're Now Running the Country's Largest Agriculture Project: I Guess That Puts the Aid Organisations to Shame'.[2] Other stories dealt with growth projections, more agriculture projects and Heineken's contribution to development.

I was suitably impressed on my first few trips. As a Dutchman, you inevitably feel a certain pride when you are far away from home and notice how popular 'our' brands are. I have very fond memories of a warm Sunday afternoon sitting in a Bujumbura restaurant, built on wooden poles, overlooking Lake Tanganyika. I was watching a herd of hippos and having a sip of a locally brewed Amstel Bock, a special beer for the autumn back home. I felt I understood what former director Marc Bolland had called 'the Heineken feeling'. 'It's that special moment when you arrive at your destination and find our green box with bottles of Heineken on sale locally.'[3]

I visited some of the poorest and least-developed countries in the world, where the government was unable to provide basic services and local business was virtually non-existent. But there was always this well-oiled commercial machine called Heineken, producing perfectly fine beers in modern factories and sending it to the remotest—but no less thirsty—areas everywhere.

The company's self-image is that of a beer brewing enterprise that has achieved success on a continent full of hurdles and obstacles. 'I compare most of our breweries in Africa with ships. Very frequently you do find yourself all at sea,' reflects De Man, in a reference to bad infrastructure and political instability.[4]

Indeed, in many countries a decent road network does not exist. Energy provision is patchy, and locally available skills levels are often insufficient for a high-tech brewery. In some markets, the company has found itself face to face with intolerant strains of Islam and Christianity, both of which promote an alcohol-free lifestyle. And then there are the political vultures, whose job it appears to be to invent one new tax after another and who are only satisfied when they have had their cut. Isn't it inevitable to take the occasional misstep in this minefield and is the company really to blame for that? Is it not, above all, a major achievement that a foreign beer brewer has managed to hold its own and produces handsome profits?

But I started having misgivings early on. As I was driven around Kinshasa for the first time, I was struck by the blueness of the city. Primus blue. Was Heineken not exaggerating here? And yes, it may be an ingrained habit in Africa to pay journalists in exchange for publicity but the deference I observed among Congolese colleagues towards the brewery's PR department struck me as unhealthy.

In the company archives, I discovered that in the early 1960s Heineken was an ardent supporter of a 'white bloc' of southern African countries, including Rhodesia, South Africa and the two Portuguese colonies Angola and Mozambique, as a barrier to 'the pressure from the black race'. I learnt that in South Africa the company was advised not to act 'in opposition to the letter/ spirit of apartheid', and I also read about the enormous amounts of money that were 'pumped' from Africa into Switzerland. If this wasn't sabotage of the work of newly independent nations, then what was?

I heard about the free crates of beer given to the elites, including the minister for good governance and several judges, and I was told about the sleepover parties of President Kabila. I saw the little schools with the beer logos painted on the walls, and the misery of Soweto's drinking dens. These issues turned out not to be incidental but formed part of a pattern.

My mental switch came when I began to regard Heineken as a subject, not an object. In other words: this is not the story of a country simultaneously granting opportunities to and setting the bounds within which Heineken can operate. Instead, this is the story of a company and its attempts to influence the government of a country and its people to such an extent that it is able to create the ideal circumstances for maximising profits. Heineken's investment in Mozambique is a clear example of this.

An essential insight came when I realised that these African hurdles, however real, form part of a narrative in which the company's own achievements are enlarged and responsibility for its wrongdoing lies elsewhere. The message is that it is actually nothing short of a miracle that this beer brewer can operate under such difficult circumstances and, along the way, does so many good things for the people and planet.

What is absent from the narrative is that those African hurdles can often benefit Heineken. Look at weak governments, for example, that fail to maintain roads and healthcare, obliging the company to find costly solutions. Clearly an obstacle for business, one would think. But at the same time, the lawlessness in many countries enables Heineken to sell its drinks without limitations, advertise its wares to its heart's content and devise its own ways to combat alcohol abuse. Levels of education are low and can be a hindrance when looking for qualified personnel, but low education levels are a blessing in disguise when there is information to be spread about the positive properties of beer. The company complains about the levels of taxation in some countries but keeps mum about the fiscal advantages it manages to negotiate, often on the basis of impact studies containing dubious data.

We also saw how Africa offers an excellent habitat for shadowy organisations like Ibecor and its predecessor Interbra. For the past fifty years, these have been used to transfer large sums of money into Europe—in the case of Interbra, these were illicit financial flows. A vicious circle continues: scarce foreign exchange disappears abroad, African governments are faced with dwindling financial resources and depend increasingly on donor countries and development organisations.

I had to think about Mama Lusamba, the upbeat beer distributor from Uvira, who sent Primus all over eastern Congo, never mind the state of the roads or the insatiable armed gangs. She was happy that over the past few years the road had improved and the presence of armed 'toll gates' has diminished. But she also said that the route was at its most lucrative when the situation was at its worst, in 2010, when she had to part with large sums of money and merchandise. Since she was the only transporter left standing, she could ask twice the normal price for her beers.

Heineken is in some ways the story of Mama Lusamba's transport business writ large. The barriers this continent erects for business are so enormous that potential competitors think twice before wading in. The Big Four (three if you consider partners AB InBev and Castel as one) jointly control 93 per cent of the African beer market, and despite the noisy 'beer wars', there is virtually no competition. Africa is a beer brewer's paradise.

It is often said that governments would be more efficient, more decisive if they ran their countries like businesses. But if there is one thing I have learnt in the past five years it is that multinational corporations can be as laborious to deal with as public institutions. Of course, when there is a surge in demand, Heineken wastes no time and can create a new bottling facility in a matter of months. But on the shadier side of the business, change can take years, even decades to arrive.

When it comes to murkier subjects, Heineken claims it is permanently working on improvements, and this may well be the case. But it seems as if the objective here is to make sure these improvements are kept to the barest minimum. That way, you can show the stakeholders that you are serious about criticism and continue to take baby steps in the right direction without too much effort.

In the late 1990s, Heineken already had in place a series of guidelines for virtually all areas related to human rights. It had the opportunity to make a giant leap forward but elected to wait until 2012. In the near future, the company should also have guidelines for doing business in conflict areas as part of the soul-searching exercise that was triggered by my research. But here again we now know that this had already been done almost twenty years ago.

Multinationals can also re-invent the wheel.

Freddy Heineken, the company's legendary CEO, used to say: 'People don't drink beer. They drink marketing.' Like no one else, he understood that selling beer successfully is a matter of psychology. In terms of taste, the different lagers on offer are almost indistinguishable, even for experts. It's about image and an emotion. 'What I'm selling is a lovely atmosphere.'[5]

Thanks to Heineken's successful marketing, a beer with no distinct taste is now called 'premium' all over the world (except in the Netherlands) and is being sold at a 'premium' price. And cherishing this image works in other areas as well. Heineken manages to package malpractice expertly; after the Geneva meeting, I am almost inclined to say it re-packages it as something pleasant.

Let us recall that peculiar conversation about human rights at Heineken Head Office with Rutger Goethart and his former colleague. The latter said:

> I can tell you from the bottom of my heart that here at Heineken we want to improve things and want to contribute positively to the soci-

eties where we operate. We try to stick to all the rules, however difficult that may be. I am hurt that this is trivialised with remarks that suggest it is all just commerce and marketing to us. It is very difficult to be an island of perfection in a sea of misery, but please, do not doubt our sincerity.

Heineken as an island of perfection. And Africa? Where Heineken has made billions in the past one hunderd-and-some years? 'A sea of misery.'

But do not doubt our good intentions.

EPILOGUE

THE BOSS AND THE PROMOTION GIRL

This book was published in the Netherlands in the spring of 2018, and this time there were more serious consequences for Heineken. While television programmes were still reluctant to invite an author holding such critical views about a shining star of Dutch industry, the new revelations incited indignation on a larger scale than before.

The story that received the most attention by far was the abuse of promotion girls. The Dutch parliament passed a motion calling on the current minister for development and foreign trade, Sigrid Kaag, to get tough on abuses within or by Dutch business abroad. Parliament is of the opinion that conditions for granting subsidies to business must be made more stringent, so that taxpayer-funded support can be reclaimed from companies that transgress.

The abuse of promotion girls had direct consequences for the company. The Global Fund, supported by Bill Gates, suspended cooperation with Heineken because of the scandal, and the Dutch ASN Bank, following a third inquiry, decided that it had had enough. The bank removed Heineken from its sustainable investment fund and has halted all other financial involvement with the company until further notice.

Heineken revised an earlier declaration in which it had claimed that the company employed just 200 girls in two countries. Internal inquiry now revealed an estimated 4,000 girls in thirteen countries.[1] The company announced a series of measures: clear and unambiguous rules, training, dress codes, no alcohol on the job and transport home after work. These are almost word for word the same measures that were put in a policy paper in 2004, which remained an empty promise.

But this time things really would be different, Heineken said. So in March 2018, the company made a firm promise that reassured some politicians and stakeholders. 'If we can't guarantee good working conditions for our promoters in certain markets by the end of June we'll stop employing them there.'

In the summer of 2018, I went to Kenya to see for myself if Heineken had kept its word this time. Was I even surprised? I met with six promotion girls, who all told me the same stories: nothing had changed. They still had to accept sexual harassment as part of the job, their uniforms were so short it made them feel like prostitutes, and some of them were forced to sleep with their bosses.[2]

In an interview with a Dutch newspaper a few months later, CEO Jean-François van Boxmeer called my reporting on the promotion girls 'exaggerated', without specifying why. 'We cannot be responsible if a customer treats a promoter inappropriately. We can't control everything.'[3]

In the meantime, I made another discovery, that shed new light on Heineken's indifference towards the promotion girls. It emerged that Van Boxmeer himself, member of the Board of Directors since 2001 and CEO since 2005, had been in a relationship with a promotion girl during his time in what was then Zaire (1990–6). Several internal sources confirm that the African subsidiaries are saturated with a culture that condones transgressive behaviour up to the highest echelons. As a result, offences are not dealt with, and misbehaviour goes unpunished.[4]

EPILOGUE

At the annual shareholder meeting, in a theatre in Amsterdam, Van Boxmeer saw no other option than to publicly recognise this revelation to be true. Yes, he had gone beyond the bounds of moral behaviour. But, said the CEO, this was exclusively related to the fact that he had been cheating on his wife, not to the relationship with the promotion girl, which was, he claims, a mutually consensual love affair.[5]

Oh well, here's to that island of perfection, then—in a sea of misery.

ACKNOWLEDGEMENTS

This book is based on more than five years of research in thirteen countries, an extensive study of the archives and the relevant literature and about 400 interviews with sources within and close to Heineken. My travels took place between October 2012 and July 2018. In each country, I stayed between two weeks and two months. I visited Nigeria five times, the Democratic Republic of Congo four times, Rwanda three times, Burundi and South Africa twice. The following countries I visited once: Algeria, Tunisia, Ethiopia, Kenya, Sierra Leone, Congo-Brazzaville and Mozambique. Given the time invested in the research, it is possible that situations have changed since I last visited a given country.

For balance, I had nine interviews with a total of eleven managers and directors at Heineken Head Office. Moreover, the company received my manuscript a few months prior to publication and was asked to comment and point out any inaccuracies. Heineken accepted the offer but added this: 'We are responding to certain texts and subjects. However, the fact that we do not comment on other passages should most certainly not be understood as tacit agreement on our part.'

For this book, I have received grants from the Fonds voor Bijzondere Journalistieke Projecten (a Dutch fund for special projects in journalism, financed by the Ministry for Education, Culture and Science), Free Press Unlimited (supported by the Dutch postcode lottery) and the Muckraker Foundation for independent investigative journalism. No third party was involved in the financing of this book. No person has been paid for information, but I did sometimes cover drinks, a meal, travel expenses or telephone credit.

Heineken in Africa was warmly received in unexpected quarters (at least to me), namely, organisations that criticise alcohol use and campaign for much stricter laws, including the Dutch group STAP and the international Global Alcohol Policy Alliance. The Norwegian organisation Forut said it was looking forward to the English translation and wanted to know what it could do to support it. To me, sponsoring was a bad idea, and instead I replied to them saying that everyone was free to order copies of the book when published, which is what happened.

My thanks first of all to the almost 400 people I had conversations, talks and interviews with during these past years. Former and current sources within Heineken were prepared to take risks by passing information on to me, as were suppliers and partners. I greatly appreciate these contributions.

I also want to thank Heineken, especially John-Paul Schuirink of the Communications Department and Tom de Man, former Africa director. It has taken some time, but I very much appreciate the fact that in the end Heineken took the decision to contribute to the book.

Thanks to all the fellow journalists across the continent who helped me, thanks to Michael Dwyer and his colleagues at Hurst for their confidence, and many thanks to James Ireland for his great support. And most of all: thanks and love to Merel and Emilia.

(Former) Heineken employees or other sources willing to share information are welcome to contact me via the website www.heinekeninafrica.com.

NOTES

HA indicates the document comes from the Heineken Archives, which is stocked in the city archives of Amsterdam.

HC indicates that the document comes from the Heineken Collection, accessible at https://heineken.memorix.nl

KB indicates that the document comes from the online databank of the Koninklijke Bibliotheek (the Royal Library in The Hague).

FOREWORD: IT WILL HAPPEN HERE

1. In this book, 'Congo' means the Democratic Republic of Congo, while Congo-Brazzaville refers to its smaller neighbour.
2. 2014 figures. In 2015 Heineken merged the Africa/Middle East region with Eastern Europe. From that moment on, disaggregated figures concerning only Africa have not been made public.
3. Jaco Maritz, 'Africa Needs More Dangotes, Says Heineken CEO', How We Made It in Africa website, 13 May 2014.
4. They are Roland Pirmez (Africa director), Tom de Man and Jean Louis Homé (his predecessors), Jan-Willem Vosmeer, Obbe Siderius, Paul Stanger and Rutger Goethart. Until 2015, the regional director for Africa was also responsible for the Middle East. That year, Eastern Europe was merged with this region (see also note 1). For ease of reference, I refer to this function as 'Africa director' in this book.
5. Room for Discussion (UvA), 'Brewing a Better World?, 23 January 2017; https://www.youtube.com/watch?v=opzxsqxftfm (accessed November 2017).

6. Hans Jacobs, 'Koningin Máxima ziet vooruitgang in Afrika' (Queen Máxima sees African progress), ANP, 13 December 2015; Speech by Prime Minister Mark Rutte at the United Nations Sustainable Development Summit, 26 September 2015; https://www.government.nl/documents/speeches/2015/09/26/speech-by-prime-minister-rutte-at-the-united-nations-sustainable-development-summit (accessed November 2017).

7. 'Heineken is VOC anno nu' (Heineken is the Dutch Each Indies' Company of our days), *De Telegraaf*, 20 August 2015.

8. Olivier van Beemen, 'Heineken is in Tunis het bier van de macht' (In Tunis, Heineken is the beer of the regime), *Het Financieele Dagblad*, 2 February 2011.

9. AFP, 'En Côte d'Ivoire la "guerre" de la bière est déclarée', *Jeune Afrique*, 13 August 2017.

1. ETHIOPIA: TURBULENT BEER PARADISE

1. Nexus Investment Solutions 2012: 5; Access Capital Research 2010.

2. Kapuscinski 2006: 31.

3. Lem, Van Tulder and Geleynse 2013: 11.

4. Luigi Robecchi Bricchetti. Source: Jeancolas 2014: 287.

5. 'Reactie op Zembla uitzending van 23 maart over Ethiopië' (Response to the 23 March Zembla broadcast on Ethiopia), 24 March 2016; http://www.heinekennederland.nl/nieuws/2016/3/24/heineken-reactie-op-zembla-uitzending-van-23-maart-over-ethiopie (accessed November 2017).

6. Meredith 2014: 431; Bulcha 2005: 1.

7. Hallelujah Lulie, 'On Teddy Afro and His "Holy War" Remark', *Horn Affairs*, 4 January 2014; Andrea Dijkstra, 'Heineken midden in Ethiopisch wespennest' (Heineken in Ethiopian hornet's nest), *TPO Magazine*, 29 December 2013; 'Boycott Bedele Campaign Catches Fire on Social Media', OPride, 27 December 2013.

8. See note 7 (Lulie); 'Ethiopia Music Sponsorship Update', January 2014; http://www.theheinekencompany.com/notifications/2014/01/ethiopia-music-sponsorship-update (accessed November 2017).

9. Natalie Righton, 'Ploumen: hier wordt iedereen beter van!' (Ploumen: this benefits everyone!), *de Volkskrant*, 2 March 2013.

10. Esrael Yohannes and Bereket Getaneh, 'Walia Takes Over: Heineken's Domination of the Ethiopian Beer Market', *Addis Fortune*, 14 December 2014.

11. Fasika Tadessa, 'Tough Bargain Leads Favour to Heineken's 40m Forex Access', *Addis Fortune*, 30 January 2018. In response, Heineken writes that the money is needed for further expansion. The company emphasises that it has made major investments in Ethiopia since 2011. Heineken does not deny its cordial relationship with the authorities but claims its preferential treatment is due to the fact that it works in the productive sector.

2. HISTORY: THE CONQUEST OF AFRICA

1. Van der Zijl 2014: 89, 120, 121; Korthals 1948: 151–3.

2. H. Ivens, 'Vestiging van brouwerijen in sommige gebieden van Afrika' (On the establishment of breweries in some parts of Africa), March–April 1947, HA 1081

3. Heap 2010: 113–14.

4. Smit 1996: 72.

5. Sluyterman and Bouwens 2014: 179.

6. Stikker 1966: 21, 22.

7. Jacobs and Maas 1991: 184, 185.

8. Smit 1996: 31, 75.

9. Dirk Stikker, 'Reisrapport' (Travel report), June 1945, quoted in Smith 1996: 75.

10. Minutes Executive Board, 30 November 1954, HC.

11. Jacobs and Maas 1991: 245.

12. Jacobs and Maas 2001: 8.5, 8.6.

13. 'Leopoldville', travel report by Dr Emmens, April 1949, HA 1082.

14. 'Rapport Ir. J.A. Emmens reis Belgisch-Congo van 21 februari tot 16 maart 1953' (Report by Dr J.A. Emmens, travel [in] Belgian Congo from 21 February to 16 March 1953), HA 1082.

15. Sluyterman and Bouwens 2014: 222.

16. Smit 1996: 76, 77.

17. Jacobs and Maas 2001: 8.10.

18. 'Export 1950–'51', HA 1980; Smit 1996: 80.

19. 'Rapport van de heer Timmer, Goldcoast en Nigeria 20 november tot 14 december 1956' (Report by Mr Timmer, Gold Coast and Nigeria, 20 November to 14 December 1956), HA 1082.

20. Smit 1996: 85; Jacobs and Maas 2001: 8.14.

21. J.H. Burger, 'Rapport over reis naar Brits West-Afrika van 24 november tot 17 december 1955' (Travel Report British West Africa, 24 November to 17 December 1955), HA 1058.

22. Smit 1996: 77, 78.

23. Dr J.A. Emmens, 'Verslag van mijn bezoek aan Belgisch Congo van 29 januari tot 14 februari 1956 ter gelegenheid van de opening van brouwerij te Usumbura op 31 januari 1956' (Report on my visit to Belgian Congo, from 29 January to 14 February 1956, for the inauguration of the Usumbura brewery, 31 January 1956), HA 1082; Plooij, 'Wanneer je verre reizen maakt' (When you travel far), *Vers van 't vat*, March 1955, HC; Nairobi; 'Nairobi 14/10/1954 Dhr (Mr) Plooij', HA 1056.

24. O. Kamerling, 'Reisrapport X Mozambique' (Travel report X Mozambique), 1961, HA 1066.

25. 'Reisrapport no 9. Reisrapport van R. van Duursen inzake zijn bezoek aan Mozambique' (Travel report no. 9 by R. van Duursen concerning his visit to Mozambique), 9 February 1964, HA 1066.

26. Jacobs and Maas 2001: 8.14.

27. Vallée 2004: 146; Willame 1990: 37, 38.

28. Van Reybrouck 2011: 259.

29. J. Ch. Cornelis, 'Rapport over bezoek van de heer Cornelis aan Ghana in november 59' (Report on visit by Mr Cornelis to Ghana, November 1959), HA 1062.

30. Sluyterman and Bouwens 2014: 347; Van der Werf, 'Verslag bezoek Cairo 3–7 september 1963' (Report visit Cairo, 3 September to 7 September 1963), HA 1086; 'Nationalisatie van Brasseries, Limonaderies et Malteries Bralima sarl en van Bouteillerie de Kinshasa sarl 14/8/75' (Nationalisation of Bralima and Bouteillerie de Kinshasa, 14 August 1975), HA 1191; Jones 2010.

31. 'Memo. Annexe 2. Bénéfices consolidés du Groupe Interbra', 17 July 1967, HA 1132.

32. 'Reisnotities Drs. A. Miedema inzake bezoek aan Congo van 25–30 januari 1971' (Travel notes Dr A. Miedema concerning visit to Congo, 25 January to 30 January 1971), HA 1087.

33. A. Miedema, 'Wat Interbra voor ons betekent' (What Interbra means to us), 19 October 1970, HA 1134.

34. Minutes Executive Board, 26 September 1962, HC; Annual Report 1962–3, HC.

35. Minutes Executive Board, 3 June 1965.

36. 'Notitie naar aanleiding van het bezoek van Van der Werf, Nijman en Klomp aan de Banque Lambert, Brussel, op donderdag 20 juli 1967' (Memo concerning the visit by Van der Werf, Nijman and Klomp to Banque Lambert, Brussels, on Thursday, 20 July 1967), HA 1132.

37. J. van der Werf, 'Kort verslag van het gesprek met de Heer Bodart op donderdag 17 augustus 1967' (Brief report of the conversation with Mr Bodart, on Thursday, 17 August 1967), HA 1132.

38. J.W. Beyen, 'Korte notitie betreffende de Interbra-aangelegenheid' (Brief memo concerning the Interbra affair), 27 October 1966, HA 1134.

39. J. van der Werf, 'Interbra', Brussels, 9 March 1967, HA 1134.

40. 'Wat is en wat doet het Technisch Beheer Buitenland' (Technical overseas management, what it is and what it does), *Vers van 't Vat*, November 1961, HC.

41. A. Miedema, 'Notities naar aanleiding van een gesprek met de heren Despret en Bodart op 13 februari 1969' (Memo on the conversation with Mssrs Despret and Bodart, held 13 February 1969), HA 1134.

42. 'De absorptie van Interbra' (The absorption of Interbra), 19 October 1970, HC; J. van der Werf, 'Interbra. Alternatieven, die bij verdere besprekingen met Lambert als leidraad kunnen gelden' (Alternatives, which can serve as guidelines during further discussion with Lambert), 14 December 1967, HA 1132.

43. Burnby Atkins et al., 'South Africa', Johannesburg, 12 September 1962, HA 1081.

44. Minutes Executive Board, 29 August 1963, HC.

45. 'Whitbread (South Africa) Pty. Ltd.', 28 February 1964, HA 1081.

46. 'The Brewery Project: South Africa; Appendices', March 1962, HA

1184; Oscar Wittert, 'Enige notities met betrekking tot bezoek Zuid-Afrika' (A few notes concerning visit [to] South Africa), March 1965, HA 1081.

47. Minutes Executive Board, 26 February 1987, HC; 'Nederlandse bedrijven op zwarte lijst Wereldraad' (Dutch businesses blacklisted by World Council [of Churches]), *De Telegraaf,* 23 January 1973 KB; 'Investeerders Zuid-Afrika medeschuldig aan apartheid' (Investors in South Africa complicit in Apartheid), *Het Vrije Volk,* 14 September 1973, KB; 'FNV wil af van "besmette" aandelen' (FNV wants to shed 'tainted' shares), *De Telegraaf,* 5 October 1979, KB; 'Interne post' (Internal messenger service), 7 April 1987, HC.

48. Sluyterman and Bouwens 2014: 356.

49. 'Vergaderstukken' (meeting notes), 29 March 1977, HC

50. Van Reybrouck 2011: 355; US Department of Commerce 1983: 175.

51. 'Reisverslag van het bezoek aan Interbra van R.J. Ankersmit van 15 t/m 17 april 1970' (Report on travel and visit to Interbra, by R.J. Ankersmit, 15 April to 17 April 1970), HA 1134

52. Van Reybrouck 2011: 371.

53. 'Notities naar aanleiding van het bezoek van Drs. A. Miedema aan Afrika van 24–29 februari 1972' (Notes on Dr A. Miedema's visit to Africa, from 24 to 29 February 1972), HA 1191.

54. 'Over ons beleid t.a.v. Bralima' (Regarding our Bralima policy), 4 December 1973, HA 1191.

55. Persmededeling' (Press announcement), 7 February 1975, HA 1191; 'Brief van Max Litvine (Compagnie Bruxelles Lambert) aan Jan Ton (Heineken), 13 januari 1975' (Letter from Max Litvine (Compagnie Bruxelles Lambert) to Jan Ton (Heineken), 13 January 1975), HA 1191; 'Note pour le conseil d'Ibecor: Relation chronologique de la prise de controle de la Bralima par les autorités zaïroises', 25 March 1975, HA 1191.

56. See note 30 ('Nationalisation ...').

57. 'Bralima', 30 May 1975, HA 1191.

58. 'Reisnotities (E.W. Wits: Zaïre)', 5 February to 18 February 1976, HA 1191.

59. See note 57.

60. Sluyterman and Bouwens 2014: 356; 'Notitie aan de heer Van der Werf' (Memo to Mr Van der Werf), 28 February 1983, HC.
61. 'Memo to Mr Van der Werf', 28 February 1983, HC.
62. Ibid.
63. 'Notitie voor de leden van de raad van bestuur' (Memo to the members of the Executive Board), 16 April 1985, HC.
64. Minutes Supervisory Board, 17 June 1988, HC.
65. In a written explanation, Heineken stresses that these subsidies not only concerned barley but also milk powder, butter and meat products. 'This was an entirely normal and approved state of affairs'.
66. 'Notitie voor de leden van de raad van bestuur' (Memo to the members of the Executive Board), 4 May 1984, HC; Annual Report, 1984 HC.
67. Minutes Supervisory Board, 23 June 1987.
68. 'Vuursteen maakt kennis met Afrika' (Vuursteen gets acquainted with Africa), *Vers van 't Vat*, May 1994, HC.
69. Karel Vuursteen, 'President's Letter for the Planning Period 1996–1998', 4 January 1995, HC.

3. NIGERIA: INTEGRATION, IN EVERY POSSIBLE WAY

1. Gerbert van der Aa, 'Ik houd van een international omgeving' (I love an international environment), *Elsevier*, 31 March 2017. The conversation took place in February 2017.
2. Euromonitor, 'Beer in Nigeria', September 2017; Annual reports Nigerian Breweries 2013 and 2014; Eigbe 2013: 4.
3. I worked on this case in collaboration with Femke van Zeijl, a Dutch journalist based in Lagos.
4. Evelyn Usman, 'NB/TMDK Feud: Police Invite NB Managers', *Vanguard*, 25 January 2017; Paul Wallace, 'Heineken's Nigeria Unit Says It's under Police Investigation', Bloomberg, 24 January 2017.
5. 'Nigerian Breweries MD Set for New Role in Heineken Group', *This Day*, 4 May 2017.
6. Limitless Mind Africa website, http://limitlessmindafrica.com/index2/ (accessed November 2017).
7. Heineken responds: 'The investigation into payment of bribes to

controllers, of which mention is being made, has been conducted at the initiative of Nigerian Breweries, following a complaint from the supplier. After an internal inquiry four staff have been dismissed.'

8. Heineken responds: 'In part as a result of the complaint by Mr. Sule concerning alleged corruption at Nigerian Breweries relating to the allocation of an energy contract, the subsequent police investigation and Nigerian media reports, a series of inquiries were conducted as instructed by Nigerian Breweries and Heineken. Those involved have always denied corruption. Heineken has an Integrity Commission, which meticulously examines accusations (or suspicions) of corruption and other fraudulent practices. The Commission can request the Global Business Conduct Department and/or Internal Audit to conduct such an inquiry, which was done in this case. The Integrity Commission issues its advice and based on this the Executive Board then determines what happens with the individual(s) involved. The findings of these inquiries provided no cause for disciplinary measures against Nico Vervelde. However, as a result of the situation that had developed it was not possible for Nico Vervelde to continue working for Nigerian Breweries. Early May 2017, he resigned as CEO, following consultations with Heineken and the president of the Supervisory Board at Nigerian Breweries. In view of his experience and previous services rendered, Heineken has offered him another position in another region.'

9. An internal source at Heineken in Nigeria confirms that these are common practices at the subsidiary, but Head Office in Amsterdam contradicts the assertion by a source at the Nigerian police. 'This is not correct, there is no question of tax evasion. No withholding tax is levied on the local delivery of goods, in this case diesel/petrol. Withholding tax is only levied on certain services and this was applied because TMDK delivered diesel but also rendered services. These accusations are therefore baseless.'

10. Two other internal sources confirm this story, but Head Office has issued a denial: 'Clémentine Vervelde has never been awarded a contract for beer transports in Rwanda "after intervention by the Executive Board". Her small two-truck company did indeed tender for a distribution contract in Rwanda in 2009, but this contract was then awarded to another transporter.'

11. Heineken responds: 'It is true that Jean-François van Boxmeer and Nico Vervelde have known each other for a long time. Both started at Heineken in the 1980s and worked for the company in Africa for a considerable amount of time. However, the same applies to various other managers and none of this implies that Nico Vervelde enjoys a privileged position or protection as a result of this. It is correct that Nico Vervelde is a member of the Supervisory Board at Forte Oil. His appointment was approved beforehand by both Heineken and Nigerian Breweries.'

12. Annual Report Nigerian Breweries 2016, 15 February 2017.

13. 'Weinig begrip voor besluit Brunel' (Little understanding for the Brunel decision), *Het Financieele Dagblad*, 27 August 2015.

14. Richard Smit, 'Grote bierbrouwers storten zich op Afrika nu westerse markt stagneert' (Large beer brewers invade Africa while markets in the West stand still), *Het Financieele Dagblad*, 3 December 2010.

15. Numerous sources in Nigeria and elsewhere confirm this informal arrangement, yet former Africa director Tom de Man denies they exist.

16. Odimegwu has a well-known talent for exaggeration. Yet every one of his major statements that I mention here—blocking SABMiller, stopping the cancelled increase of excise duty, the strategic grain reserve and the PR money—have been confirmed by at least one other source.

17. Ogunbiyi 2007: 128.

4. SALES AND MARKETING: AFRICAN BEER WARS

1. See Foreword, note 2.

2. Plato, *Logic*, quoted in Diageo Investor Conference, 'Reigniting Growth on Guinness', November 2013.

3. De Man says that the extra capacity was more than welcome at the time.

4. Kaziboni and Das Nair 2014.

5. McKinsey 2003: 12.

6. Wangui Maina, 'Heineken Sparks Beer Wars with Nairobi Office', *Business Daily*, 29 November 2011; 'Beer War in Nigeria, Who Wins?', Nairabrains, 3 October 2011; Baudelaire Mieu, 'Brassivoire lance les hostilités plus tôt que prévu contre Castel', *Jeune Afrique*, 15 November 2016.

7. Van Reybrouck 2011: 500.

8. Erik Stelwagen, 'Erik in Congo: De eerste dagen' (My first days in Congo), 7 January 2006; http://stelwagen.blogspot.com/2006/01/ (accessed November 2017).

9. Gerard Reijn, 'Drabdrinkers opgelet: bier wordt helder' (Message to those who drink opaque hooch: clear beer is coming), *Volkskrant*, 21 December 2012.

10. Melle Garschagen, 'Geliefd bij de snelle jongens' (Popular with the cool guys), *NRC Handelsblad*, 14 November 2014.

11. Lyumugabe 2012: 524.

12. 'The Beer Factor in Human Nutrition: Facts over Fiction', *Daily Independent*, 23 November 2014.

13. Poikolainen 2014.

14. Fabian Odum en Paul Adunwoke, 'The Beer Debate: How Much Is Good for the Body, Health?', *The Guardian* (Nigeria), 24 January 2015.

15. 'Beer and Health: Experts Preach Modest Consumption'; http://www.promptnewsonline.com/beer-health-experts-preach-moderate-consumption (accessed November 2017); see note 12.

16. Kunle Aderinokun, 'Experts Reveal Amazing Health Benefits Derivable from Moderate Beer Consumption', *This Day*, 11 November 2015; see note 12.

17. See note 14.

18. 'When Experts, Socialites Shared Experience on Brewing', *Vanguard*, 9 December 2014.

19. '8th Nigerian Golden Pen Awards Open'; http://nbplc.com/news/?p=470 (accessed September 2017).

20. Jessica Hatcher, 'Africa's Drinking Problem: Alcoholism on the Rise as Beverage Multinationals Circle', *Time Magazine*, 9 August 2013.

21. De Bruijn 2011: 37.

22. Odejide 2006: 28; Jernigan and Obot 2006: 65, 66; Dumbili 2014: 15; De Bruijn 2011: 9.

23. Dumbili 2014: 16.

24. Gordon et al. 2010.

25. Heineken Responsible Marketing Code (2008); Sustainability Report, 2004/5.

26. Heineken Alcohol Policy.
27. Jernigan and Obot 2006: 69.

5. SIERRA LEONE: THE MYSTERIOUS GODFATHER

1. Saidu Bah, '2015 Was Challenging for Sierra Leone Brewery with Almost Le 50. Billion Loss', *Awoko*, 15 July 2016.

6. IMPACT: ARTISTIC ARITHMETIC

1. See Chapter 1, note 9; Chapter 3, note 13; and Chapter 6, note 5; Scheherazade Daneshkhu, 'African Farming: Global Companies Help Boost Small Farms', *Financial Times*, 21 January 2011; Liedewij Loorbach, 'Met Heineken de wereld verbeteren' (A better world with Heineken), *OneWorld*, 24 February 2014; 'Heineken en Bavaria brouwen voor dorstig Ethiopië' (Heineken and Bavaria: brewing beer for thirsty Ethiopia), *Nieuwsuur*, 31 January 2015; 'Hollandse Handel' (Dutch trade), *Zembla*, 23 March 2016.
2. Jonathan Witteman, 'Heineken is top, zegt Rutte bij VN' (Rutte tells UN Summit: Heineken is the best), *de Volkskrant*, 30 September 2015.
3. Teun Lagas, 'Koopman en hulpverlener' (Salesman and aid worker), *Trouw*, 11 February 2013.
4. Van Gerwen and Van Ede 2014: 109.
5. Joël Roerig, 'Junglebier: "Wij runnen het grootste landbouwproject van het land, best beschamend voor hulporganisaties"' (Jungle beer: 'We're now running the country's largest agriculture project. I guess that puts the aid organisations to shame'), *De Telegraaf*, 13 November 2010.
6. Sustainability Report 2009. This report was published in 2010.
7. Information from local sourcing director Paul Stanger. He adds that in 2012 this figure was revised downwards to 45 per cent.
8. Heineken responds: 'We are convinced that the effects of local sourcing are mostly positive, for small-scale farmers, local agriculture, the economy as a whole and for Heineken. But we admit that until now we have focused mainly on the advantages of local sourcing without paying sufficient attention to the possible negative side-effects. This is the reason we are currently setting up a research project in cooperation with the African Studies Centre at Leiden University, which will look into all aspects, positive and negative, of locally sourcing raw materials in Africa.'

9. Information from the Dutch Ministry of Foreign Affairs, the Common Fund for Commodities, Heineken, EUCORD and the German Corporation for International Cooperation (GIZ). Heineken responds: 'On the "state subsidies" we receive for the local sourcing projects we would like to remark that the subsidies allocated to these projects always and fully benefit the local sourcing projects, the farmers involved and the projects' NGO partners. These subsidies do not go to Heineken. One would also do well to realise that Heineken's investments in the local sourcing projects usually outstrip the size of the subsidy awarded.'

10. In Burundi, one hectolitre of locally brewed beer attracts a 36,000-franc tax, soft drinks 30,000 and Nyongera 7,200. Source: 'Loi no. 1136 portant fixation du budget général de la République du Burundi pour l'exercice 2015'; http://www.finances.gov.bi/images/download/budgets/budget-gnl-2015-signe-pdf (accessed November 2017).

11. 'Hollandse Handel' (Dutch trade), *Zembla*, 23 March 2016.

12. 'Alle neuzen dezelfde kant op' (All eyes on the same prize), 16 October 2013; http://www.departnership-verkiezing.nl/houdt-alle-neuzen-dezelfde-kant-interview-jurriaan-middelhoff-collega-ministerie-buitenlandse-zaken (the post has since been removed).

13. Bakan 2004: 108.

14. Bitzer 2011.

15. Carlijne Vos, 'Arme koffieboer niet beter van hulp' (Poor coffee farmer does not benefit from aid), *de Volkskrant*, 24 February 2011.

16. Henk Knipscheer, 'Business Case #1', 20 April 2011; http://local-sourcing.com/content/business-case-1-sierra-leone (accessed June 2015); 'Heineken Shares "Groundbreaking" Sourcing Projects'; http://www.theheinekencompany.com/media/features/sourcing-inspiration/heineken-shares-groundbreaking-sourcing-projects (accessed November 2017); see Chapter 6, note 1.

17. 'Report by A.B.A.', 1 December 1966, HA 1081.

18. Annual Report 1987, HC.

19. 'Corporate Social Responsibility: Heineken in Africa', *World of Heineken*, August 2005, HC.

20. Conversation with Paul Stanger; http://www.indexmundi.com/Agriculture/?commodity=sorghum&graph=production (accessed November 2017).

21. 'Minutes, Annual Shareholders Meeting Heineken N.V.', 1 April 2018; https://www.theheinekencompany.com/-/media/Websites/ TheHEINEKENCompany/Downloads/PDF/AGM-2018/Verslag-2018-Heineken-AvA-notulen.ashx

22. 'Ibecor in Brussels: An Import Link in Contacts with Africa', *Heineken International Magazine*, 1 January 1987, HC.

23. Meredith 2014: xvi.

24. OECD 2011: 54. Heineken responds: 'The amounts Ibecor charges for its services are fully in line with the relevant international guidelines.'

25. Ibecor 2013 Annual Report, Heineken 2013 Annual Report, HC.

26. Minutes Executive Board, 13 April 1989, HC.

27. See Foreword, note 5.

28. 'We Enabled Heineken to Understand and Manage Its Impact on Local African Economies'; http://www.stewardredqueen.com/en/track-record/ cases/cases-item/t/we-enabled-heineken-to-understand-and-manage-its-impact-on-local-african-economies (accessed November 2017).

29. Triple Value 2009.

30. Triple Value 2009; Steward Redqueen 2013; Presentation by René Kim.

31. 'Creating a Real Impact on Local Economies and Communities'; http:// www.theheinekencompany.com/sustainability/case-studies/creating-a-real-impact-on-local-economies-and-communities (accessed February 2018).

32. Jean-François van Boxmeer at WEF Africa; http://www.theheineken-compa-ny.com/media/features/jean-francois-van-boxmeer-at-wef-africa (accessed November 2017).

33. Flexnews, 'AgriVision 2013: Siep Hiemstra, President Africa & Middle East', Heineken, 20 June 2013; http://www.flex-news-food.com/con-sole/Page-Viewer.aspx?page=49227&str=Beer%20Heineken (accessed November 2017).

34. René Kim responds by saying that he does not consider his research educated guesswork. According to him, the model's limitations are exaggerated in this text. 'The model offers insights that can help with the decision-making process regarding ways to strengthen the local economy.'

35. Chris O'Brien, 'The Perils of Globeerization', *Foreign Policy*, 24 October 2006.

36. Jernigan 2002: 4.

7. SOUTH AFRICA: TEH FIGHT FOR POWER IN THE TOWNSHIPS

1. Mager 2010.

2. Heineken internal documentation.

3. In 1980, South Africa had 30 million inhabitants. Of those, 72 per cent were black, 16 per cent white and 9 per cent coloured. The latest census was held in 2015, and South Africa was found to have 55 million inhabitants, distributed as follows: 80 per cent black, 9 per cent coloured and 8 per cent white. Sources: Foreign Policy Study Foundation 1981: 42; Mager 2010: 54; Demographics of South Africa; http://en.wikipedia.org/wiki/Demographics-of-South-Africa   (accessed November 2017).

4. Krige 2010: 232, 233.

5. Haworth and Acuda 1998: 30; Thalia Holmes, 'It's Time for Shebeens to Sober Up', *Mail & Guardian*, 12 April 2013.

6. Norman Adami, 'SAB Zenzele Full Terms Announcement', 8 December 2009; http://www.sab.co.za/sablimited/action/media/downloadFile?media-fileid=599 (accessed February 2015; the post has since been removed).

7. Annaleigh Vallie, 'SAB Declares Victory in Local Beer War', *Business Day*, 15 February 2012.

8. Joël Roerig, 'Lastercampagnes tegen Heineken in townships' (Campaign of false rumours against Heineken in townships), *De Telegraaf*, 25 March 2010.

9. See note 7.

10. 'Amstel Lite Container Will Not Be Replaced', *Business Day*, 6 May 2015.

8. CORPORATE SOCIAL RESPONSIBILITY: ALCOHOL AND CHARITY

1. According to figures from research by KPMG in 2001. The results have been adapted for 2012 and completed with data from the Dutch Ministry of Public Works. Source: 'Kosten van alcoholmisbruik';

http://www.gratisstoppenmetdrinken.nl/nieuws-publicaties/12-kosten-van-alcoholmisbruik.html (accessed July 2015; post has since been removed).
2. WHO 2011: 37.
3. See, for example, Andersson 2008, Room et al. 2002.
4. AfDB 2012: 44, 45. The costs are itemised as 'alcoholic beverages, tobacco and narcotics'. In most countries south of the Sahara, smoking is not widespread in relative terms and drug abuse is limited.
5. Matzopoulos et al. 2014: 127, 128; Econex en Quantec Research 2010: 4. There is more research in Budlender 2010.
6. Dumbili 2014: 4, 5, 15; Brasseries du Cameroun; http://en.wikipedia.org/wiki/Brasseries-du-Cameroun (accessed November 2017).
7. Bakke and Endal 2010: 23, 24.
8. Bruggink 2014: 239.
9. Yoon and Lam 2013: 3, 4; Heineken Alcohol Policy; Sustainability Report 2013.
10. Heineken Alcohol Policy.
11. Jernigan 2002: 5; Bakke and Endal 2010: 25.
12. See note 10.
13. Dumbili 2014; Eisenberg 1984; De Bruijn 2011: 71; Smith et al. 2006; Sustainability Report 2013.
14. Dumbili 2014: 12.
15. 'Launching Underage Alcohol Responsible Consumption'; http://www.bra-lirwa.com/cms/index.php/press-room/178-launching-underage-alcohol-responsible-consumption (accessed November 2017); David Dusabirane, 'Bralirwa Mobilizes the Prohibition of Alcohol Consumption to Teens under 18!'; Iny-arwanda.com, 16 August 2014.
16. Homé 2006: 16.
17. Sustainability Reports 2004/5 to 2014.
18. Van Dalen and Kuunders 2003.
19. See Foreword, note 5.
20. Christopher Ingraham, 'Think You Drink a Lot? This Chart Will Tell You' (Wonkblog), *Washington Post*, 25 September 2014; Sarah Boseley, 'Problem Drinkers Account for Most of Alcohol Industry's Sales, Figures Reveal', *The Guardian*, 22 January 2016.

21. Charles Parry, Pamela Trangenstein and Neo Morojele, 'Heavy Drinking among Adults in Tshwane: Findings from the First International Alcohol Study (South Africa)' (Presentation at Global Alcohol Policy Conference 2017), South African Medical Research Council, 2017.

22. WHO 2018.

23. See, for instance, 'Bralirwa Moving Like Express Train', *Heineken International Magazine*, December 1991, HC.

24. Mark van Assen, 'Alle macht aan het bier' (To beer all the power), *De Pers*, 5 October 2010.

25. Pauline Bax, 'Een miljoen kratten bier, 800 vrachtwagens vol' (One million crates of beer, 800 full lorries), *NRC Handelsblad*, 1 August 2009.

26. Yoon and Lam 2013: 6.

27. Braeckman 2012.

28. Bais and Huijser 2005: 42, 43.

29. Kate Hodal, 'Not Remotely Refreshing: Global Health Fund Criticised over Heineken Alliance', *The Guardian*, 2 February 2018.

30. Heineken Africa Foundation, 'Report 2010/2011'.

31. Van Cranenburgh and Arenas 2014: 530–2.

32. Ibid.

33. Sustainability Report 2004/5.

9. BURUNDI: DICTATORS COME AND GO, HEINEKEN STAYS

1. Lemarchand 2002; United States Institute for Peace, 'International Commission of Inquiry for Burundi: Final Report', 13 January 2004; http://www.usip. org/sites/default/files/file/resources/collections/commissions/Burundi-Report.pdf (accessed November 2017).

2. This section is based in part on the author's articles in *NRC* and *Le Monde*.

3. 'Burundi: la Cour constitutionnelle valide la candidature de Nkurunziza', RFI, 5 May 2015.

4. Human Rights Council, 'Rapport de la Commission d'enquête sur le Burundi', 11 August 2017; Nick Cumming-Bruce, 'U.N. Group Accuses Burundi Leaders of Crimes against Humanity', *The New York Times*, 4 September 2017; 'Burundi Becomes First Nation to Leave International Criminal Court', *The Guardian*, 28 October 2017.

5. Heineken denies crates were sent to the court.

6. Homé 2006: 80.

7. Ibid., 84, 85.

8. Geert van Asbeck, 'Hutu's in Burundi: Heineken steunt oorlogsmis-dadiger' (Hutus in Burundi: Heineken backs war criminal), *NRC Handelsblad*, 8 March 1997; Geert van Asbeck, 'Moordpartij Burundi achtervolgt Heineken' (Killing spree in Burundi haunts Heineken), *NRC Handelsblad*, 14 March 1997.

9. Homé 2006: 90.

10. Resolution no. 1072, adopted by the UN Security Council on 30 August 1996.

11. 'Ohne Bier wäre der Krieg in Burundi längst zu Ende', *Die Welt*, 25 July 1996.

12. Michela Wrong, 'Heineken Refreshes Parts Other Burundi Taxes Fail to Reach', *Financial Times*, 14 June 1996.

13. Ibid.

14. Chris McGreal, 'Beer That Fuelled Genocide', *The Guardian*, 19 August 1996.

15. 'Burundi dwingt Heineken tot brouwen' (Burundi forces Heineken to brew beer), ANP, 8 January 1997; Homé 2006: 125, 126.

16. Philip de Wit, 'Heineken kan in Burundi niet om politiek heen' (In Burundi, Heineken cannot ignore politics), *Algemeen Dagblad*, 10 January 1997; see note 15.

17. Homé 2006: 134, 135.

18. 'Heineken brouwt zelf weer in Burundi, negeert embargo' (Heineken brews its own beer again in Burundi, ignores embargo), *NRC Handelsblad*, 10 March 1997; 'Conflict Heineken met Hutu's escaleert' (Heineken's conflict with Hutus escalates), ANP, 9 March 1997; 'Burundi Army Admits It Killed 126 Hutu Refugees', *The New York Times*, 12 January 1997.

19. See notes 8 and 16.

20. See note 8.

21. 'FNV vreest voor veiligheid Heineken-werknemers in Burundi' (FNV fears for Heineken workers' safety in Burundi), ANP, 10 March 1997.

22. Geert van Asbeck, 'Heineken in Afrika: vredesduif of collaborateur?'

(Heineken in Africa, a force for peace or a collaborator?), *NRC Handelsblad*, 20 March 1997.

23. Arjen van der Ziel, 'Wat verder ter tafel komt: Jean Louis Homé; "De charme van Afrika is dat je nooit alles zult begrijpen"' (Jean Louis Homé: 'Africa's charm is that you will never understand everything'), *FEM Business*, 27 July 2002.

10. WORKING FOR HEINEKEN: THOSE WOMEN WERE RAPED

1. 'Hutu's houden vast aan sluiting Burundese brouwerij Heineken' (Hutus insist on closure of Heineken's Burundi brewery), *de Volkskrant*, 14 January 1997; 'Heineken-brouwerij als modelbedrijf in Burundi' (Heineken brewery, a corporate model in Burundi), *De Telegraaf*, 4 August 2001.

2. Heineken Code of Business Conduct.

3. Ogunbiyi 2007: 185.

4. Jacobs and Maas 1991: 255.

5. At the time of writing 9 out of 13 African subsidiaries are headed by Europeans, 4 by Africans.

6. Annual Report, Nigerian Breweries, 2014.

7. 'Een Hollands biertje in Afrika' (A Dutch beer in Africa), RTL4, 15 April 2009.

8. John van Schagen, 'Bier verkopen in hartje Afrika' (Selling beer in the heart of Africa), *Management Team*, 28 April 2011.

9. See Chapter 6, note 5.

10. 'Je moet zo flexibel zijn als een kameleon' (You have to be flexible, like a chameleon), *Vers van 't Vat*, January 1997, HC.

11. Van der Borght 2011: 28.

12. Minutes Executive Board, 23 July 1987, HC.

13. Marc Doodeman, 'In ieders belang' (In the interest of all), *Het Financieele Dagblad*, 8 April 2006; Van der Borght 2011: 30; Elske Schouten, 'Aidsremmers voor de drie vrouwen van de chef' (Antiretrovirals for the chief's three wives), *NRC Next*, 17 August 2006.

14. Van der Borght 2011: 106, 107.

15. Sustainability Reports 2004/5 to 2014. Heineken responds (in July

2017): 'The actual percentage for Africa as regards on site incidents and accidents (minor+serious+fatal) on our Africa plants as it relates to the total worldwide figure is 26 per cent.'

16. Sarah Smit, 'Heineken Issue Ferments: Labour-Broking Shows Few Signs of Disappearing', *Mail & Guardian*, 1 November 2017. Heineken responds: 'After the situation had been brought to our attention we took immediate action by establishing the facts and, where necessary, correcting matters.' The supplier who was in breach of the law was replaced by a competitor who, according to Heineken, is in compliance, and thirty-four workers who had been temping for more than three months were given a fixed contract.

According to Ronald Wesso of the Casual Workers Advice Office that supports the workers, Heineken's claim that the issue has been resolved is wrong. He makes the point that the issue is still under consideration at the Commission for Conciliation, Mediation and Arbitration. He also gives little credence to Heineken's assertion that the company knew nothing about the working conditions. He says: 'They themselves created a system that keeps the workers at arm's length. If Heineken had been serious about solving this issue, they would have offered fixed contract to all workers involved, just like the law prescribes.'

17. Van Cranenburgh 2016: 102.
18. Ibid.
19. Heineken internal documentation.
20. Joop Bouwma, 'Biertje', *Trouw*, 23 May 2003.
21. Heineken internal documentation.
22. Giel ten Bosch, 'Biermeisjes bezorgen Heineken hoofdpijn' (Beer girls, a headache for Heineken), *De Telegraaf*, 10 May 2008.
23. See, for instance, Dumbili, 2016.
24. Heineken responds: 'We do not recognize ourselves in the image given of the Heineken Head Office as a hostile place for women.'

11. CONGO: IF YOU CAN MAKE IT THERE, YOU CAN MAKE IT ANYWHERE

1. Homé 2006: 34.

2. This section is based in part on the author's articles in *NRC Handelblad*, *Vrij Nederland*, *Follow the Money* and *Le Monde*.

3. Heineken's estimate is about 150 former workers.

4. The conquest of Congo and the takeover by Laurent-Désiré Kabila, who removed Mobutu from his throne in 1997, are referred to as the First Congo War.

5. Human Rights Watch 2003.

6. Bralima's website features a report on this visit to the prime minister. 'Le président de la région Afrique-Moyen-Orient et Europe de l'Est de Heineken en visite en RDC'; http://bralima.net/fr/au-revoir-m-siep-hiemstra-et-bienvenue-m-roland-pirmez/le-president-de-la-region-afrique-moyen-orient-et-europe-de-lest-de-heineken-en-vis-ite-en-rdc (accessed September 2017).

7. Augustin Matata Ponyo was asked for a reaction but according to one of his close collaborators does not want to make any comments. Heineken also declined to comment.

8. By that time, the RCD had split in RCD-Goma, which controlled the area around Bukavu and RCD-Kisangani. The source who gave me this document assures me that a similar agreement existed for Bukavu.

9. Schouten 2013.

10. Jason Miklian and Peer Schouten, 'Fluid Markets', *Foreign Policy* (September/October 2013).

11. Koch 2014: 152.

12. See note 10.

13. See Chapter 8, note 24.

14. These names are fictitious.

15. Olivier Rogeau, 'Kabila perd son Mazarin', *Le Vif/L'Express*, 17 February 2012.

16. This was part of the extensive training Heineken organised for 750 African managers, mentioned by Jean Louis Homé in Chapter 2.

17. See note 10.

18. 'Brewery Flourishes in DRC's Difficult Climate', WikiLeaks, 20 November 2006; https://wikileaks.org/plusd/cables/06kinshasa1770-a.html (accessed November 2017).

19. Latest reports put the number at 1,200.

12. CONFLICT ZONES: WAR, TYRANNY AND BUSINESS ETHICS

1. OECD, African Development Bank, 'Perspectives économiques en Afrique', 2006.
2. Heineken internal documentation.
3. 'The World's Worst Dictators'; https://parade.com/36356/parade/the-worlds-worst-dictators-hosni-mubarak (accessed November 2017).
4. http://www.theheinekencompany.com/sustainability/brewing-a-better-world/united-nations-global-compact (accessed November 2017).
5. https://www.unglobalcompact.org/what-is-gc/mission/principles/principle-2 (accessed November 2017).
6. Schouten 2013: 20.
7. Van Reybrouck 2011: 483. This is a general remark he makes; it does not specifically refer to Heineken.
8. Heineken responds: 'We reject any and all accusation or suggestion that Heineken were involved or complicit with crimes against humanity or human rights abuses.'
9. '"Lokaal investeren maakt het verschil"' ('Investing locally makes the difference'), nuzakelijk.nl, 15 November 2013.
10. See also Bakan 2004: 50.
11. Jeurissen 2009: 43.
12. Bais and Huijser 2005: 41.
13. Heijn 2014: 56, 57.
14. Barbara Rijlaarsdam, 'Bonussen bij Heineken zorgen weer voor heibel' (Bonuses at Heineken cause another row), *NRC Handelsblad*, 25 April 2014.
15. Lenfant and Van Cranenburgh 2018.
16. Bais and Huijser 2005: 92, 93.
17. Ronald Jeurissen, 'Heineken kan regime in Birma juist ondermijnen' (Heineken is in a position to undermine the Burma regime), *de Volkskrant*, 2 February 1996.
18. Tabaksblat 1997: 20, quoted in Jeurissen 2009: 279.
19. Schwartz and Gibb 1999: 41.
20. 'Heineken stopt activiteiten in Myanmar' (Heineken halts Myanmar activities), *Vers van 't Vat*, July 1996, HC.
21. Bais en Huijser 2005: 51.

22. 'Corporate Human Rights Benchmark 2017: Company Scoresheet; Heineken'; www.https://www.corporatebenchmark.org (accessed January 2018).
23. Heineken responds: 'The beer promoters still have our attention. They have shared Asia's best practices with the HR managers in the relevant African countries.'
24. Heineken has written an extensive response, in which it says that the Business Conduct Department in Amsterdam started an investigation in August 2013, when the company was informed by *Foreign Policy* journalist Jason Miklian about the road blocks. 'As a precautionary measure all transport in the area was halted immediately and all payments to transporters (third parties) of Bralima products were suspended. The inquiry brought to light that the depots in Bunia, Beni and Butembo were normally supplied from Kisangani by road but that this had become impracticable since a number of bridges on that route were weakened by rainfall and had subsequently collapsed under the weight of tanks and heavy lorries. This was the reason lorries contracted by Bralima took another route, from Goma, as a result of which they were exposed to road blocks manned by rebels who were active in the area. Once Heineken learnt of this, the company gave further instructions to Bralima to avoid transports in that region and if necessary take alternative routes via Rwanda and Uganda. The inquiry revealed that M23 rebels had been on sanctions lists issued by the European Union and United States and confirmed that between April and August 2013 a very limited number of forced toll payments had been made to M23 by transporters of Bralima products under contract. It is important to note here that this does not concern human rights abuses but toll payments made under threat of force from the rebels by transporters of Bralima products under contract. The one million dollars mentioned are vastly exaggerated and may be a fabrication.

All relevant measures and instructions came from Heineken's regional president for Africa and the Middle East at the time, acting under advice from the Business Conduct Team. They were given in writing and confirmed by Bralima's management and the directors of the breweries.

Kisangani, Bunia, Goma and Bukavu were visited in the week of April 21, 2014, with the objective to provide training for a large number of the Bralima workforce. The visit was effected by the Bralima management team and representatives of the Business Conduct Team from Amsterdam. Mid-December 2014, representatives of the Business Conduct Team visited Congo again. This time, a large number of Bralima staff in Kinshasa received training, from the brewery as well as the Boukin bottle plant. In short, precautionary measures were taken immediately, an inquiry was conducted and aftercare was provided locally. It is unclear to us where the cover-up story emanates from. It is equally unclear to us from where the story originates that negotiations should have taken place with RCD-Goma or other armed groups. Nothing from the Business Conduct inquiry and subsequent visits suggests that any of this has taken place.'

25. Van Cranenburgh refers to this case: AP, 'Nestlé Admits to Forced Labour in Its Seafood Supply Chain in Thailand', *The Guardian*, 24 November 2015.

26. Heineken responds: 'We do not recognise ourselves in the image provided.'

27. Heineken responds: 'The human rights policy is an integral part of the Heineken Code of Conduct. Compliance is verified annually by way of Heineken's risk management process. In addition to this we have various programs that are geared towards avoiding or minimising risks relating to human rights. Apart from the Code of Conduct these include our Health&Safety program, the Supplier Code process and the sustainability programs under Brewing a Better World. In the past year we have also worked with Shift, a not-for-profit organisation with human rights experts who work for all relevant stakeholders, including governments, NGOs and business. Based on our work with Shift we have identified our main human rights issues and developed a three-year program, which is aimed at further embedding respect for human rights in the organisation and includes updating our current human rights policy. We will continue working with Shift and together map further (potential) human rights issues and ensure that our operating companies develop practical and effective plans of action in order to

deal adequately with human rights issues, in other words: in line with the UN Guiding Principles.'

13. RWANDA: BREWING BEER FOR MASS KILLERS

1. See Chapter 8, note 23.
2. Homé 2006: 91–3.
3. Homé 2006: 92. Homé uses the term *musumbo* for 'white person'. This is probably due to an error on his part or Boreel's. The common word in Swahili is *muzungu*.
4. Homé 2006: 95.
5. Gourevitch 1998: 3.
6. 'Rwanda Genocide'; https://en.wikipedia.org/wiki/Rwandan-Genocide#Death-toll (accessed November 2017); Straus 2004: 95.
7. At different moments, *The New Times* mentions thirty, sixty or sixty-six victims. 'Bralirwa Opens Staff Memorial Site', *The New Times*, 27 April 2006; 'Bralirwa Remembers Fallen Staff', *The New Times*, 29 April 2008; 'Bralirwa Honours Colleagues Killed in 1994', *The New Times*, 26 April 2011.
8. Homé 2006: 100.
9. Kees Broere, 'Lekkerder dan een klamme sandwich' (Tastier than a musty sandwich), *de Volkskrant*, 27 October 2011; Homé 2006: 100.
10. Brauman 1994: 13; see Chapter 9, note 14.
11. Gourevitch 1998: 18.
12. 'Etienne Nzabonimana'; http://www.trial-ch.org/fr/ressources/trial-watch/trial-watch/profils/profile/327/action/show/controller/Profile.html (accessed May 2015; post has since been removed).
13. Fletcher 2007: 38.
14. Hatzfeld 2003: 27, 28, 33, 69, 73, 105, 107, 109, 213, 214, 220.
15. Homé 2006: 97.
16. Wilma Kieskamp, 'In bloedig Rwanda brouwt Heineken lustig voort' (In blood-stained Rwanda, Heineken merrily keeps on brewing), *Trouw*, 17 June 1994.
17. See Chapter 8, note 24.
18. 'Rwanda het bier en de dood' (Rwanda, beer and death), *Leeuwarder Courant*, 20 June 1994, KB.

19. See note 16.

20. Lolke van der Heide, 'Drijven op hulp' (Kept afloat by aid), *NRC Handelsblad*, 23 November 1999.

21. 'Voorraad Heineken droogt langzaam op na 5e stakingsdag' (Heineken stocks slowly running dry as strike continues for a fifth day), *De Telegraaf*, 26 April 1994, KB.

22. Rob Hoogland, 'Bier', *De Telegraaf*, 27 April 1994, KB.

23. This is Heineken's full statement: 'We insist that the Gisenyi brewery at the time of the genocide was out of Heineken's control as a result of the great panic and chaos in the country and the region. During the genocide, Bralirwa's directors were abroad or had fled the killers. This was the situation in which the brewery's manager [Sinayobye] led the brewery without instructions, requests, plan or strategy provided by the Bralirwa directors. Some time later two of the directors were indeed in Goma in order to obtain clarity about the situation in Rwanda. Do not forget that there were no mobile telephones at the time and that internet and e-mail were non-existent. Radio stations like RFI were the most important source of information. A number of Bralirwa workers crossed the border, were accommodated in Goma and given sustenance and some money. In Goma there were a few talks with people from the brewery but the fact that there was occasional contact does not imply in any way that Heineken controlled the brewery. Once again, it was virtually impossible to get an impression of the situation on the ground, let alone make a precise assessment of what exactly was going on in Gisenyi. As far as we know, Heineken has not delivered yeast to the brewery during the genocide. Having said that, a brewery is certainly able to continue working for three months without new yeast supplies by cultivating the yeast that is present on site. Finally, we have no knowledge of the alleged replacement of Tutsi drivers with Hutus by the Bralirwa management.'

24. Homé 2006: 110, 111.

25. Minutes Executive Board, 1 December 1994, HC.

26. Homé 2006: 20.

27. See note 20.

28. Questions by a member of the Dutch Second Chamber (Parliament),

submitted on 25 November 1999; http://parlis.nl/kvr10786 (accessed November 2017).

29. This report is based on separate conversations with three survivors, Alphonse Bahati, Jean-Bosco Karoretwa and Jonathan Habimana, and the passage Homé dedicates to the event in his book (2006: 169–73).

30. Homé 2006: 172.

31. Geke van der Wal, 'Karel Vuursteen', *de Volkskrant*, 20 April 2002.

32. Mark Schenkel uses a similar wording in: 'Op de biermarkt van Rwanda ontspint zich een wedstrijdje Nederland-België' (Match between Holland and Belgium on the Rwandan beer market), *Het Financieele Dagblad*, 11 November 2013.

14. WHAT ABOUT HEINEKEN? RESPONSES AND STRATEGY

1. 'Ons standpunt over Heineken in Afrika' (Our position on Heineken in Africa); http://www.theheinekencompany.com/samen-groeien-in-afrika/het-boek-heineken-in-afrika (accessed January 2016; post has been removed).

2. See Foreword, note 5.

3. De Man and I exchanged a few more emails, discussing the extent to which the local turnover of a Heineken subsidiary benefits the local economy. Earlier, I had made calculations with a top manager in Nigeria, and the outcome was that at least half of the money went abroad. De Man says it is much less, but the evidence he produced was too limited and selective to be convincing.

4. See note 1.

5. Van Beemen 2015: 327.

6. Roderick Mirande, 'Heineken komt weer met heuse productreclame: Heineken's Heerlijkheden' (Heineken returns with a real product-related advert: Heineken's Delights), *Adformatie*, 17 November 2015.

7. Those professors are Ton Dietz of the Africa Studies Centre (Leiden University), Paul Hoebink (development economy) at Radboud University in Nijmegen and Joost Jonker (history) and Brian Burgoon (political economy) of Amsterdam University.

8. Heineken Annual Report 2016. At the book presentation of *Heineken in Afrika*, Ton Dietz received the first copy. He was not involved in the production of the book.

9. This amount is mentioned in the Africa Studies Centre research proposal, which the author has seen. Heineken responds: 'We have not yet received, let alone approved the budget proposed by Leiden University for the research project. It is, therefore, entirely premature to quote an amount related to this research project in the book.'

15. MOZAMBIQUE: TAX BREAKS FOR PROPAGANDA

1. https://en.wikipedia.org/wiki/List-of-countries-by-gdp-(nominal)-per-capita
2. See, for instance, 'The Lion Kings?', *The Economist*, 6 January 2011.
3. Cyril Bensimon, 'Un eldorado en péril', *Le Monde*, 11 March 2016.
4. Hanneke Chin-A-Fo and Bram Vermeulen, 'Miljoenenroof Mozambique liep deels via Amsterdam' (Theft of millions from Mozambique: a part went through Amsterdam), *NRC Handelsblad*, 1 June 2016.
5. 'Fraude mag handel niet in weg staan' (Fraud should not impede trade), *NRC Handelsblad*, 16 May 2017.
6. Heineken denies this. 'The embassy has assisted in establishing contact between the two parties and inform us about the Mozambican government's trade delegation to the Netherlands.' The Dutch Ministry of Foreign Affairs however, recognises it has lobbied for Heineken. It claims the aid programmes mostly mentioned in this context were the future agricultural projects that should provide the brewery with grains.
7. Olivier van Beemen, 'Belastingvoordeel en politieke inmenging. Heineken gaat nu ook naar Mozambique', *Follow the Money*, 31 October 2018.
8. Adérito Caldeira, 'Governo vai conceder benefícios fiscais para nova fábrica de cerveja em Moçambique e aumenta incentivos às CDM' (Government to hand fiscal benefits to new beer factory in Mozambique and increases incentives to CDM), *Verdade*, 14 November 2017.
9. *Boletim da República*, 6, 202 (27 December 2017).
10. Heineken further responds: 'Brewing beer is capital intensive. In the initial phase, new breweries do not have the economic advantages of scale that existing breweries dispose of. What this means is that for a brewer the "entry costs" to a new market are high, also because substantial investments must be made in brand placement and building a

distribution network. The law the Mozambican authorities adopted last year lowers these obstacles in the first few years.'

11. According to a yet to be published report, https://twitter.com/Action Aid/status/959068150129156097

POSTSCRIPT: AN ISLAND OF PERFECTION IN A SEA OF MISERY

1. A report of this session was also published on the website Follow the Money. 'Mensenrechtenschendingen in Afrika—het kan ook "leuk" zijn' (Human rights abuses in Africa can be 'fun'), 29 January 2018.

2. 'Heineken helpt' (Heineken is helping), *Elsevier*, 6 July 2002; see Chapter 4, note 9, and Chapter 6, note 5.

3. Sluyterman and Bouwens 2014: 402.

4. Clementine Fletcher, 'Heineken Should Target Ethiopia, Congo for Growth, De Man Says', Bloomberg, 8 July 2011.

5. René Zwaap, 'Freddy Heineken', *De Groene Amsterdammer*, 6 November 1996; Smit 2014: 273.

EPILOGUE: THE BOSS AND THE PROMOTION GIRL

1. 'Working with Brand Promoters'; https://www.theheinekencompany. com/Working-with-Brand-Promoters, 4 July 2018.

2. Olivier van Beemen, 'De biermeisjes van Heineken vergaat het nog niet veel beter' (Heineken's beer girls are not much better off), *NRC Handelsblad*, 3 September 2018.

3. Jeroen Bos and Henk Dheedene, 'Ik heb moordpartijen gezien. Dat doet wel iets met je' (I have witnessed the mass killings. That touched me somehow), *Het Financieele Dagblad*, 24 November 2018.

4. Olivier van Beemen, 'Een bus vol schaars geklede meisjes voor de Heineken-staf' (A bus full of scantily clad girls for Heineken's staff), *NRC Handelsblad*, 20 April 2018.

5. See Chapter 6, note 21.

BIBLIOGRAPHY

From the archives

Material from the Heineken Archives in the Amsterdam City Archives (referenced HA in the notes):

Travel reports from Africa (archived under numbers 1052–92), Cobra and Interbra (1129–37), correspondence, documents and reports on participation in Africa (1180–91F), Cobra (1819–2031).

Heineken Collection, accessible via https://heineken.memorix.nl (referenced HC in the notes):

Annual reports (1936–2017), minutes from Executive Board meetings (1931–95) and Supervisory Board meetings (1957–95), documentation for meetings (1918–87), President's Letters (1989–95), *Vers van 't Vat* (1950–2005), *Heineken NL Magazine* (2005–14), *Heineken International Magazine* (1984–92), *World of Heineken* (1989–2014).

Reports and policy documents accessed from websites (Heineken and subsidiaries):

Sustainability Reports (2004/5–2014), Water Policy Statement (1999), Company Environmental Policy Statement (1999), Energy Policy Statement (1999), Alcohol Policy (2004), Terms of Reference Integrity Committee (2006), Supplier Code (2008), Global Distribution Policy (2010), Global Occupational Health and Safety Policy (2011), Policy on Employees and Human Rights (2012), Code of Conduct (2013),

BIBLIOGRAPHY

Brewing a Better Future: What's Brewing seminar (2013), Speak Up Policy (2014), Responsible Marketing Code (2008 and 2016).

Nigerian Breweries and Bralirwa's Annual Reports, sustainability reports and fact sheets from Algeria, Burundi, the Democratic Republic of Congo, Egypt, Ethiopia, Nigeria, Rwanda and Sierra Leone.

Books, reports, scientific articles and publications

Access Capital Research, 'Sector Report Beer: Investing in Ethiopia', May 2010.

AFDB, 'A Comparison of Real Household Consumption Expenditures and Price Levels in Africa', 2012.

Alcohol Justice, 'How Big Alcohol Abuses "Drink Responsibly" to Market Its Products', May 2012.

Amnesty International, 'Human Rights Principles for Companies', January 1998.

Anderson, Peter et al., 'Impact of Alcohol Advertising and Media Exposure on Adolescent Alcohol Use: A Systematic Review of Longitudinal Studies', *Alcohol & Alcoholism*, 44, 3 (2009), pp. 229–43.

Andersson, Pierre, *Global Hangover: Alcohol as an Obstacle to Development*, Stockholm: IOGT-NTO International Institute, 2008.

Apotheker, Roos, 'Heineken in Sierra Leone: The Local Sourcing of Sorghum by the Sierra Leone Brewery Limited (SLBL)', KIT, 2012.

Bais, Karolien and Mijnd Huijser, *The Profit of Peace: Corporate Responsibility in Conflict Regions*, Sheffield: Greenleaf Publishing, 2005.

Bakan, Joel, *The Corporation: The Pathological Pursuit of Profit and Power*, London: Constable, 2004.

Bakke, Øystein and Dag Endal, 'Vested Interests in Addiction Research and Policy: Alcohol Policies Out of Context; Drinks Industry Supplanting Government Role in Alcohol Policies in Sub-Saharan Africa', *Addiction*, 105 (January 2010), pp. 22–8.

Beemen, Olivier van, *Heineken in Afrika*, Amsterdam: Prometheus, 2015.

Berghezan, Georges, 'Groupes armés actifs en République Démocratique du Congo: Situation dans le "Grand Kivu" au 2ème semestre 2013' (Armed groups active in the Democratic Republic of Congo: situation in Grand Kivu in the second half of 2013), Groupe de recherche et d'information sur la Paix et la Sécurité, November 2013.

BIBLIOGRAPHY

Bernstein Research, 'The Bernstein Global Beer Guide, Second Edition: Which Regions and Countries Drive Industry Profits and Why?', April 2013.

Bitzer, Verena, 'Partnering for Change in Chains: The Capacity of Partnerships to Promote Sustainable Change in Global Agricultural Commodity Chains', University of Utrecht, 2011.

Borght, Stefaan van der, 'Making HIV Programmes Work: The Heineken Workplace Programme to Prevent and Treat HIV Infection 2001–2010', University of Amsterdam, 2011.

Boxmeer, Jean-François van, 'Etude du marché gabonais des bières et soft-drinks: proposition d'une stratégie et d'une tactique commerciales pour les Brasseries Artois' (A study of the Gabonese beer and soft drinks market: proposal for a commercial strategy and tactic for the Artois Breweries), Université Notre-Dame de la Paix de Namur, 1984.

Braeckman, Colette, *Le dinosaure: le Zaïre de Mobutu* (The dinosaur: Mobutu's Zaire), Paris: Fayard, 1992.

——— *Rwanda: histoire d'un genocide* (Rwanda: history of a genocide), Paris: Fayard, 1994.

——— *L'homme qui répare les femmes: violences sexuelles au Congo; le combat du docteur Mukwege* (The man who repairs women: sexual violence in Congo; Doctor Mukwege's fight), Brussels: André Versaille, 2012.

Brauman, Rony, *Devant le mal: Rwanda, un génocide en direct* (Face to face with evil: Rwanda, a live genocide), Paris: Arléa, 1994.

Bredoux, Lénaïg and Mathieu Magnaudeix, *Tunis connection: enquête sur les réseaux franco-tunisiens sous Ben Ali* (Tunis connection: an inquiry into the Franco-Tunisian networks under Ben Ali), Paris: Seuil, 2012.

Bruggink, Jan-Willem, 'Ontwikkelingen in het aandeel rokers in Nederland sinds 1989' (Developments in the percentage of smokers in the Netherlands since 1989)', *Tijdschrift voor Gezondheidswetenschappen*, 91, 4 (2003), pp. 234–40.

Bruijn, Avalon de, 'Monitoring Alcohol Marketing in Africa: Findings from the Gambia, Ghana, Nigeria and Uganda, WHO Regional Office for Africa/STAP', Utrecht, July 2011.

Bryceson, Deborah Fahy (ed.), *Alcohol in Africa: Mixing Business, Pleasure, and Politics*, Portsmouth: Heinemann, 2002.

BIBLIOGRAPHY

Budlender, Debbie, 'Money Down the Drain: The Direct Cost to Government of Alcohol Abuse', Soul City, 2010.

Budlender, Debbie et al., 'National and Provincial Government Spending and Revenue Related to Alcohol Abuse', Soul City, November 2009.

Bulcha, Mekuria, 'Genocidal Violence in the Making of Nation and State in Ethiopia', *African Sociological Review*, 9, 2 (2005), pp. 1–54.

Burke, T.R., 'The Economic Impact of Alcohol Abuse and Alcoholism', *Public Health Reports*, 103, 6 (November 1988), pp. 564–8.

Butcher, Tim, *Chasing the Devil: On Foot through Africa's Killing Fields*, London: Vintage, 2011.

Carmody, Pádraig, *The New Scramble for Africa*, Cambridge: Polity Press, 2011.

Crane, Andrew and Dirk Matten, *Business Ethics*, New York: Oxford University Press, 2007.

Cranenburgh, Katinka van, 'Money or Ethics? Multinational Corporations and Religious Organisations Operating in an Era of Corporate Responsibility', Erasmus University Rotterdam, 2016.

Cranenburgh, Katinka van and Daniel Arenas, 'Strategic and Moral Dilemmas of Corporate Philanthropy in Developing Countries: Heineken in Sub-Saharan Africa', *Journal of Business Ethics*, 122, 3 (July 2014), pp. 523–36.

Crisafulli, Patricia and Andrea Redmond, *Rwanda Inc.: How a Devastated Nation Became an Economic Model for the Developing World*, New York: Palgrave Macmillan, 2012.

Dalen, Wim van and Monique Kuunders, 'Don't Ask a Bird to Clip Its Own Wings: Analysis of Self-Regulation of Alcohol Marketing in the Netherlands', STAP, 2003.

Davis, Peter, *Corporations, Global Governance, and Post-Conflict Reconstruction*, Milton Park: Routledge, 2013.

Deloitte, 'The Rise and Rise of the African Middle Class', *Deloitte on Africa Collection*, 2012.

Deutsche Bank, 'Castel: The Key to SABMiller's African Growth Strategy', London, 5 October 2010.

Dowden, Richard, *Africa: Altered States, Ordinary Miracles*, London: Portobello, 2008.

BIBLIOGRAPHY

Draulans, Dirk, *Handelaar in oorlog* (Wartime merchant), Amsterdam/ Antwerp: Atlas, 2003.

Dumbili, Emeka, 'Changing Patterns of Alcohol Consumption in Nigeria: An Exploration of Responsible Factors and Consequences', *Medical Sociology Online*, 7, 1 (February 2013).

——— 'The Politics of Alcohol Policy in Nigeria: A Critical Analysis of How and Why Brewers Use Strategic Ambiguity to Supplant Policy Initiatives', *Journal of Asian and African Studies*, 49, 4 (June 2014), pp. 473–87.

——— '"She Encourages People to Drink": A Qualitative Study of the Use of Females to Promote Beer in Nigerian Institutions of Learning', *Drugs: Education, Prevention and Policy*, 23, 4 (2016).

——— 'Heightened Hypocrisy: A Critical Analysis of How the Alcohol Industry-Sponsored "Nigerian Beer Symposium" Jeopardises Public Health', *Drugs: Education, Prevention and Policy*, 2018.

Econex and Quantec Research, 'Working for South Africa: The Contribution of SAB to the South African Economy', September 2010.

Ederveen, Sandra, 'Malt Barley: A Short-Term Cash Crop or Sustainable Investment? A Study on the Impact of the CREATE Project on the Livelihood and Food Security of Contracted Smallholders in Ethiopia', University of Utrecht, 2016.

Eigbe, Esili, 'Nigeria and East-Africa's Beer Market', SBG Securities, 21 January 2013.

Eisenberg, Eric M., 'Ambiguity as Strategy in Organizational Communication', *Communications Monographs*, 51, 3 (1984), pp. 227–42.

Fick, David, *Africa: Continent of Economic Opportunity*, Johannesburg: STE Publishers, 2006.

Fieldgate, Ilse et al., 'Economic Impact of an Advertising Ban on Alcoholic Beverages: For Industry Association for Responsible Alcohol Use', Econometrix Ltd, 2013.

First, Ruth, Jonathan Steele and Christabel Gurney, *The South African Connection: Western Investment in Apartheid*, London: Temple Smith, 1972.

Fletcher, Luke, 'Turning Interahamwe: Individual and Community Choices in the Rwandan Genocide', *Journal of Genocide Research*, 9, 1 (2007), pp. 25–48.

BIBLIOGRAPHY

Foreign Policy Study Foundation, *The Report of the Study Commission on US Policy toward Southern Africa: South Africa; Time Running Out*, Berkeley/Los Angeles: University of California Press, 1981.

Fort, Timothy L., *Business, Integrity and Peace: Beyond Geopolitical and Disciplinary Boundaries*, New York: Cambridge University Press, 2007.

French, Howard W., *A Continent for the Taking: The Tragedy and Hope of Africa*, New York: Random House, 2004.

Games, Dianna (ed.), *Business in Africa: Corporate Insights*, Johannesburg: Penguin, 2012.

Gerwen, Frans van and Sharon van Ede (eds), 'Evaluation of Schokland and Millennium Agreements 2008–2013', 17 March 2014.

Gordon, Ross, Anne Marie MacKintosh and Crawford Moodie, 'The Impact of Alcohol Marketing on Youth Drinking Behaviour: A Two-Stage Cohort Study', *Alcohol and Alcoholism*, 45, 5 (2010), pp. 470–80.

Gourevitch, Philip, *We Wish to Inform You That Tomorrow We Will Be Killed with Our Families: Stories from Rwanda*, New York: Picador, 1998.

Granvaud, Raphaël, *Areva en Afrique: une face cachée du nucléaire français* (Areva in Africa: a hidden face of France's nuclear industry), Marseille: Agone, 2012.

Haley, Usha, *Multinational Corporations in Political Environments: Ethics, Values and Strategies*, Singapore: World Scientific, 2001.

Hatzfeld, Jean, *Une saison des machettes* (Machete season), Paris: Seuil, 2003.

Hausse, Paul La, *Brewers, Beerhalls and Boycotts: A History of Liquor in South Africa*, Johannesburg: Ravan Press, 1988.

Haworth, Alan and S.W. Acuda, 'Sub-Saharan Africa', in Marcus Grant (ed.), *Alcohol and Emerging Markets: Patterns, Problems and Responses*, Philadelphia: Brunner/Mazel, 1998, pp. 19–90.

Heap, Simon, 'Beer in Nigeria: A Social Brew with an Economic Head' in Steven van Wolputte and Mattia Fumanti (eds), *Beer in Africa: Drinking Spaces, States and Selves*, Zürich: Lit Verlag, 2010, pp. 109–29.

Heijn, Dennis, *Je kan bomen alleen ontwijken als je vaart hebt: Anders handelen door anders te kijken* (You can only evade trees when you're going fast: Acting differently by looking differently), Amsterdam: Prometheus/Bert Bakker, 2014.

BIBLIOGRAPHY

Homé, Jean Louis, *Le businessman et le conflit des grands lacs* (The business-man and the Great Lakes conflict), Paris: L'Harmattan, 2006.

Howard, Philip H., 'Too Big to Ale? Globalization and Consolidation in the Beer Industry', University of Michigan, May 2013.

Huesken, Bastiaan, 'Brewing a Better Future in the Democratic Republic of Congo: An Impact Assessment of Heineken's Local Sourcing Initiative', European Cooperative for Rural Development, July 2013.

Human Rights Watch, 'World Report', 2003.

Ikime, Obaro, *Fifty Years of Brewing Excellence: A History of Nigerian Breweries PLC 1946–1996*, Lagos: Nigerian Breweries, 1999.

Jacobs, M.G.P.A. and W.H.G. Maas (in collaboration with J. van der Werf), *Heineken 1949–1988*, Amsterdam: Heineken NV, 1991.

——— *De magie van Heineken* (Heineken's magic), Amsterdam: Heineken NV, 2001.

Jeancolas, Claude, *Rimbaud l'Africain. 1880–1891*, Paris: Textuel, 2014.

Jernigan, David, 'Alcohol in Developing Societies: A Summary of Room and Others', 2002.

Jernigan, David and Isidore Obot, 'Thirsting for the African Market', *African Journal of Drug and Alcohol Studies*, 5, 1 (2006), pp. 57–70.

Jeurissen, Ronald (ed.), *Bedrijfsethiek een goede zaak* (Corporate ethics good business), Assen: Van Gorcum, 2009.

Jones, Geoffrey, 'Multinational Strategies and Developing Countries in Historical Perspective', working paper 10–076, Harvard Business School, 2010.

Kapuscinski, Ryszard, *The Emperor: Downfall of an Autocrat*, London: Penguin, 2006 [1978].

Kaziboni, Lauralyn and Reena Das Nair, 'The Beer Industry in Africa: A Case of Carving Out Geographic Markets?', *Quarterly Competition Review*, Centre for Competition, Regulation and Economic Develop-ment, November 2014.

Koch, Dirk-Jan, *De Congo codes: Een persoonlijk verhaal over de zin en onzin van ontwikkelingssamenwerking* (The Congo codes: a personal story about the sense and non-sense of development cooperation), Amsterdam: Prometheus/Bert Bakker, 2014.

Kolk, Ans and François Lenfant, 'MNC Reporting on CSR and Conflict in Central Africa', *Journal of Business Ethics*, 93 (2010), pp. 241–55.

BIBLIOGRAPHY

Korthals, H.A., *Korte geschiedenis der Heineken's Bierbrouwerij Maatschappij N.V. 1873–1948* (A brief history of Heineken's Beer Brewing Company N.V. 1873–1948), Amsterdam: Allert de Lange, 1948.

Krige, Detlev, 'Inequality and Class through the Drinking Glass: An Ethnography of Men and Beer Consumption in Contemporary Soweto', in Steven van Wolputte and Mattia Fumanti (eds), *Beer in Africa: Drinking Spaces, States and Selves*, Zürich: Lit Verlag, 2010, pp. 223–55.

Lem, Marjolein, Rob van Tulder and Kim Geleynse, *Doing Business in Africa: A Strategic Guide for Entrepreneurs*, Utrecht: Berenschot, 2013.

Lemarchand, René, 'Le génocide de 1972 au Burundi' (The 1972 genocide in Burundi), *Cahiers d'études africaines*, 167 (2002), pp. 551–68.

Lenfant, François and Katinka van Cranenburgh, 'Business Responsibilities in Times of War and Peace: The Case of Heineken in Central Africa', *Journal of Business, Peace and Sustainable Development*, 2018 (planned publication).

Lubek, Ian, 'Cambodian "Beer Promotion Women" and Corporate Caution, Recalcitrance or Worse?', *Psychology of Women Section Review*, 7, 1 (2005), pp. 2–11.

Lyumugabe, François et al., 'Characteristics of African Traditional Beers Brewed with Sorghum Malt: A Review', *Biotechnologie, Agronomie, Société et Environnement*, 16, 4 (2012), pp. 509–30.

Mager, Anne Kelk, *Beer, Sociability, and Masculinity in South Africa*, Bloomington: Indiana University Press, 2010.

Malyon, Stephanie, *SLBL 50 Years: Wi briwri Wi Salone*, Freetown: Sierre Leone Brewery Ltd, 2012.

Matzopoulos, Richard et al., 'The Cost of Harmful Alcohol Use in South Africa', *South African Medical Journal*, 104, 2 (February 2014), pp. 127–32.

McKinsey, 'McKinsey on Finance: Perspectives on Corporate Finance and Strategy', 2003.

——— 'Lions on the Move: The Progress and Potential of African Economies', June 2010.

Meredith, Martin, *The Fortunes of Africa: A 5,000-Year History of Wealth, Greed and Endeavour*, London: Simon & Schuster, 2014.

Nexus Investment Solutions, 'Ethiopian Beer and Soft Drink Market Profiling', May 2012.

BIBLIOGRAPHY

NCDO, 'Economic Assessment Model: Local Economic Impact of the Sierra Leone Brewery Limited, a Heineken Operating Company', 2006.

Obot, Isidore and Akanidomo Ibanga, 'Selling Booze: Alcohol Marketing in Nigeria', *The Globe*, 2 (2002), pp. 6–10.

Odejide, Olabisi, 'Alcohol Policies in Africa', *African Journal of Drug & Alcohol Studies*, 5, 1 (2006).

Ogunbiyi, Yemi, *Sixty Years of Winning with Nigeria: The History of Nigerian Breweries 1946–2006*, Ibadan: Bookcraft, 2007.

Olusanya, Olaoluwa, 'Armed Forces, Alcohol Abuse and Responsibility for Wartime Violence: Applying the Attention-Allocation Model', *Psychiatry, Psychology and Law*, 20, 1 (2013), pp. 105–22.

OECD, 'Herziene OECD richtlijnen voor multinationale ondernemingen. Aanbevelingen voor verantwoord ondernemen in een mondiale context' (2011 update of the OECD Guidelines for Multinational Enterprises), 2011.

Poikolainen, Kari, *Perfect Drinking and Its Enemies*, Minneapolis: Mill City Press, 2014.

Quaak, Lizet, Theo Aalbers and John Goedee, 'Transparency of Corporate Social Responsibility in Dutch Breweries', *Journal of Business Ethics*, 76 (2007), pp. 293–308.

Rehm, Jürgen et al., 'Alcohol and Global Health 1: Global Burden of Disease and Injury and Economic Cost Attributable to Alcohol Use and Alcohol-Use Disorders', *Lancet*, 373 (2009), pp. 2223–33.

Reybrouck, David Van, *Congo. Een geschiedenis* (Congo: The epic history of a people), Amsterdam: De Bezige Bij, 2011.

Room, Robert et al., *Alcohol in Developing Societies: A Public Health Approach*, Finnish Foundation for Alcohol Studies (in collaboration with WHO), 2002.

Ruster, Willem and Rene Kim, 'The Socio-Economic Impact of Brarudi in Burundi in 2010', Steward Redqueen, 5 August 2011.

Schouten, Peer, 'Brewing Security? Heineken's Engagement with Commercial Conflict-Dependent Actors in the Eastern DRC', CCDA Project, September 2013.

Schwartz, Peter and Blair Gibb, *When Good Companies Do Bad Things: Responsibility and Risk in an Age of Globalization*, New York: John Wiley, 1999.

BIBLIOGRAPHY

Sluyterman, Keetie and Bram Bouwens, *Heineken: 150 jaar: Brouwerij, merk en familie* (Heineken: 150 years; Brewery, brand and family), Amsterdam: Boom, 2014.

Smit, Barbara, *Heineken: Een leven in de brouwerij* (The Heineken story: The remarkably refreshing tale of the beer that conquered the world), Nijmegen: Sun, 1996.

———— *Heineken. Een leven in de brouwerij* (The Heineken story: The remarkably refreshing tale of the beer that conquered the world), Amsterdam: Prometheus Bert Bakker, 2014.

Smith, Sandi W., Charles K. Atkin and JoAnn Roznowski, 'Are "Drink Responsibly" Alcohol Campaigns Strategically Ambiguous?', *Health Communication*, 20, 1 (2006), pp. 1–11.

Sonneville, Francois, 'Beer on the New Frontier: Opportunities for Brewers on the African Continent', Rabobank Industry Note 429, March 2014.

Stikker, Dirk U., *Memoires: Herinneringen uit de lange jaren waarin ik betrokken was bij de voortdurende wereldcrisis* (Memoirs: recollections from my long years of involvement with the ongoing global crisis), Rotterdam/The Hague: Nijgh & Van Ditmar, 1966.

Stirling, Trevor, Jean-Marc Chow and Nicole Thain, 'MegaBrew Revisited: Why We Still Think the Acquisition of SABMmiller by AB INBEV Is Unlikely, But Not Impossible', Bernstein Research, 14 March 2012.

———— 'Africa: The World's Most Attractive Beer Region?', Bernstein Research, 19 March 2013.

Straus, Scott, 'How Many Perpetrators Were There in the Rwandan Genocide? An Estimate', *Journal of Genocide Research*, 6, 1 (March 2004), pp. 85–98.

Tabaksblat, Morris, *Dialoog binnen de samenleving: Unilevers visie op verantwoord ondernemen* (A society-wide dialogue: Unilever's vision of corporate social responsibility), Rotterdam: Unilever Corporate Relations, 1997.

Triple Value Strategy Consulting, 'Economic Impact of Heineken in Sierra Leone', Amsterdam, 23 November 2006.

———— 'Serving the Planet, Serving Nigeria: The Socio-Economic Impact of Nigerian Breweries', The Hague, May 2009.

US Department of Commerce, Bureau of the Census, *World Population*

BIBLIOGRAPHY

1983: Recent Demographic Estimates for the Countries and Regions of the World, December 1983.

Vallée, Olivier, 'Brassage de soi(f)s?' (Mixing drinks and selves?), in Jean-François Bayart and Jean-Pierre Warnier (eds), *Matière à politique: Le pouvoir, les corps et les choses* (Political material: power, bodies and objects), Paris: Karthala, 2004, pp. 129–49.

Vermeulen, Stefan, *Heineken na Freddy: De strijd van een Nederlands wereldconcern* (Heineken after Freddy: the battle of a Dutch multinational), Amsterdam: Prometheus, 2016.

Volleman, Katrien, 'Combining Stakeholders' Strengths in the Fight against Food Insecurity: Public–Private Partnerships as Legitimate Actors of Global Governance', University of Oslo, 2015.

WHO, 'Global Strategy to Reduce the Harmful Use of Alcohol', 2010.

———— 'Global Status Report on Alcohol and Health', 2011, 2014 and 2018.

Wijk, Jeroen van and Herma Kwakkenbos, 'Beer Multinationals Supporting Africa's Development? How Partnerships Include Smallholders into Sorghum-Beer Supply Chains', in: Meine Pieter van Dijk and Jacques Trienekens (eds), *Global Value Chains: Linking Local Producers from Developing Countries to International Markets*, Amsterdam: Amsterdam University Press, 2011, pp. 71–88.

Willame, Jean-Claude, *Patrice Lumumba: La crise congolaise revisitée* (Patrice Lumumba: the Congolese crisis revisited), Paris: Karthala, 1990.

Willis, Justin, *Potent Brews: A Social History of Alcohol in East Africa 1850–1999*, London: British Institute in Eastern Africa, 2002.

Wolputte, Steven van and Mattia Fumanti (eds), *Beer in Africa: Drinking Spaces, States and Selves*, Zürich: Lit Verlag, 2010.

Yoon, Sungwon and Tai-Hing Lam, 'The Illusion of Righteousness: Corporate Social Responsibility Practices of the Alcohol Industry', *BMC Public Health*, 13 (July 2013).

Zijl, Annejet van der, *Gerard Heineken: De man, de stad en het bier* (Gerard Heineken: the man, the city and the beer), Amsterdam: Querido/Bas Lubberhuizen, 2014.

BIBLIOGRAPHY

Audio-visual sources

Een Hollands biertje in Afrika (A Dutch beer in Africa), documentary on Dutch television, RTL4, 15 April 2009.

'Heineken en Bavaria brouwen voor dorstig Ethiopië' (Heineken and Bavaria: brewing beer for thirsty Ethiopia), *Nieuwsuur*, 31 January 2015.

'Hollandse handel' (Dutch trade), *Zembla*, 23 March 2016.

'Maatschappelijk verantwoord ondernemen: Heineken in Afrika' (Corporate social responsibility: Heineken in Africa), *TweeVandaag*, 22 August 2005.

Mobutu roi du Zaïre (Mobutu king of Zaire), Belgian documentary, 1999.

'Promotiemeisjes Heineken nog steeds slachtoffer seksuele intimidatie', *EenVandaag*, 4 September 2018.

INDEX

INDEX

INDEX

INDEX

INDEX

INDEX

INDEX

INDEX

INDEX

INDEX

INDEX

INDEX

INDEX

INDEX

INDEX